To God be the glory
George D Miller

THE DEACON'S
BEACON

"Things I Never Learned in Seminary"

GEORGE MILLER

To: Pastor Evan
From: The Bandy's

TATE PUBLISHING, LLC

Published in the United States of America
by Tate Publishing, LLC
127 East Trade Center Terrace
Mustang, OK 73064
(888) 361–9473

ISBN: 1–9332900–4-8

TABLE OF CONTENTS
NUMBER LIST

TABLE OF CONTENTS
BIBLE LIST

BEAM 1

WHAT A BIBLE STUDY

LUKE 24:27

What is this book all about anyway? If some alien from the planet Krypton came down to earth, what would he think? He may think we do not think much of it because so many earthlings do not bother with the Book. But there is a rather large group of earthlings that do carry this book around with them, especially on Sundays. He might think that it is some kind of a good luck piece, a rabbit's foot, something to ward off evil. So he might want to ask the earthlings just what is this book you carry around with you? What is it for? What would you say to him? What is this the book all about?

The central theme of the book is Jesus Christ the Son of God. Everything in the book is centered around Him. The Old Testament gives the preparation for His coming. The New Testament tells about what happened when He came. It ends with what will happen later at His second coming. Sure, there are historical books and what we call the poetical books and prophetical books. But they are all about Him. I wish I could have heard His Old Testament Bible Study that He gave to those two who were walking on their way to Emmaus (Luke 24:13–31). He held back their perception so He could give them this Bible study. He started with Moses and went through the Scriptures. What a study!

He may have started with the first promise of the Messiah. This was in Genesis 3:15 where it states that the seed of the woman, the Messiah, would bruise, or break, the head of the serpent, Satan that is. This was the promise for all times. An anointed One, the Messiah, would defeat Satan and break his chains upon mankind. There would be a deliverer from sin.

He could have told them about how God asked Abraham to give up his son and then how God spared Abraham and yet spared not His own Son, Who went to the cross for sinners. He may have told them about how the manna that came down from heaven to feed Israel was only a picture of the Messiah, who was the true manna. He may have told them how, when Moses struck the rock at Horeb, and the water came gushing out to save the dying people, that also was another picture of the Messiah. He was like that innocent rock and He was struck to give life to the guilty.

He could have gone through all of the Law of Moses to show that no one ever could keep that law until He came and fulfilled it. He became a curse for sinners so that sinners could be saved from the curse. He might have told them about how the blood which was sprinkled on the Mercy Seat that covered the Ark was a picture of His blood shed on the cross for sinners who had broken the law. They could now approach a Holy God and live. His blood shed on the cross was what the Day of Atonement was all about. His blood opened up a new way of approach to God. There is a new Mercy Seat for us now in heaven. He could have told them about how the veil of the temple was to keep sinners from approaching a holy God, but now that veil was done away with and any sinner can approach God, if he comes through the sacrifice Messiah made for us on the cross. The veil kept sinners out. The cross welcomes them in.

He could have pointed out how Joseph was another picture of the Messiah. How Joseph was hated by his brothers, and sold by them. How Joseph married a Gentile woman, like He would marry a Gentile Church. He may have pointed out how Joseph was later exalted and saved the very brothers who sold him.

And Ruth? How she was redeemed by Boaz, a wealthy and powerful Goel, who also was another picture of Him. He was the Jacob's ladder of the Old Testament. He was the Melchizedek who came to Abraham's aid. He was the Stone that smote Nebuchadnezzar's image in Daniel 2:25, which would rule over the entire earth without end. He was the Mediator that Job asked for. He was the Good Shepherd that David spoke of in Psalm 23. Hundreds of years before crucifixion was practiced, David said Messiah would not be stoned to death, the normal way for a Israelite to be executed (Psalms 34:20). And it all came to pass. The Messiah was crucified

He could have told them that Isaiah 53 was a picture of Him, the Messiah, who when we had gone our own sinful ways, the Lord laid on Him the iniquities of us all. And on and on and on. What a Bible Study! I wish we could have had a recording of it, and a translation so we could understand it. What a lesson! And think how many arguments it would have solved, too.

What is it all about? It is about God's Son and how God so loved the world that He gave His only begotten Son, that whosoever believes in Him should not perish but have everlasting life (John 3:16). That's what it's all about. Have you read it? Have you received Him? No better time than right now!

BEAM 2

GOD, GIANTS, AND GRASSHOPPERS

NUMBERS 13:33

The majority report said it couldn't be done. There were giants over there and we were like grasshoppers. What can a grasshopper do against a giant? Get out of the way! What does a giant do to a grasshopper? He squashes it. The majority report came back with an overwhelming vote of "No! We can't do it."

But there was a minority report also. Joshua and Caleb said "We can do it. Let's go! God has given us the land. There is nothing too hard for us, if God is with us." God was in their report. Even grasshoppers can defeat giants when God is on their side. Who was right here? Both were. If we leave God out, we can't do it. Grasshoppers don't have a chance against giants. If we put God in, giants don't have a chance against grasshoppers. If we leave God out of our lives we are defeated by giants.

Let's look at some of those giants.

Financial-giants. "How can we afford to give, and live on the rest of our salary? We need retirement money. I am going to need a new car soon."

There are Fear-of-the-Future Giants, who rob us of our peace. So we go to a psychiatrist to help us. Who knows what tomorrow will bring? We tell him problems, we think. He listens, and listens, and listens.

We pay him to hear us talk. (Your wife listens to your talk for nothing.)

There is that health giant. "I'm not as young as I used to be. Who is going to care for me as I get older? Will I be able to care for my Honey? Will Honey be able to care for me? What if I lose my driver's license?"

There is the job giant. "I may lose my job if I live like a Christian should. I've already been passed over for promotions. How will I get another job at my age? It isn't fair."

There is the guilt giant. "I know I did wrong back there but I was a young Christian. I'm sorry now, but what can I do about it?

There is the aging giant, the discouragement giant, the temptation giant. Lots of giants."

There is that greatest giant of all, the death giant. He is the one we fear most because of the unknown, the pain we may suffer, the place where we will be forever, the loved ones we may never see. Death is still an enemy, even for the believer. But one day he will be put away forever (1 Corinthians 15:26).

There are truly many giants in this world and we are but insignificant little grasshoppers. What can we do against giants? Yes, without God we don't have a chance. But we don't need to put God out of our lives. Put God in our lives and everything is changed. We can do anything God wants us to do. Only God can defeat Giants. Put Him in our lives and we can say, "I can do all things through Christ, which strengtheneth me" (Philippians 4:13). And He will lead us all the way. The Majority Report kept Israel out of the promised land for another 38 years. What a shame. But Joshua and Caleb were given passes to live till they entered the land. But what a waste of time!

Ah! What a beautiful story that such weak and helpless creatures can defeat the forces of darkness, if God is on our side. And He wants to be on our side. Have we let Him? "We are more than conquerors through Him that loved us' (Romans 8:37). "Resist the devil, and he will flee from you." But there is something you must do first. "Submit yourselves therefore to God" then you can resist the devil (James 4:7). Don't try the second part until you have done the first part. "For whatsoever is born of God overcometh the world: and this is the victory that overcometh the world, even our faith" (1 John 5:4).

"But be of good cheer; I have overcome the world" (John 16:33).

BEAM 3

JOHN SMITH

WHO BEGAT, WHO BEGAT, WHO BEGAT

1 CHRONICLES 6:4,5,6,7, etc.

A very unusual name that is, John Smith. Almost as unusual as John Doe. I wonder how many John Smiths were born in Baltimore last year? Or Cleveland? And who cares?

Well, God cares and God knows how many John Smiths were born in Toledo, and Birmingham, and which one was born on October 23. So what?

Many so-called Bible students get weary reading about all of the begats. Even some seminary students, who have sworn to preach the whole Word, skip over these begats. Shame on them.

It may not sound interesting or even theological, and certainly not as romantic as other portions of the Scriptures, but they are there for a purpose. Look at some of these verses. "Eleazar begat Phinehas, Phinehas begat Abishua, and Abishua begat Bukki, and Bukki begat Uzzi" (1 Chronicles 6:4–5). This may sound monotonous to some of us but there is a good reason for these begats to be in Scripture. We are not numbers. We are not a crowd that God looks on. He could have said, "There were a lot of people born from Adam's day to Abraham's time. And, there were a multitude of people born from Abraham's time to David's time." No! God names names. We are not just a part of a crowd. We are not just a number. Remember how many times you have seen a prisoner who had just a number on his uniform. God does not see us like that.

If the name is John Smith, or Jane Doe, He knows which one was born in Cincinnati on the 4th of March 1998. And if there were three such John Smiths born at that time, He knows each one separately from the others.

And, God gave His Son to die for the John Doe, or John Smith, or Abishua who begat Bukki. He loved the Jane Doe and the Jane Smith born in Topeka on the 14th of September and sent His Son to die for her. Not just a number, not just one of a crowd, but for each one in the crowd that He knows by name.

Some have said that Jesus called Lazarus by name to come forth out of the grave (John 11:43) so that all of the dead in the graveyard did not come forth in a resurrection. Perhaps so. One day the graves will be opened and all who have trusted Jesus will come forth in new and glorious bodies that will never know pain, sickness, suffering, sin, or death (John 5:28–29). John tells us what the Lord Jesus said about His sheep. "The sheep hear His voice, and He calleth His own sheep BY NAME" (John 10:3).

He knows us by name. Yes, the begats are there for a purpose. Remember we are not just numbers. When He comes for His own, He will know His own by name. It will not be "Hey You" or "Hey You all." It will be Fredericka, or Wilbur, or Susannah. If the very hairs of our head are numbered (Matthew 10:30), it is not a hard thing for God to know our names. What is hard for God anyhow?

He knows intimately. What a love story! "Bless the Lord, O my soul: and all that is within me, bless His holy name. Bless the Lord, O my soul, and forget not all His benefits" (Psalm 103:1–2).

"Notwithstanding in this, rejoice not that the spirits are subject unto you; but rather rejoice because your names are written in heaven" (Luke 10:20). Is your name there? It should be.

BEAM 4

EXCUSES, EXCUSES, EXCUSES

EXODUS 3:11, 4:1–18

Of all the men in the scriptures, not counting the Lord Jesus, who is in a separate category in almost everything, there are two that stand out. One is in the New Testament. He wrote thirteen of the books of the New Testament. No one did so much for the church as the Apostle Paul. He suffered perhaps more than any other disciple. But he was a special instrument in the Lord's hands. He was called for a special purpose and he fulfilled that purpose.

You may have guessed who the other one was. There were great men of God in the Old Testament but one stands out as unique. He was a mighty instrument in God's hands. He was the one who brought out God's people from Egypt. He has five books named after him, in a way. The Law of Moses we hear over and over again. He is forever identified with that Law that God gave him on Mount Sinai. However, when God called Moses to deliver His people, Moses did not want to go. He wanted nothing to do about going back to that land that he left some forty years before. He was content to stay where he was. "Send someone else, Lord, send anybody else Lord, not me."

He had all kinds of excuses. Look at some of them.

WHO AM I? That was the first one. He is looking at THE SPEAKER. God said He had come down to deliver His people. He heard their cry and saw their persecution. He said He would bring them into a land flowing with milk and honey. Their cry had come up to Him. And Moses says "Who am I?" Well who was this man? He had been in Egypt forty years ago and was born there. He lived there as Pharaoh's daughter's son. He knew all about Egypt. He may have been a bit more hot headed then. He killed an Egyptian for smiting one of the Hebrews. He is a bit older, by forty years, an eighty year old man. But did he think God would not go along? God said He had come down to deliver Israel. God says I will be with thee (3:12).

That should be enough for any man to know that God is with him. Not Moses. Now he is thinking of THE CONGREGATION. He then says when I come to the people of Israel and tell them this they will ask who sent me. What shall I tell them? What is your name? Then God says He is the Great I AM. This is the message he is to tell them.

Then he has another excuse. He then thinks about THE RECEPTION. Suppose they don't believe me? Then what? He has a message from God to deliver and he is thinking about how well it will be received.

Then what shall I do? Suppose they don't like it, Lord?

Then he goes into HIS INABILITIES. He says "I am not eloquent" (Exodus 4:10). Now he is looking at the strength of the speaker, instead of the message. He says, "I am tongue tied. I do not speak well." Or maybe he said "I, I, I, ca ca can cannot sp sp spe speak wah wah well, uh, Luh Luh Lord." And the Lord said "Who hath made man's mouth . . . or the dumb or the blind? Have not I the lord?" (Exodus 4:10–11). Moses has made enough excuses that we read the anger of the Lord kindled against Moses (Exodus 4:14). Excuses, excuses, excuses. Send somebody else Lord. Send anyone. I don't want to go. That is what he was really saying. But, Moses did go. And look what happened. He delivered God's people out of bondage.

Well, we must look at ourselves and see what is our excuse. We have a message. "Believe on the Lord Jesus Christ and thou shalt be saved" (Acts 16:31). "Neither is there salvation in any other for there is none other name under heaven given among men whereby we must be saved" (Acts 4:12). This is the message the world needs to hear. And they will not hear it if we do not go. "And how shall they believe in Him of whom they have not heard? And how shall they hear without a preacher? And how shall they preach, except they be sent? As it is written, How beautiful are the feet of them that preach the gospel of peace, and bring glad tidings of good things!" (Romans 10:14–15). You want beautiful feet? Go!

"Go ye into all the world and preach the Gospel to every creature" (Mark 16:15). Have we? What is our excuse? It is the message that counts, not the messenger. And Lo He is with the messenger. What excuse do we have? Are we tongue tied, or are we afraid, are we uneducated? So what? There is no excuse. God said go. I am with you and I will stay with you. Let's go. God does not ask us to do what we cannot do but will open up the way for us to do what He asks.

BEAM 5

EAGLES' WINGS

EXODUS 19:4

This is the way God said He brought Israel to Himself. This was from Egypt to Mount Sinai. Along the way Israel murmured, complained, and was bitter about the whole thing because it was not what they had expected or wanted.

In Exodus 14:11–12 we read "Because there were no graves in Egypt" you have brought us out here to die in the wilderness. It had been better to serve the Egyptians than to die in the wilderness. In Exodus 15:23–24 they came to Marah, which means "bitter," because the waters there were bitter and they could not drink them. And again they murmured against Moses. God showed Moses a tree. When it was cast into the waters the waters were made sweet. (This is another Old Testament picture of the New Testament cross. The tree, or the cross of Christ, sweetens the bitter things of life). In Exodus 16:3 they complain again that they could fill their bellies at the fleshpots of Egypt, but were now hungry in this wilderness. So God gave them "manna," which means "what is it?" because they did not know what the thing was. It also was a type of Christ, the Living Bread, Who came down from heaven.

In Exodus 17:3 they murmured again because they were thirsty and Moses says the people were ready to stone him to death (v.4). So God told Moses to go to the Rock at Horeb where God said He would stand before Moses and Moses should hit the rock with the rod he used in Egypt, where he hit the river and did miraculous things before Pharaoh. Water came gushing out of the rock. Here again is another Old Testament picture of the New Testament Christ. The innocent Rock was smitten by the rod of Moses, a picture of the Law, and life came out to save the guilty, who deserved to be smitten, instead of the innocent Rock.

They murmured, complained, were backbiting, and wanted to stone Moses at various times. Yet in all of this there is no record of anyone being slain by God for all of their complaining and backbiting. Now they come to Sinai and are given a choice to keep this new thing, called the Law, or go on in grace, being carried on eagles' wings. They chose the Law. They had a preview of the Law and said OK, we will do all that the Lord hath said (Exodus 19:8). Before Moses got through hearing all of the Law, they broke it, and made a golden calf. A Holy and Righteous God must judge sinners. The result from this was that "there fell of the people that day about three thousand men" (Exodus 32:28).

Where is the love story here? When we come to "grace," which is the way God saves sinners, and in the New Testament preaching of the first grace sermon by Peter, we read "There were added unto them about three thousand souls" (Acts 2:41). Could this be a coincidence? Hardly. Even the same word is used in both places. "About" three thousand. What a beautiful way for the New Testament message to start out. The Law of Moses, in its first sermon, cost "about" three thousand deaths; the grace of the Gospel in its first sermon saved "about" three thousand souls.

Yes, He sweetens bitter things in life. He, the innocent Rock, is struck for the guilty ones' sins and life comes forth to save the guilty. He is the Manna, the true Manna, that came down from heaven. The Gospel of grace, being carried on eagles' wings, is far better than the Law of Moses, which no sinner has been able to keep. They made the wrong choice. But we do, too. However, God is gracious when we do and gives us another chance to be carried on eagles' wings.

"Being justified freely by His grace through the redemption that is in Christ Jesus" (Romans 3:24).

"Grace that is greater than all our sins."

BEAM 6

PREACHING SHEEP OR PARTIAL OBEDIENCE

1 SAMUEL 15:14

Saul was sent on a mission by God. He was to utterly destroy the Amalekites, spare none, not even cattle, but destroy all (1 Samuel 15:3). That nation laid wait for Israel when they came out of Egypt and God said they should not live. Saul was to destroy.

After the battle Samuel came to see Saul. After the customary greetings, Saul says "I have performed the commandment of the Lord" (15:13). Oh yeah! Then some sheep start bleating, or is it preaching? Samuel says "What is this bleating in my ears, and this lowing of the oxen?" (15:14). "Oh," Saul says, "I just spared a few people, like Agag the king, and some animals. We can sacrifice them to the Lord." Then Samuel gives us that wonderful statement.

"Behold, to obey is better than sacrifice and to harken than the fat of rams" (15:22). God would rather have us obey Him than to be sorry afterward and do some kind of penance.

Saul's partial obedience leads to horrible consequences. This may not be evident to everyone who partially obeys God, but we should learn a lesson from this Sermon by Sheep. The king of these Amalekites was Agag. He is killed by Samuel. However, he had some heirs that were spared by Saul's partial obedience. I am sure that Samuel did not know about them.

The Amalekites wanted to destroy Israel completely, not sparing any Israelite. We read about this same hatred later in the book of Esther. In that book is a man named Haman, who hated Jews so much he wanted to destroy all of them. A Hitler before his time. One Jew named Mordecai did not bow to Haman, so Haman wanted to kill all of them. In Esther 3:1 we read that Haman was "the Agagite." After nearly 600 years they still hate all Jews and want to destroy them, all of them. And they would have if God had not intervened. This would never have happened if Saul had obeyed the Lord.

Sometimes we think it does not matter if we don't go all the way, like the Lord told us. After all we did get some of it done. That should count for something. Even if it is not disastrous, we still may lose many of God's blessings by only doing part of what He said.

It was not disastrous for Peter when the Lord told him to "let down your nets" (Luke 5:4). Peter says "Master, we have toiled all night, and have taken nothing: nevertheless at Thy word I will let down the net" (Luke 5:5). Notice, Peter said **NET** while the Lord said **NETS**. One net could not hold two nets full of fish. So the net broke. Then Peter falls down before Jesus and says "Depart from me for I am a sinful man, O Lord" (Luke 5:8). He lost fish. Perhaps that taught him to be more obedient to the Lord later when he was fishing for men instead of fish. It was good that the Lord did not depart from Peter. Peter needed Him. So do we.

What a beautiful story though. The Lord did not depart from Peter. And, He does not leave us when we do the same thing. But, we lose some fish. Or more? Why lose some fish by going part way? Let's go all the way. The fish we are fishing for are souls that He died for. He has said "I will never leave thee, nor forsake thee" (Hebrews 13:5). What a wonderful promise He has given us. A promise from One Who cannot lie. We need to give Him complete obedience. He will supply all that we need to carry out the obedience. It's better to hear His "Well done, thou good and faithful servant," than to hear sheep telling on us. Let's not lose fish.

BEAM 7

WHY ME? WHY SO LONG?

GENESIS 41:1

Here is a love story that may make us wonder. Why was this innocent man forgotten by the butler after Joseph interpreted his dream and begged him to remember him when he got out of jail (Genesis 40:14)?

Why did two years go by without any release, parole, etc? I can see Joseph asking why. "Any word from the White House? You mean all those pardons were given out and I didn't get one? Why me, O Lord?"

These two years are the longest two years in the Bible. But there was a reason for it. Where would Joseph have been if he had been given a pardon? He may have gone back to his father's house. But then there were those brothers who hated him. Would they try it again, only this time make it permanent? He could have gone back, trusting the same Lord Who preserved him to protect him.

Or, he could have gone into Egypt, to get lost in the crowd. Why bother to go back where you are not wanted, by the brothers anyway? Then what would have happened when Pharaoh had his mysterious dream? The butler says "I do remember my faults this day" (Genesis 41:9). Not sins? What would he have said if Joseph had been released? "Oh, Pharaoh, I forgot to tell you about this young Hebrew. This man could interpret dreams like no one you ever heard. I am sorry that I didn't tell you this before."

Pharaoh most likely would hanged the butler's head like he hanged the chief baker's head.

It was a long two years for Joseph, an innocent man, suffering in a foreign country and accused of a crime he did not commit. But God had His purpose. God had Joseph right where Pharaoh could find him easily, in the jailhouse. Yes, right where he could lay his hands on Joseph. Much easier than sending out a search party all through Egypt to find this young foreigner.

And why? So Joseph could save many lives in Egypt and in the surrounding countries. So Joseph could save the very brothers that sold him into slavery. So Joseph could be exalted as the second in command throughout all of Egypt. So Joseph could be an Old Testament type of Christ who was sold by His brothers and later highly exalted. So Joseph could be married to a Gentile bride just as Jesus will be.

Yes, a love story of God's way to turn trials into triumphs. His experience is an Old Testament fulfillment of a New Testament Scripture that Paul gives us in Romans 8:28. When things like that happen to me I want to think that "***many*** things work together for good to them that love God." I might even think that ***"most*** things work together for good to them who love God." But all things?

But the Scripture states "***All*** things work together for good to them that love God" (Romans 8:28).

Do you mean "all," even this, is to be worked out for good? Do I love God? Can I trust His Word? I do wonder "Why me, Lord?" But can I trust His love? One day I will understand. Maybe it will be longer than two years, but some day I'll understand it all, bye and bye.

He loves Joseph, and me, and you, even though we may wonder "Why me, Lord?" In His good time we will know. "For now we see through a glass darkly, but then face to face" (1Corinthians 13:12). Those two years seemed like ages to Joseph while he was in jail. Later, he could look back on them and understand why it happened that way. He told his brothers, "As for you, ye thought evil against me, but God meant it unto good, to bring to pass, as it is this day, to save much people alive" (Genesis 50:20). So will we look back and understand. God loved Joseph in jail and loves us too while we say "Why, Lord?" He desires to do us good, in Christ, for His glory.

BEAM 8

GOD'S PULSE BETTER THAN PORK CHOPS

DANIEL 1:12

Daniel and his three friends were captive in a foreign land, Babylon. It was an honor to stand before the King, Nebuchadnezzar. Even though he was the one who killed your people and took you prisoner you were supposed to be honored to work in his palace, like one of his cabinet members. But you had to look good. No sad faces, no anemic looking people, and no skinny run down runts. You were to look healthy and happy like you enjoyed just being in his presence. Nehemiah heard the bad news about the walls of Jerusalem being broken down and the gates to the city being burned. He wept and was sad when he thought about it. He came into the presence of his king Artaxerxes. The king noticed it and Nehemiah was sore afraid (Nehemiah 2:2). You did not look sad in the presence of royalty, not in that day. NO! They were treated like gods.

To work in Nebuchadnezzar's administration you had to be healthy and wise and happy. But the problem was that the king wanted to feed these Jewish men unclean food, unclean according to the Law of Moses. Probably pork chops which were forbidden by the law. It could have been ham sandwiches. Daniel made up his mind that he would not defile himself with the king's meat, or wine. The three friends go along with him. Now the problem shifts to the man who was put in charge of feeding these four men, Melzar.

He is afraid. If these four men look skinny and weak and not healthy and happy, he will get in trouble with Nebuchadnezzar and it might be his head that comes off. Then he will really look sad and unhealthy. What can he do. God has brought Daniel into favor with Melzar, but friendship is not something to lose your head over. So Daniel makes a deal with Melzar. He says feed us pulse, that is beans or lentils, some vegetarian meals, perhaps soup made out of other seeds, but not pork chops. Daniel says he should give them ten days of this gruel, I mean, vegetarian soup and salad and then look them over. If they are not healthy and happy Melzar wins the contest. Then I don't know what Daniel would have done. But Daniel had great faith in his God. "Test us," he says. "Give us pulse, or tofu, and see what happens."

Ten days go by and it's inspection time. What do you know? Daniel and his three friends appear fairer and fatter in flesh than the children that ate the pork chops (Daniel 1:15). I do not believe they were overly fat, for they would not be all that healthy looking then. So now they can go to school and learn the Chaldean tongue and be servants around the palace. This seems like a little thing, but God has greater plans for Daniel later on, and also for the three Hebrew children.

What is the lesson here? Here were some men who determined in their hearts that they would not defile themselves. Yes, they stuck their necks out, but so be it. We are asked to be faithful to Him Who went to the cross for us. What does He promise? "If they have persecuted Me, they will also persecute you" (John 15:20). Paul, who knew a lot about persecution, writes "All that will live godly in Christ Jesus shall suffer persecution" (2 Timothy 3:12). If the world loves us, maybe it is because we are not living a godly life in Christ. Maybe we are not willing to take a stand like Daniel did. Maybe we would rather be polluted, or defiled, by this world's offerings than take a stand. We want to be liked.

Jesus also said, "Whosoever therefore shall be ashamed of ME and of MY words in this adulterous and sinful generation, of him also shall the Son of man be ashamed when He cometh in the glory of the Father with the holy angels" (Mark 8:38). How can we be ashamed of One Who loved the world so much He laid down His life for sinners so they could be saved and have eternal life? Let's be like Daniel, who determined in his heart to not defile himself. Pork chops are OK today for anyone who likes them. The spiritual lesson is to not be contaminated by the sinful world we must live in. Keep oneself clean. Don't be dirtied by what the world offers in food, or entertainment, or magazines, or books, or movies et al.

There is much that the world calls "entertainment" that is polluting to a believer.

"Pure religion and undefiled before God and the Father is this, To visit the fatherless and the widows in their affliction, and to keep himself unspotted from the world" (James 1:27). How about visiting those widows, instead of that movie?

BEAM 9

JONAH THE POUTING PROPHET 1–2

Jonah has been the subject of controversy for generations, even though there have been other cases of men being swallowed alive by fish or whales and living to tell about it. Unbelief does not want you to be told of such things. But first, take a good look at this man.

In the first chapter we find a PROTESTING PROPHET. God says "Go East young man," and Jonah goes West. He absolutely refused to go where God sent him. Why? Fear? Hardly. He offers himself as a sacrifice when he is on board the ship. Prejudice, not wanting to help those dirty Gentiles at Nineveh? But he is gracious toward those Gentile sailors. Jealousy? His reputation as a prophet might be soiled if what he said was not fulfilled. Hardly, from the story. He tells us later why he did it. He knew God was a gracious God and a forgiving God who would spare Nineveh, if it repented. Wow! Angry because God is gracious. He did not want Nineveh spared. Why? He knew Nineveh was a rising world power and was already making forays into the land of Israel, perhaps into Jonah's own neighborhood.

Assyria was noted for its cruelty. They would pull tongues out from men's mouths. Men were skinned alive inch by inch and their skins stretched on city walls. Amos tells us "Surely the Lord will do nothing, but He revealeth His secret unto His servants the prophets" (Amos 3:7). So why should Jonah be a foreign missionary and go to these wicked people? Because God said so.

God wanted Jonah in Nineveh. God said go East. Jonah went West. So God prepares a great storm that frightens the veteran sailors. They never saw such a storm. They believe something must have made the gods angry. Jonah? He's asleep below deck. His conscience did not bother him a bit. So they wake him up to call on his God, whoever he might be. The storm rages on, so they cast lots to find out who did it. Who was the sinner that did this evil deed that has made the gods angry? Jonah wins the lottery.

He confesses that it was all his fault and he offers the solution. "Cast me into the drink," he says. The heathen sailors pray to the God of Jonah to not hold it against them and they throw Jonah overboard. The sea immediately calms down and these heathen sailors are converted to the God of Jonah. Even in his disobedience God uses him to reach others. What a gracious God!

In Chapter two we have the PRAYING PROPHET. Inside the fish Jonah prays. But he says he is praying from the "belly of hell" (2:2). Which brings up the question, did Jonah die? It sure looks like it. In the Old Testament we have books that teach about God's redemption (Ruth), God's sovereignty (Esther), God's deliverance (Exodus). Where is one that teaches the resurrection? 1 Corinthians 15:3 states that Christ was raised the third day "according to the Scriptures." Which Scriptures? In Matthew 12:39–40 we are told that the only sign given to the Scribes and Pharisees was the prophet Jonah. "For as Jonas was three days and three nights in the whale's belly, so shall the Son of man be three days and three nights in the heart of the earth." It certainly looks like Jonah is an Old Testament picture of the resurrection.

So God hears this disobedient prophet when he prays. "And the Lord spake to the fish," we read. "and it vomited out Jonah upon dry land" (2:10). I guess we could say that the whale said "Jonah you make me sick." So here we go again. God says "Go East, young man." This time Jonah goes East. He did not want to spend another night in "Whale Inn." He is a stubborn prophet. But God is a gracious God. He has a message for Nineveh and he wants Jonah to deliver it. It is gracious of God to put up with this prophet, but we read in chapter three that He gives Jonah a second chance. "The word of the Lord came unto Jonah the second time, saying arise, go unto Nineveh" (3:1–2). That is another story. That time it is the preaching prophet. But what a wonderful God we have. He gives a second chance, a third chance, a fourth chance. But His patience runs out. Let's not count on an endless number of chances. Turn to Him now.

BEAM 10

JONAH THE POUTING PROPHET 3–4

Chapter three–the PREACHING PROPHET. Jonah decides that Nineveh is better than the Whale Inn so the prophet goes East as God told him to. He may have looked somewhat different now. Dr. Rimmer, President of the Research Science Bureau of Los Angeles, tells about a sailor who fell overboard in the English Channel. He was swallowed by a shark. Forty eight hours later the same shark was captured and cut open. They found the sailor alive and unconscious. He was rushed to a hospital but was found to be suffering from shock. He was OK, except he lost his hair and had patches of yellowish brown skin over his entire body. He was on exhibit in London as the Jonah of the Twentieth Century. Of course the skeptics do not want you to know that. Jonah may have looked somewhat ghostly also. Whether or not, he came to Nineveh and he had a ready audience. Remember the crew had to go back to port because they threw their cargo overboard. What a message they had to tell about their passenger, Jonah. And here is that same Jonah with a message from the God of Israel.

This disobedient prophet preached one sermon over and over again. One message, "40 days and Nineveh shall be overthrown." The message hit home. The people believed God and repented. The king laid aside his robes and proclaimed a fast for all, both men and animals, and no water was to be drunk either. They turned from their sins and I am sure they prayed. They were wondering if God would turn from His judgment and spare the city. And God saw their repentance and did turn from His anger. This does not mean that God changes His mind about sin. It is just that God cannot stand to allow sin to go unpunished or punish some sinner who has turned from his sin. God is still unchanging. If God destroyed Nineveh after the people turned away from their sins He would be a different God. So God spared Nineveh. Now He had to deal with His prophet

Chapter four–the POUTING PROPHET. Jonah had the greatest revival in history. The whole city, thousands and thousands of people, believed his message and turned from their sins. This was greater than any evangelist in history. But was Jonah happy? No indeed. "It displeased Jonah exceedingly, and he was very angry" (4:1). He still did not want Nineveh spared. So he sits down outside the city in a booth and waits for the fire to come down. What a man! After his preaching has turned a city around, he still wants to see if God will send down fire like He did on Sodom and Gomorrah. But God is gracious. He says later that He has 120 thousand children in the city, "persons that cannot discern between their right hand and their left" (4:11). What can He do to get Jonah to see that?

Jonah says he "knew that thou art a gracious God, and merciful, slow to anger" (4:2). So God prepares something else, just for Jonah. He prepared a storm in the first chapter. He prepared a fish for Jonah. Now He prepares a gourd to grow up and give shade for Jonah's head. He was probably bald from that whale's belly so it felt so good out there in the hot sun. After Jonah gets some joy and pleasure from the shade of this gourd, God prepares a worm. Yes, the Almighty God of creation is God of His universe and God of little things, like a worm. The worm kills the gourd and there goes Jonah's shade. Jonah wishes to die. Now God speaks again to Jonah. He tells Jonah that he had nothing to do with growing that gourd. It came up in a night and perished in a night. But God had everything to do with the creation of man, including these men, women, and children of Nineveh.

If Jonah could have pity on that gourd why cannot God have pity on His creation? God is gracious and kind and tender hearted and merciful. He asks us to repent, to turn from our wicked ways as He did Nineveh. Did Jonah learn his lesson? I believe so. He wrote the book. It is not easy to tell the world how bitter you were and how you pouted because someone else was saved from their sins. Jonah saw the light. Nineveh saw the light too. Have we seen the light? We cannot go on in our sins. We must give an account for our deeds. He is gracious and merciful to all who turn to Him. Even a Jonah needs His mercy. So does John Doe and Jane Doe, or Smith, or whatever my name is. Praise God for His mercy.

BEAM 11

WHAT DO YOU WANT?
IF YOU COULD HAVE ANYTHING YOU ASKED FOR
1 KINGS 3:5

Well what would you say? Here we read that God comes to Solomon and gives him a free choice. It's like the proverbial blank check we hear so much about. God says "Ask what I shall give thee." What a gracious offer on God's part. Whatever it is, no restriction, money, fame, honor, whatever, just ask Me. Not many people have this opportunity. We read about the genie in the bottle and having three wishes, but that is a fairy tale. This is the real thing.

So what would you choose? Perhaps health? What would come first? The world puts its whole energy in getting fame and fortune. Not very enjoyable if you are not healthy. Solomon makes a wise choice. He chooses wisdom. He says he is not able to judge these people (of Israel). "I am but a little child. Give me wisdom" (1 Kings 3:7–9). A good choice. The request pleased the Lord. He says that Solomon did not ask for long life, a good choice, nor riches, another good choice, but you can't take it with you as they say. Neither did he ask for the life of his enemies, something that Hitler would have liked. He asked for wisdom to rule over God's people.

So God gave him an understanding heart, a heart of wisdom. So much wisdom that God said there was never anyone as wise before Solomon, neither should there ever be anyone as wise after Solomon (1 Kings 3:12). No, not even the Apostle Paul would be as wise. No Nostradamus or anyone else would have such wisdom. Einstein may have been a genius but never would there be one as wise as Solomon.

And God was gracious also in giving Solomon those things that he did not ask for, the things that men usually ask for. God says in verse 13 "I have given thee that which thou hast not asked, both riches, and honour: so that there shall not be any among the kings like unto thee all thy days." Most people have heard something about the wisdom of Solomon. Many are also aware of all the riches, the gold and silver that he heaped up. We read that silver became as stones (1 Kings

10:27). In other words, gold and silver became so plentiful they were like dirt. A great choice, wisdom.

But was it the best choice? Yes, God was pleased with that choice, but was it the best? We read that Solomon loved many strange women, that is foreigners, women who were not of Israel and did not serve the God of Israel (1 Kings 11:1). He played politics and married the daughters of foreign kings to keep the peace. He had 700 wives and 300 concubines (1 Kings 11:3). He built altars for them, which God commanded not to build. He built high places and worshiped these idols of his wives. All to keep peace? No, wisdom did not keep him from going astray from God. There were three things that God said a king of Israel should not do. They were not to heap up gold, not to gather lots of horses, not to multiply wives. Solomon did all three. Wisdom does not keep one from going astray.

It would have been much better if Solomon had made another choice. What would that be? Why not ask God to help me be an obedient person, good in His sight, not what the world calls "good." Far better for us if we can be a truly obedient person and love God throughout our lives. This we cannot do by ourselves, but God gave Solomon a blank check. Ask of Me and I will grant it. I wonder if Solomon regretted his choice later in life? I wonder. Maybe we can learn a little from Solomon. May this be our prayer and desire, to be a good person always seeking to do God's will and to reflect God and represent Him here on earth. I wonder! Help me, Lord, to be obedient and love You Who first loved me.

"The fear of the Lord is the beginning of wisdom; and the knowledge of the holy is understanding" (Proverbs 9:10).

BEAM 12

WHAT SHALL I DO WITH JESUS? AND YOUR ANSWER?

MATTHEW 27:22

This is the question that without a doubt is the most important question in life. It is what life is all about. Even those who do not have any kind of belief in this Jesus, Who is called the Messiah, still have to sign their documents with an AD or, if they are writing a history, a BC. Pilate asked "What shall I do then with Jesus which is called Christ?" ***We*** must answer this question also. Who is He? And depending on Who He is in our minds and lives, will determine what we do with Him.

Pilate tried to excuse himself from the whole affair. He did not have enough backbone to set Jesus free.

When they said crucify Him, Pilate said "Why, what evil hath He done?" (27:23). He had no evidence of wrong doing but he did not set Him free. So what does this weakling do? He asks for some water and then in Roman style washes his hands. This is supposed to wash away any guilt. Then he says "I am innocent of the blood of this just person: see ye to it" (27:24). How about that. He says Jesus is a just person but he still does not set Him free.

If I remember my Shakespeare correctly it was Lady Macbeth who said "All the perfumes of Arabia cannot sweeten this little hand." Not one bit. She took part in a murder. Perfume does not take away the guilt. And Pilate? He said he was washing his hands, he was not guilty of any wrongdoing concerning this one Jesus, called the Messiah. How about that! Not guilty, I am clean, I have washed my hands. Aha! Nearly 2000 years later the church, at least in some places, says the Apostles' Creed. And after nearly 2000 years we say "He (that is Jesus) suffered under Pontius Pilate." Two thousands years have not cleansed Pilate from the guilt he bears.

But we also must answer the question. What shall I do with Jesus, Who is called Christ, that is Messiah?

I believe it would be fitting to call Him Messiah rather than Christ. They mean the same thing in the Scripture but so many think of Jesus as His first name and Christ as His last name. Messiah means "anointed one" in the Hebrew, the same as Christos, the Greek word, means "anointed one" in the New Testament. What shall I do with Him? If I try to avoid the question, as Pilate did, I will never rid my hands and heart from the stain, just as Pilate never did either. One thing is certain. This one Person changed the world forever. Even if one does not believe in Him as Savior we must account for His coming into the world, dying by being crucified, and being raised from the dead. Even if we do not believe He rose from the dead, we have to account for the multitudes who saw Him and for all the multitudes that gave their lives for Him and swore that they had seen His resurrection body.

Paul says this was not some vision seen by some children. This was not a dream or some other kind of hoax. He says that there was a time when more than 500 people at one time saw His resurrection body and most of those were still alive when Paul wrote about it in 1 Corinthians 15:6. I know of no apostle, or evangelist, or deacon, who got rich preaching the Word and telling the world about the risen Messiah. Most of them died horrible deaths for His sake. They knew He had risen from the dead.

And how do you account for the church, the true church, which preaches His word and tells the Good News? How do you account for the millions of lives that are changed because they have believed and have received a new birth? And what are WE doing with this Jesus Who is called Messiah? What WE do with Him now will determine what HE will do with US later. What shall I do with Jesus? And you? What are you doing with Him? We have to answer this question some time. No better time than now!

"But put ye on the Lord Jesus Christ, and make no provision for the flesh, to fulfill the lusts thereof" (Romans 13:14).

BEAM 13

RUTH CHOOSING

CHAPTER 1

The first chapter of the book of Ruth tells us the story of a backsliding family from Bethlehem that went off to the land of Moab, because the grass looked greener over there. This was contrary to the Law of Moses. The nation of Israel was joined to the land of Israel that was once the land of the Canaanites. This was the easy road to take. When things got tough they left. Later, when they return, their friends are still alive in Bethlehem, so God provided a way for them to make it through the famine.

So the woman, Naomi, and her husband and two sons go east to Moab. The father was Elimelech, which means "My God is King." If God is King He should be king when there is a drought or famine or any other kind of trouble. These are tests for us to learn to trust Him. Now Elimelech dies in Moab. So instead of going home, Naomi does something else that was forbidden under the Law. She allows her sons to marry heathen girls, Oprah, oops, Orpah and Ruth. This was strictly forbidden by the Law of Moses "An Ammonite or Moabite shall not enter into the congregation of the Lord; even to their tenth generation shall they not enter into the congregation of the Lord for ever" (Deuteronomy 23:3). The sons' names are Mahlon and Chilion which mean "sickly" and "pining." I have once in my life met a man who was named "Mahlon." I was surprised when I learned his name. Maybe it sounded good to his parents but I wonder if they knew what the name meant? I don't believe they did. I think of these two boys as a couple of sick twins We are not surprised to learn that they did not live long over in Moab. There are now three graves in Moab filled by this family.

Now Naomi thinks it is time to go back where she came from and where she should have stayed. But what shall she do with these daughters in law? To take them back would declare to her neighbors that they had been a prodigal family. We have a prodigal son in the New Testament. Here is the prodigal family of the Old Testament. She tries to persuade them to stay in Moab. She is actually asking them to stay with their heathen gods of Moab (verse 15). Orpah says OK, kisses her mother-in-law and goes back to her people and her gods (verse 15). Ruth says "No way." Ruth has fallen in love with the God of Naomi, even though Naomi has left His appointed land, Israel.

Verse 16 might sound like a romantic episode of a mother-in-law evangelizing her daughter-in-law. But Naomi knows she will be the talk of the town if she returns to Bethlehem with a heathen Moabite daughter-in-law. But Ruth insists on going with Naomi. When they come into Bethlehem she is the talk of the town. The "they" in verse 19 is feminine, so I can see the women hanging up their clothes to dry and eyeing this woman coming to town with an obvious heathen (you could tell by her clothes). I can hear them saying, "Who is that? Is that Naomi? My how she has aged. And who is that with her? Where are her husband and sons? Is that really Naomi?"

Now Naomi gets bitter, and says don't call me Naomi (which means "pleasant"), but call me "mara " (which means "bitter"). Then she starts blaming God for her trouble. She says "I went out full, and the Lord hath brought me home again empty" (verse 21). Yes, but He brought you home, Naomi. That is where you belong.

That's the way. God did not drive her out. She went out on her own. God did bring her back, but He had to empty her to do it. Would the prodigal son ever come back home if he had prospered over in that far off land? He had to lose everything and come down to where he was ready to eat pig's food before he "came to himself." So with Naomi. God wanted her back, full or empty. Since she would not come back full, He had to bring her back empty. But He brought her back.

This wonderful little book has everything in it. This first chapter gives us a picture of what we have in this world. There are three woman who represent mankind. Orpah represents the person who hears the Gospel and says "No thanks. I like it where I am. Maybe later. I have plenty of time. I am still young yet. No hurry. All of my friends are here too. I think I'll stay."

Naomi represents what some would call the backslidden saint. One who is a believer but is out of the will of God. She cannot be in fellowship with Him while in the land of Moab. She wants the easy life, no trials, no famine. And she does not want anyone to know what she has been up to. There are some saints that have said, in deeds if not words, "I want to live my own life." That is the person who has not yet given it all to the Master.

Then there is Ruth. She represents the one who has heard the wonderful message about a Redeemer, Who went to the cross to pay for the sins of others. The One who says He is the only Door, the only Way, the only Truth. She falls in love with this One and says "Don't try to persuade me otherwise. Don't entreat me to go back to my old life. I am going on with you to this new life. I have fallen in love with the God of Israel."

What a beautiful story. Which of these three women best describes you? And me? Wait till you see what happened after she made this decision. That's the word, decision. We must make a decision.

"Choose you this day whom ye will serve, . . . but as for me and my house, we will serve the Lord" (Joshua 24:15). There is no better choice!

BEAM 14

RUTH LABORING

CHAPTER 2

When one is given a new life, as Ruth was given, the next thing you read about is that she works. This is the norm for the saint. We labor for the Master from the dawn to setting sun. Oops! From dawn to dawn. Ruth and Naomi are poor. They have no income. Their house and land is in hock. How can they make it? Naomi has told Ruth enough about the Law of Moses so she desires to go into the fields and labor by gleaning. As a newcomer to a farm I had to learn what gleaning was. I did not know what those cows were eating out in a field that was already harvested. The corn had been cut. What were they doing out there? Even the finest harvesting machine by Deere and Co., or some other company, left some grain on the ground. Picking up the little bits that were left behind was gleaning.

In the Law of Moses there was provision for the widows, the stranger, and the fatherless. When an Israelite harvested his grain he was not to go back and pick up the few stalks that he left behind. When the grapes were harvested, he did not go back over the vines a second time and pick more grapes. The same was done with his olive tree. All the olives did not ripen at the same time, nor did all the grapes. This was left for the widows, the orphans, the foreigners. This was God's welfare program. He did not simply pour out an abundance like the manna of old. He did not send a welfare check to them either. He expected them to work. He provided for them, but they had to work for it. (Deuteronomy 24:19–22). Even in the New Testament Paul says "If any would not work, neither should he eat" (2 Thessalonians 3:10).

Naomi tells Ruth of a relative, Boaz, a mighty man of wealth. She is to go into his fields and glean. Glean she does. Boaz comes out to see the harvest and it is love at first sight. "Who is this?" he asks. She is the Moabitish damsel that came back with Naomi. You can see love working already. Boaz tells Ruth to not work in any other field but his. He tells her he will protect her and tells her to come into the house at mealtime and eat. He even gives her some parched corn. Isn't love grand? This again is an Old Testament picture of our New Testament Boaz. Our Boaz, Jesus, feeds, protects and loves us. He is a mighty man of wealth. Everything that the Father has is given to the Son. He shelters us, He protects us, He gives us rest and feeds us with the bread of life. He is the true manna which came down from heaven.

Ruth can scarcely believe her ears that this wealthy and powerful man would care to give aid to a foreigner, a Moabite. But he does more. After lunch, when Ruth goes back into the field to continue gleaning, Boaz tells his crew to let her glean even among the sheaves, which was not something the Law of Moses said a stranger could do. Boaz says let her do it and reproach her not. Then he adds something that is really a beautiful picture of what the Lord Jesus does for His saints. He says "Let fall also some of the handfuls of purpose for her" (Ruth 2:16). This explains just how it is that under trying circumstances, when the saints may wonder why this is happening to them, suddenly blessings unforeseen come. That sudden turn of events, that person or thing or happening that makes the saints wonder how it could be, may be explained as our Great Boaz, Jesus, letting fall some handfuls of blessings on purpose. Did you ever receive some unexpected blessing, some unexpected gifts of grace? Perhaps He was letting some handfuls of purpose fall for you. It has happened to me.

What a beautiful story. We are "Saved by grace through faith." But we are then told that "we are His workmanship created in Christ Jesus unto good works, which God hath before ordained that we should walk in them" (Ephesians 2:8–10). Let us glean, let us work, for the night is coming when no man can work. "The harvest is truly plenteous, but the labourers are few" (Matthew 9:37). After work comes rest. That is what we see in the next thrilling episode of Ruth.

BEAM 15

RUTH RESTING

CHAPTER 3

The harvest season is over. No more gleaning for Ruth. What is she to do? How will they live? Naomi knows the law of the kinsman-redeemer. She says, "Shall I not seek rest for thee" (3:1). My how she has changed. In chapter one she said "the Lord grant you that ye may find rest"(1:9). Now she says she will seek rest for Ruth. This is Naomi's council. She then tells Ruth to get herself all cleaned up. Put away her garments of mourning for her dead husband and get dressed up because you are going to propose. Sprinkle on some "Evening in Moab." Fix up you hair. You're going courting tonight.

Under the Law of Moses there was a provision for certain widows, those who lost a husband and had no children. The land was tied to the family and if a son died without some heirs, the family name would be lost, along with the family farm. The word for this kinsman-redeemer was "Goel." He was to redeem his brother's property, if the poorer brother had to mortgage his property. He could buy back his property and he was also to avenge his brother's blood, if his brother had been killed. He did not have to be a brother from the same father, but a near relative. The closest relative had first choice. Leviticus 25:47–49, Deuteronomy 25:5–10; 19:5–6, 11, 12.

He was also able to take his dead relative's wife and marry her to raise up children for his brother's name. No, God did not teach polygamy. This law was only under certain conditions and for a definite purpose. It was to keep his brother's name alive and his property in the brother's family by having children in his brother's name. But he was not required to do this. *This was a voluntary act.*

Boaz is a near kinsman. Naomi tells Ruth to get dressed and go down to the threshing floor that night and after all the celebrating is over place herself at Boaz's feet. This was her way of saying she was a widow, which Boaz already knew, and that she would like him to fulfill his duties and marry her. It would be embarrassing if Boaz refused. Under the Law that was given by Moses, the widow was to ask for the man's shoe as proof that he turned her down, and then she was to spit in his face. Perhaps this was no longer being done in Ruth's day. But this way, just in case he turned her down, nobody would know about it.

Boaz is thrilled at the idea. He was in love with Ruth from the first time he saw her but perhaps he thought he was a little too old for her, and there was another kinsman who was even nearer. That one had first choice. So he tells Ruth to wait until the next day. He will talk to this brother about it and see what he says. Then he sends her home loaded with more corn. Six measures. Why not seven, that complete or perfect number? He, himself, will be number seven.

She goes home to Naomi and Naomi wants to know how it went. In 3:16 she asks who Ruth is. It is not that she didn't recognize her in the dark. She wants to know if she is engaged to be Mrs. Boaz. Then she says sit still, my daughter, Boaz will not rest until he has finished the matter (3:18).

This is another beautiful picture of the cross in the Old Testament. Boaz is that mighty wealthy man of power who is a picture of the Lord Jesus, the only begotten Son, Who has all things given to Him by the Father. He is our near kinsman, a true man born of a woman, and true God from eternity. He alone can pay the price and buy us unto Himself. He loved sinners so much that He laid down His life for them to buy them back from sin. He went to the cross to purchase His bride. Jehovah is married to Israel (Jeremiah 3:14) while the church is called the bride of Christ, engaged now but to be married later (2 Corinthians 11:2). He is our Boaz, our kinsman-redeemer. He will not rest until He has finished the transaction. What He starts, He will finish. What a love this is. "Faithful is He that calleth you, Who also will do it" (1 Thessalonians 5:24).

BEAM 16

RUTH MARRYING

CHAPTER 4

This little book is so full of New Testament teachings. What is the order of our life and growth? It is right here. First we make the decision to receive the Savior God has provided for us. Then we work for Him. We cannot work until we are made alive so this work is not for salvation but for service to Him, Who gave all for us. After we labor from the dawn till setting sun we then rest. Oops! There I go again. From dawn to dawn. Now our labor is over and wc wait for the promised reward like Ruth did. Then comes the promised wedding of the bride, the church. But back to the story of Ruth.

Boaz wants to marry the girl he fell in love with. He wants to redeem her and her husband's property. Aaah, but there is a nearer kinsman who gets first choice. Boaz calls the city council together. The gate was the courthouse in those cities and he calls ten elders to hear his case. This is a legal matter. After he gets them all seated he tells the kinsman of the land that was Elimelech's and is now in hock. Does this unnamed kinsman want to redeem it? Mr. Unnamed says yes, he will redeem it. This word "redeem" is to buy back by paying the price. This is how the Lord Jesus redeemed us, by paying the price. So far, so bad for Boaz. But Boaz is not stupid. He holds off until the last to tell Unnamed that when he buys the land back he also gets this Moabite woman, Ruth (4:5). Unnamed does not want to do this. So Boaz gets just what he wanted all along. Unnamed then takes off his shoe (4:8) and this serves as a witness to the court that he has given up his rights to the land of Elimelech, and Ruth the foreigner. Nothing is said about spitting in his face. Maybe the custom stopped or Ruth did not want to do it. Ugh!

What do we learn about the kinsman redeemer, or Goel? There are several things in this book that relate to the New Testament teaching of redemption.

In order to redeem a land or person the redeemer had to have THE RIGHT TO DO IT. Some stranger could not do it even if he were made of gold. Jesus had the right because He was the God-man. He was a near kinsman being fully man as well as fully God.

Secondly, the redeemer had to have THE ABILITY TO REDEEM IT. Even if he were a true brother, but broke, he could not get his brother out of hock. Jesus had the power to redeem for He alone had the sinlessness that was required to redeem sinners. He who knew no sin became sin for us that we might have His righteousness imputed to us (2 Corinthians 5:21).

Lastly, the redeemer HAD TO BE WILLING TO REDEEM IT. Mr. Unnamed in this story did not want to do it. Boaz was ready and willing to do it. Jesus not only had the right to claim us, and the power to do so, but He wanted to do so. He said, concerning His life, "That no man taketh it from Me, but I lay it down of Myself" (John 10:18). He willingly laid down His life for us. He wanted to do this. What a beautiful story.

This book tells us why Jesus was born in Bethlehem. It tells us that Boaz became the great-grandfather of David. Bethlehem was David's city. That is where Joseph and Mary had to go to pay there taxes.

Perhaps Mr. Unnamed stands for the Law which shuts out sinners while Boaz stands for grace which opens the door to let sinners come in. Whether or not, this story tells how a Moabite, who is shut out by the Law, who could never, ever come into the congregation of Israel, is brought in by grace. What the Law could not do, grace did. We also, who are shut out because of our sins, for ever and ever, are now by His blood brought in to live with Him, for ever and ever. What a love story! Is He your Boaz? He is in love with us. He wants to redeem us. "Let every thing that hath breath praise the Lord" (Psalm 150:6).

BEAM 17

IN THE FULNESS OF TIME

GALATIANS 4:4

Did you ever wonder why He was born when He was born? We are told that the calculators of the calendar made some mistakes. One of them was they forgot about the year Zero. They made up a BC and they followed it with an AD but forgot about Zero. From 1 BC to AD 1 would be two years, mathematically speaking. There should be a zero in there somewhere. Then you would get one year from 1 BC to 0 and another from 0 to AD 1. Other errors were made about the reign of Caesar Augustus the emperor of the Roman Empire and Cyrenius the governor of Syria, so we end up with Jesus being born around (?) 4 BC. That might sound rather weird for Him to be born four years before Christ, that is, BC.

Be that as it may, we can do nothing about it now. But why was He born at that time, or during that era?

Galatians 4:4 says that it was when the "fulness of time" came that God sent forth His Son. Why at this time? What was so different about this time that it could be called "full?" What difference would it have made if Jesus had been born 600 years sooner, or 800 years later? Why at this time?

There are three nations that must be considered. One is the nation of Israel and the other two are the two empires that came into existence, and what they contributed. Israel had come back from its 70 years captivity with a new thing that had developed while they were captive in Babylon. They had synagogues now where they gathered to hear the Word read. They also had some new religious parties. There were Sadducees. These could be classified as the Modernist Movement. They did not believe in the hereafter, in spirits, or resurrection. "For the Sadducees say that there is no resurrection, neither angel, nor spirit" (Acts 23:8). Then there were the Pharisees. These could be classified as the Legalists. They not only insisted that the Law of Moses be kept but they added their own rules and "traditions" and made them superior to the Law of God. They prepared the nation, which sat in darkness, for the coming Light of the World. Religion was a failure. Israel needed a Savior and so did mankind.

But what about the Greek empire? It was not ruling when Jesus came, but it had a great deal to do with how the Gospel was spread. When Alexander the Great conquered the world, he was quite lenient with those he conquered. He allowed them much freedom in their law, and allowed them freedom in their worship. One thing he was not tolerant with was the language. They had to learn Greek. This was the "common language" or the koine, and it was the official language of the empire. Everyone had to learn Greek and be able to speak Greek even if they knew four other languages. Greek was the common tongue. It was the language used to give us the New Testament. Yes, the Greeks have a word for it. Greek best describes God's Word to us. Yes, it's all Greek to me, too!

The Romans came along after the Greeks and they added something to make the time "full." They were master builders. They learned the secret of laying under-water cement. There are buildings still standing in Rome and other places that they built over 2000 years ago. But their roads were masterfully constructed. There are some of them still in use today. What does all this have to do with the Gospel? Just think of the disciples, like Paul, or Peter, or Barnabas, trying to get the message of the Gospel out to the world. What problems there would be if they had to have an interpreter to go along for every new nation they entered?

Think of the problems if they had to have passports, or visas, before they could enter another nation, or perhaps be shut out from entering another nation. And think how convenient for those travelers who walked from one end of the empire to another to have roads built for them. Yes, the Romans built them so they could move their armies from one end of the empire to another in case there was a rebellion. But God was using the Roman road building crews to build for Paul and Silas, so they could go on foot from one end of the empire to another carrying the Gospel message. "The Greeks have a word for it." Yes, and wherever they went they would be understood. And the Romans had a road for it. This was the fullness of time when it was just right for the Savior to be born so that the world could hear the "good news" of salvation.

Now the Gospel message can be broadcast all around the world and even the speakers can be seen on TV anywhere in the world. Have you heard the message? We have no excuse now. Tune in and hear. Hear and live–for ever, with no sin and no condemnation. He paid it all for us. What a gracious God!

BEAM 18

"NOT SO, LORD"

ACTS 10:14

What a contradiction this is! We may say "Not so" and we may say "Lord" but how can we put them together and say "Not so, Lord?" But the Apostle Peter is always a teaching character to all of us. We may not say it the way Peter did but we may also say in our acts, if not in our words. If Jesus is our Lord, then we cannot say "No" to Him when He asks us to do something. Understanding what the Lord is trying to say to us is another matter. We all need to pray for wisdom when it comes to guidance.

Peter was a Spirit-filled Apostle now, not like he was before Pentecost. He preached the first sermon about the resurrected Jesus and brought thousands to the Lord, "about three thousands souls" (Acts 2:41).

But those of us who are Gentiles can hardly fathom the great change that was about to take place. We go to church and hear the sermons and go home and try to live by the Word of God, little aware of the great gulf that once divided us from Israel.

Paul tells us that in times past when we were Gentiles that we "were without Christ" and "having no hope" and "without God in the world" (Ephesians 2:12). Of course many Gentiles then and now would not believe that they were without God in this world. Isaiah tells us how foolish it is for man to cut down a tree and burn part of it to be warm, burn part of it to bake his bread, and then he uses part of it to make a god. He falls down and worships this piece of a tree that he just cut down (Isaiah 44:14–17). But man is willing to worship the creature instead of the Creator if he will not accept God's Light, the Lord Jesus.

So there was this great gulf separating the Jew from the Gentiles. Peter is a new born Christian, although they were not called that yet. He was a Jew who believed the Messiah had come in the person of Jesus. However, Peter still had the teaching of the Law of Moses in him which was taught from childhood.

Gentiles were unclean and unholy and were called dogs and

Goim. You did not enter their homes and you did not eat with them. They were unclean, You would not eat in the home of a leper. God had to take some stringent steps to get Peter to see all of those things were past now, and the Gospel was to go to all people of every nation, tribe, and tongue.

So Peter has a vision. He went up on the housetop to pray and got hungry and then fell asleep. He is human. Then God gives him this vision of a great sheet with all kinds of animals in it, unclean as well as clean. Peter is hungry. God says to Peter "Kill and eat" (Acts 10:13). That is when we hear this nonsense of non sequitur from Peter. "Not so, Lord." And besides this, the Lord had to repeat this same vision two more times. After three times hearing the Lord say "What God hath cleansed, that call not thou common" (Acts 10:15), Peter saw the light. When the messengers from Cornelius' Gentile household arrived, Peter was now ready to preach, teach, eat, or do anything else with the Gentiles. He got the point.

Have we? We call Him Lord. We go to church. We pray to Him, and in His name. Do we sometimes do what Peter did? Do we say to Him, Who died for us, "No, Lord?" We may join the church and sing in the choir but above all else the Lord wants us to do what He says. It should be "Yes, Lord, if that is what You want." Or we may say "No" but not in the same sentence as "Lord," because then He is not our LORD. What we should say, if we have doubts about what He is trying to tell us, is "Whatever You want me to do, Lord." We should be ready to go where He sends us and say what He tells us and do what He asks us. "Not so, Lord," makes no sense at all. We can speak better English than that. "Yes Lord" is the proper answer from His followers. Is He our Lord? OK. Then say "Yes Lord."

"Great is the Lord, and greatly to be praised; and His greatness is unsearchable" (Psalm 145:3).

BEAM 19

A TRUE LOVE STORY

MATTHEW 1:19

There has been much controversy about the birth of Jesus. This comes from the unbelievers and theologians who can always find something in the Scriptures to have doubts about. They will discuss the word "virgin" and declare it means a young woman or maiden in Isaiah 7:14 They say the word "almah" does not mean virgin but a young woman. The translators of the Old Testament from the Hebrew into the Greek thought otherwise and translated the word "parthenos" which means virgin in the Greek. These theologians can sure mess up something that is so clear to the rest of us "unlearned." Look at the passage in Isaiah. God tells Ahaz the king of Judah to ask for a sign, that is, a miracle. He says go ahead and think of a hard one for Me.

"Ask thee a sign of the Lord thy God; ask it either in the depth or in the height above" (Isaiah 7:11). Now would a young woman giving birth to a child be any kind of a miracle? Of course not. So God gives Ahaz a sign, a miracle. A virgin shall give birth to a child. Besides this, you have the New Testament stating it was a fulfillment of what Isaiah spoke. "Now all this was done, that it might be fulfilled which was spoken of the Lord by the prophet saying, Behold a virgin shall bring forth a son and shall call his name Emmanuel, which being interpreted is God with us" (Matthew 1:22–23).

One party to this whole fulfillment is sometimes overlooked. That one is the husband. Joseph loved Mary. Joseph thought that somehow Mary had been unfaithful to the vows they had made. That would have been the proposal, as we call it today. Under Jewish custom, the marriage was in three parts. The first was the engagement or betrothal. This was a legal and binding act. It was usually done by the parents of the groom. Genesis 24 is a beautiful example of how Abraham sent a servant to get a bride for his son Isaac. After the proposal, there was a wedding ceremony. This is where the families of the betrothed celebrate the union of the couple. The bride is veiled and the couple is brought to the wedding chamber. This is where Laban, Rachel's father, switched women on Jacob and gave him Leah instead of Rachel, for whom he had worked seven years (Genesis 29:23). What a father-in-law! No wonder they did not get along. Then there is the final or physical union of the two. Then the wedding feast begins and may last for weeks.

Much more can be said about the wedding ceremonies in the Near East. But we want to look at this man Joseph. He was in love with Mary. He could not understand it because he was sure she loved him. How could this thing happen? How could she be pregnant? It was permissible to divorce a woman who had been unfaithful. But Joseph loved Mary. What a love this was. He loved her so much that he did not want to make their divorce public. And divorce it was, since they were legally bound in marriage after the betrothal. If she had been unfaithful, under the Law of Moses, she could have been stoned to death (Deuteronomy 22:20–21). But Joseph loved Mary. He decides to divorce her in private. What love! But an angel of the Lord brings the message from God that Joseph should take Mary to wife because "that which is conceived in her is of the Holy Ghost" (Matthew 1:20). Joseph loved Mary. I am sure he positively leaped for joy when he heard the news. He now knew that it was a virgin birth. And Mary was his loving and faithful wife.

Yes, Jesus came into this world a different way. He could not come through Adam's family for Adam's children are sinners. He came a sinless Son of God, conceived by the Holy Spirit. Mary provided the body. Jesus came a sinless savior to exchange His righteousness for the sinner's sins. He made the exchange. But we must make an exchange too. "And by Him all that believe are justified from all things, from which ye could not be justified by the Law of Moses" (Acts 13:39). We must believe on Him! Believe and receive. He is The Life. We receive eternal life when we receive Him.

BEAM 20

GIVE ME THIS MOUNTAIN

JOSHUA 14:12

It was 7 years after the conquest of the land began. Much land remained to be possessed (Joshua 13:1). But Joshua was old and it was to be divided by lot so that each tribe could finish the job of conquest. Now the two oldest men in the nation meet. They are at least twenty years older than any others (Numbers 14:29). Before the lots are to fall, Caleb makes a request that is special. It is special because Caleb was one of the two spies sent out by Moses to spy the land and he and Joshua were the two who gave a good report; that Israel could take the land. They were outvoted by the other spies so Israel disbelieved God and for punishment they were to wander in the wilderness for 38 years.

It was when they spied out the land that Caleb saw the place he wanted, Hebron. Moses swore on that day the Caleb should have "the land that thy feet have trodden shall be thine inheritance, and thy children's for ever, because thou hast wholly followed the Lord my God" (Joshua 14:9). That did not mean the people of Hebron would just get up and leave. Caleb had to take it from them. But Caleb has not lacked in faith toward God even though he is much older now. He counts every day as evidence of God's faithfulness.

He saw others about him dying in the wilderness, but God had declared that he and Joshua would be kept alive because of their faithfulness. Now he wants his possession, at 85 years of age. Caleb says he is as strong now as he was when Moses sent them out 45 years ago. What marvelous things faith can do.

It can do what may seem like the impossible. And some things are impossible without faith.

We see here the CLAIM OF FAITH. Caleb is claiming the promise made 45 years ago by God to Moses. Unbelief starts with the difficulties and reasons to give to God. Faith starts with God and reasons to go ahead and expect God to answer. Unbelief leaves God out. Caleb and Joshua saw the cities, the walls, the giants, but they also saw God as the Almighty, the conqueror of it all. Unbelief brought

God down to the level of the grasshopper. Faith saw a God who is greater than giants and could do whatever He promised.

Nothing pleases God so much as to have sinners take Him at His word, to believe God simply because God said it. Hebrews 11:6 says not only that "without faith it is impossible to please Him," but it also says "He is a rewarder of them that diligently seek Him."

We also see the CONFIDENCE OF FAITH. This claim of Caleb was kept alive and nourished by installments of fulfillment. Two promises were given; that he should be kept alive and that he should inherit this mountain. Others might be discouraged but each day gave witness to God's faithfulness. The fulfillment of one fed the fire of the other. After entering the land he fought bravely alongside Joshua for 7 years to subdue the land. All the while his heart was at Hebron. He never lost the vision of it.

Then there was the CONSUMMATION OF FAITH. Caleb says "I'll drive them out once and for all." The Anakim did not frighten Caleb. He had faith in God. We too should have faith in Him Who promised that He would finish the work He started in us. He has much to do but, He is faithful. "He which hath begun a good work in you will perform it until the day of Jesus Christ" (Philippians 1:6). We do not deserve His salvation but it is by grace apart from any works. Even so, God rewards those sinners who are faithfully serving Him. "For God is not unrighteous to forget your work and labor of love (Hebrews 6:10). Faith can do the impossible. "Give me this mountain," Caleb said. Take courage when you think of His promises, and Hebron. He is faithful who promised. "Now unto Him that is able to do exceeding abundantly above all that we ask or think, according to the power that worketh in us, unto Him be glory in the church by Christ Jesus throughout all ages, world without end. Amen" (Ephesians 3:20–21).

BEAM 21

MELCHIZEDEK, AND THE FIRST COMMUNION

GENESIS 14:17–24

Who was this Melchizedek anyway? He comes out of nowhere and goes back into nowhere. But he is a striking picture of the Lord Jesus in the Old Testament. He came to Abraham just in time. Abraham had just won a terrific battle against five kings. These five kings had won a war against four kings which included the kings of Sodom and Gomorrah. Those five kings took Lot, Abraham's nephew, prisoner. Of course they took everyone else and everything that they could carry. Abraham went after them with his own men "born in his own house, three hundred and eighteen" (Genesis 14:14).

I do not now where he learned warfare for Abraham was a peaceful man. However, he wanted to rescue his nephew. What a victory! But many times after a great victory we are most vulnerable to temptation. We may feel like we are big shots of some kind. The natural man loves himself. This is when we hear about this Melchizedek. From nowhere he comes into the story and meets Abraham just before this temptation. The king of Sodom wanted to reward Abraham for his victory. He wanted to give Abraham all of "the goods," only he would take back the people. I do not know who would want the people of Sodom, but certainly not Abraham. But if Abraham took all of the "goods," then it could be said later that Sodom made Abraham rich. That would be the temptation.

That is when this unknown Bible character comes into the picture. He meets Abraham and serves him bread and wine. That sounds like a communion to me. It looks forward to the time when the Lord Jesus will serve His apostles their first communion. Then Melchizedek blesses Abraham, who was still named Abram at this time. He blesses Abram in the name of the most high God, possessor of heaven and earth.

It is interesting that this is the title Satan used when he said he would exalt his throne above the heights and he would be like "the Most High" (Isaiah 14:14). Satan wants to be over all.

Melchizedek means "king of righteousness" and he is also

called the "king of peace" as Hebrews 7 tells us. Doesn't that sound like Jesus? The writer of Hebrews also tells us that this Melchizedek was without father or mother, without beginning or end, "made like unto the Son of God" (Hebrews 7:3). Of course he had a father and a mother. He certainly had a beginning. But the Scriptures do not give us a clue as to who they were. That is unlike other people in the Bible. Their lineage is given. This man is a type of Christ in that nothing is said about his beginning or ending or heirs or anything else. Jesus is the eternal Son of God, without beginning or end. He also is the King of Righteousness and the King of Peace.

We are told that Abraham gave him a tenth of what he had. This is a theological point here. Abraham did not have any children yet and when he did it was several generations before Levi, the son of Jacob, was born. Yet the writer says that Levi paid a tenth to Melchizedek, even though he had not been born (Hebrews 7:9). He was in the body of Abraham. That makes Romans 5:12 more clear when it states that we all sinned in Adam. Not being born, yet we sinned because we all were in the loins of Adam, just like Levi was in the loins of Abram. So we all not only have sinned in our lifetime, but we sinned in Adam because we were in Adam at the time. No wonder we are all born sinners.

But this man brought bread and wine and presented to Abraham what could be called the first communion. And just in time. Abram says "I will not take from a thread even to a shoelatchet." Why these two items? A thread is the smallest part of our clothing. A shoelatchet is the smallest part of our shoe. This is a picture of OUR STANDING before God in heaven and OUR WALK on earth before men. Our walk in this world and our clothing of His righteousness cannot have anything from Sodom added to it. If it does it would ruin it. We have His righteousness for our standing. We have His Spirit to guide us in our walk. We need nothing of this world to help in any way. What a beautiful story!

BEAM 22

MOSES STRIKES THE ROCK AGAIN WAS THAT SO BAD?

NUMBERS 20:11

Moses had been putting up with a lot. He brought out these people from the bondage of Egypt. He did not want to go there in the first place, but God chose him to go. God said to him "Come now therefore, and I will send thee unto Pharaoh, that thou mayest bring forth my people the children of Israel out of Egypt" (Exodus 3:10). He made some excuses, but he finally got it into his head that he was the one God chose to do this job of deliverance. After some tug of war with Pharaoh and many plagues, Pharaoh lets Israel go.

Then Moses has as much trouble leading Israel through the wilderness as he had with Pharaoh. They murmur and complain, they wish they were back in Egypt. They get tired of the same manna every day. This was an Old Testament symbol of Jesus, the true Bread from Heaven. They complain that they will die in the wilderness. When they had a chance to enter into this promised land they do not because they say they can't. There are giants over there. "What did you do Moses? Did you bring us out here to kill us? Weren't there any graves in Egypt that you brought us out here to bury us in this wilderness." They long for the onions, leeks, and garlic (ugh) that they had in Egypt (Numbers 11:5). They get so angry that at times they want to stone Moses to death. "Why did you do this?" It was really a complaint against God. He brought them out. He gave them manna. He led them through Moses, but it was His leading.

So they complain about water. Yes, it would take a stream, or a river, to feed more than a million people. "And the children of Israel journeyed from Rameses to Succoth, about six hundred thousand on foot that were men, beside children" (Exodus 12:37). But God is able. He did provide. He told Moses to strike the rock in Horeb with the same rod he used to smite the river in Egypt, and water would come out. And it did. It must have gushed like a fire hydrant to feed so many people. But the people complain, complain, complain. They come to the desert of Zin. Yes, they need more water. God tells Moses to gather them together with Aaron, Moses' brother, and SPEAK to the rock before their eyes and it shall give forth water (Number 20:8). Moses has had enough of their complaints. He strikes the rock twice and water comes gushing out of the rock. God says Moses shall not lead the people into the promised land.

Was that fair? So Moses lost his temper for a while. He will lead them for 40 years and not be allowed to take them across the wilderness into the land. He could go up on Mt. Nebo and look over to see the land, but he could not lead them into it. What was so bad about what Moses did? He did not listen to what God said, for one thing. But another thing is that God was painting a picture of the cross in the Old Testament. Moses spoiled what God was trying to reveal to us. The Rock was a picture of Christ. Paul tells us that in 1 Corinthians 10:4. "They drank of that spiritual Rock that followed them and that Rock was Christ." He was to speak to, not strike, the rock.

The picture was that Moses rod, representing the Law, struck an innocent Rock, which represented Christ, and from the innocent Rock came life for those sinners who were dying. He, the Rock, took the punishment the guilty ones deserved. But the Rock only dies once for sin. "So Christ was once offered to bear the sins of many" (Hebrews 9:28). By striking the Rock again, even if he struck it once the second time, Moses ruined the picture God was painting. If the offering of Christ had to be done a second time, it would teach that the first offering was not enough. It would teach that His death is not sufficient to remove all of our sins. Sorry about that Moses. It did seem like a little thing, but Jesus was a perfect sacrifice. And a perfect offering does not need to be offered a second time. Once Jesus died for the ungodly. That is sufficient to satisfy all of God's demands. What a savior! (Oh yes! Moses does get into the land–only much later. He is there with Jesus and Elijah on Mt. Transfiguration.)

BEAM 23

FILLING EMPTY VESSELS

2 KINGS 4:1–7

She was in debt. She could not pay. Her husband was a believer but he had died. The creditors, in those days, could take your children to be slaves to pay off your debt. What would it be like today if they did that?

She cried out to Elisha, the prophet of God, for help. What could she do? What could he do to help this poor widow? He told her to do something that seemed absolutely foolish. I can hear her sons now saying "That's crazy." What did he tell her? First he asked her what she had. She had just a little vial of oil.

This would be a small vial, most likely not enough to feed a lamp. It may have been used for cooking or the anointing of the head. A small bottle no doubt. Archeologists call them bill-bills, from the sound they make when your pour from them.

Now Elisha tells her to borrow vessels from her neighbors, as many vessels as she can get. He said not a few. Go to your neighbors and borrow all you can get, empty vessels. Then he tells her to pour the oil into them. Wow! Does that make sense. I can almost hear her sons. She says to them, "Yitzhak, go next door to Leah's house and ask her to lend us all the empty vessels she can spare. An Ephraim, you go to Miriam's and do the same thing. Go get all that you can carry." If they were like children I know they would have said, "Aw Mom, this is crazy. All we have is this little pot of oil. What good will it do to get more pots, and bigger pots?" "Yitzhak, do as I say. Go borrow vessels." "Aw Mom." "Yitzhak, do you want the car Saturday night?" or whatever it was that he would want. Zechariah 8:5 tells us that boys and girls played in the streets. History tells us they may have played Egyptian team games of tug-of-war, while the girls practiced juggling. Perhaps she said no more tug-of-war. So Yitzhak and Ephraim go, perhaps reluctantly. "All right. I'll go, but I'll still feel silly." Anyhow, they go. They get a house full of empty vessels. Then this widow starts pouring.

I can see her now. "Yitzhak, hand me that vessel over there in the corner." And she pours, and she pours.

"Ephraim, get me that large pot over there by the door." And then Ephraim says, "Mom, it is already full. You filled it already. Don't you remember?" And she says "Yitzhak, isn't there a vessel by your feet?"

"Mom. Every vessel is full. There are no more empty ones." Then we read that the oil stayed, that is it stopped coming out of that little vessel. What a miracle! Then she tells the prophet. He tells her to sell the oil, use the money to pay her debt, and then to live off the rest.

What a beautiful story! She does not lose her sons to the debtor, she pays off her credit cards, I mean her debts, and she still has money left over to care for her children. What a love story.

What did she have? Not much. A little oil. What did she have to do? Believe the prophet. She was responsible for bringing the vessels. God was responsible for supplying the oil. She could have been still pouring oil. God has no shortage of oil. God said to Moses, "What is that in thine hand?" (Exodus 4:2). It was a rod, that is a stick. God said cast it down. It became a serpent. God used Moses to smite Egypt until Pharaoh let His people go. We are told to bring our vessels to God, also. Our bodies are our vessels. "We have this treasure in earthen vessels, that the excellency of the power may be of God, and not of us" (2Corinthians 4:7). We are to bring them to God so He can fill them and use them for His glory. Romans 12:1.

We are responsible to bring the vessels. God is responsible to fill the vessel. And He will. What a beautiful love story. We are nothing. Empty, worthless, vessels, until He fills us.

BEAM 24

WHEN THE WORLD CAVES IN

JOB 1 - 2

Most people have heard about Job. Even those who never have read the story or anything else in the Bible. We are aware that his world suddenly collapsed and everything he had was gone. More than all the wealth he had, and he was a very wealthy man, was the loss of his children

This shows first of all that wealth in itself is not evil. It is the love of money that is evil and produces all manner of evil. Abraham also was a wealthy man who loved the Lord. But, there are not many who can worship the Lord and keep material wealth in the proper place. The Lord Jesus told us that it would be easier for the camel to go through the needle's eye, than for a rich man to enter the kingdom of God (Luke 18:25).

Job is one of those few who can be rich and also religious, if you will. A true religion realizes that all we have comes from Him. "Every good gift and every perfect gift is from above, and cometh down from the Father of lights" (James 1:17). Years ago I wondered about listening to music that may have been written by someone who was not a believer. Then this verse came to me. Whether the music is from Handel or Mozart, the gift has come down from above, and we should be thankful.

Job was made the object of a contest between God and Satan. Satan said Job did not love God for nothing. God had so richly blessed Job that He was really paying someone to love Him (Job 1:9–11).

So God gave Job over to Satan for the test. But with certain stipulations. This is also a beautiful story. When Satan tries us, God puts a limit on how far he can go. He was not to harm Job physically. So everything was taken away from Job and the world fell in on him. But Satan would not stop. He insisted that Job would curse God if he were to suffer physically. So we have the story of Job's intense suffering.

Without going into all of the theology of the book, there is a beautiful love story here. I just want to look at this one part of the book. Job had seven sons and three daughters (1:2). They all died in one terrible blow. A great wind came out of the wilderness and it blew the house down where all the children were that day, and all, all ten of them died. Not many believers could take such a disaster as that. But Job did. Job passed the test that Satan threw at him and Job blessed the name of the Lord. He said "the Lord gave and the Lord hath taken away; blessed be the name of the Lord" (Job 1:21).

At the end of the book, after Job passed the test and proved that Satan is a liar, was a liar, and always will be a liar, God doubled everything Job had. We read in Job 42:12, "So the Lord blessed the latter end of Job more than his beginning." Then we read how the Lord doubled the number of sheep, the number of camels, the number of oxen, and the number of she asses. Then we are told Job had also seven sons and three daughters (Job 42:13). Some may have imagined a mistake here. God doubled everything Job had but ONLY gave him seven sons and three daughters. Why not double? Why not fourteen sons and six daughters?

Because God did double Job's children. He is simply saying to Job, "I have half of your children and you can have the other half for a while." Remember when David's child died, David said "I shall go to him, but he shall not return to me" (2 Samuel 12:23). This is love. Letting us know that our children are safe with Him. Even the infants of non-believers go to be with Him. If we are His, then the time will come when we will see the rest of our family. Death cannot separate us from those who are with Him. God did double all that Job had. What a gracious and loving God to do that. "Bless the Lord, O my soul, and all that is within me, bless His holy name" (Psalm 103:1).

BEAM 25

PSALM 23

Walking Through the Cemetery Alone

This is probably the most familiar passage in the Bible. It is spoken at countless burials. It is quoted by many who do not believe in the inspiration of the Scripture. Countless sermons have been preached and written about this Psalm. What can I say? I do not want to go into an exposition of the Psalm. Much of it is so clear and self evident that it could be regarded as talking down to people who already can read English and know the meanings of English words. So what can I say?

There is just one thing that is sometimes overlooked. I would like to bring your attention to this love story, and a beautiful one it is. Have you noticed how the Psalm, written by a shepherd, David, goes along until the subject of death comes up? He is writing under the inspiration of the Holy Spirit. He uses the third person pronoun when speaking of God, the Shepherd.

He says "He" maketh me to lie down, "He" leadeth me, "He" restoreth my soul. Then David comes to that fearful thing called death and he then uses the second person pronoun, "Thou." Now grammarians would grasp this immediately. "Thou" is simply the King James English way of saying "you." Why is this such a beautiful story?

Years ago I read about a famous and faithful preacher in England. When he was a little lad he got a job over in the next town. This may have been his first job. That I could not find out. He had one great dread about this opportunity. He had to walk through a cemetery to get there and home again. This was in the days before Edison, before the dark and dreadful place, at least to him, was lighted up. This was also in the time when men, and boys, worked ten or twelve hours a day and six days a week.

He said to his father that he would be home Sunday. "No, Alex. You come home Saturday." "Awe Dad," I can hear him saying. "Sunday?" "No, Alex, you come home Saturday." This was also in the time when young boys obeyed their parents, even if they did not like what they were told to do. He could not dissuade his father so

Saturday it was. All week long he thought about what Saturday would bring. He was in absolute fear of going through that cemetery. Well, fear did not stop the clock. Saturday came.

He was in absolute terror as he approached that awful and dreadful place of darkness and doom. With his heart racing and his body in dread he started into that fearful place. That was not enough. When he just got started he thought he heard something in the darkness. He was terrified. Then a voice cried out. "Alex, it that you?" It was his father. His father did not tell him he would meet him. He knew how Alex dreaded that awful place so he came to meet him.

He took his son's hand and they walked through that cemetery together. Tell me, do you think Alex feared walking through that cemetery with his father holding his hand? I don't.

The Psalmist, through the Holy Spirit, is telling us something like that. He says "He" "He" "He" until he comes to that fearful enemy, and he is an enemy, death. Then he switches to the second person pronoun "You" are with me. It is like God coming to meet us personally when we fear the most and taking us by the hand to walk through the dreadful place called death. Why would we fear then with Him holding our hand? Would you fear, with God holding your hand? I think not. What a beautiful love story it is. What a loving God He is.

"I sought the Lord. And He heard me, and delivered me from all my fears" (Psalm 34:4).

BEAM 26

FOR WHOM DID CHRIST DIE?
A SIMPLE LOOK AT A DEEP SUBJECT

It is a subject that has divided believers for generations. Can we simply accept what the Scripture says about His death? From the time of Calvin there have been some theologians who have pursued the idea that Christ died only for those who are eventually saved. This has been called the "Limited Atonement Theory," although those who believe it would not call it a theory. Some knowledgeable scholars have pointed out such passages as John 3:16. "For God so loved the world that He gave His only begotten Son that whosoever believeth on Him should not perish but have everlasting life." But they are told that John 3:16 does not mean He died for all, only the saved ones who believe. It certainly sounds like He loved the world that will have some perish, and He gave His son for that world, that has some perish.

There are other passages that are perfectly clear, if we want to know the truth. But as sure as two and two are five some theologians will miss the point. If we are not willing to learn, if we are not willing to leave our prejudices, we will not learn anything. The first rule of learning is to be willing to learn.

The Day of Atonement.

This was the day when the High Priest sacrificed a bullock for his own sin offering (Leviticus 16:6) and then offered a goat for the sins of the people of Israel (Leviticus 16:15). This was a most holy day in Israel. A priest could not enter into the Holy of Holies. Only the High Priest could do this and it was only on one day in the year. The blood of one goat which was killed was sprinkled upon the Mercy Seat in the Holiest of Holies. Another goat, called a scapegoat, was set free, signifying that the sins of the people were gone, gone like that goat that was set free in the wilderness (Leviticus 16:21).

The scripture states clearly enough, if we want to hear the scriptures, that the goat which was sacrificed was killed and its blood sprinkled upon the Mercy Seat was for the sins of the people. The High Priest makes an atonement "for himself, and for his household, and for all the congregation of Israel" (Leviticus 16:17). Now the question is "Was every Israelite saved? Every one of the congregation of Israel saved?" I believe you see the point.

Now in the New Testament. In John 11 we read of a prophecy made by Caiaphas, the High Priest, about Jesus and His death. He prophesies that Jesus should die for the nation (11:51). If it seems strange that a High Priest who wanted Jesus killed should speak the truth of divine prophecy, we need to look into the Old Testament and see what happened to Balaam the greedy prophet. Balaam was hired by Balak to curse Israel. He wanted to do it, for the money. But God would not let him curse Israel. He had to bless Israel.

Balaam, like the High Priest, prophesied by the Spirit. In spite of trying to curse for the money he could not, for God made him bless. Balaam says "Behold, I have received commandment to bless, and He hath blessed; and I cannot reverse it" (Numbers 23:20). So God overrules the will of man and makes a false prophet of greed bless, even against the false prophet's will.

Likewise, in John 11 Caiaphas is overruled to pronounce a prophecy that states that "one man should die for the people" (50). The writer, the Apostle John, then states clearly, if we want to really see it, that Caiaphas spoke of Jesus Who "should die for the nation" (11:51). So Jesus died for the nation of Israel. Was every Jew saved, including Caiaphas, and Judas, and every other member of that nation? You see this point also, I believe. So Jesus died for those who were not saved, were not of the "elect." So where is this "limited atonement" theory? Where does it put the Scriptures that teach the Day of Atonement was for everyone in the nation? Or, that Jesus died for the nation, yet every Jew was not saved. Where? Tell us. And why wasn't every Jew saved? He died for all of them. Tell us.

BEAM 27

MATTHIAS

THE THIRTEENTH APOSTLE, HUH?

ACTS 1:15–26

Is Matthias one of the thirteen, I mean twelve apostles? If not, why not? Peter, and again we love this man, opens his mouth and puts his foot in it again. He feels they must choose another apostle to take the place of Judas. True, you hear little about some of the other apostles, so because we hear no more about Matthias that in itself does not mean he was not an apostle. But here are some of the other reasons to see that Peter, and the other 10 were wrong in choosing Matthias.

In the FIRST place they were told to wait until they were empowered from on high. Luke 24:49 states that the Lord Jesus said unto them that they were to wait "in the city of Jerusalem until ye be endued with power from on high." We know now what that power was. The filling of the Holy Spirit from on high at the day of Pentecost. If Peter had known then what we know now he too would have waited. He was a different man after Pentecost. What a difference a day made. What a preacher he became. And fearless, unlike he was when he denied he knew the Lord Jesus. But they did not wait. So the first thing to note is, they were disobedient to the command.

SECONDLY, would you choose your pastor or deacon by throwing out the dice to see who wins? I think not. True, there were times in the Old Testament when God told His people to cast lots, but no one told Peter to do this in Acts 1.

THIRDLY, God chose Saul, who became Paul the apostle, "a chosen vessel unto Me" (Acts 9:15). He, Paul, was sent to the lands of the Gentiles, not to the race of the Gentiles, to preach the Word. Paul always went into the synagogue and preached to the Jews first that Jesus was Messiah, but in the Gentile lands. If, and when, the Jews rejected Paul's preaching, then he preached to the Gentiles. Peter, however, was sent to the land of Israel to preach the Word, not to a racial people, but a geographic people. Peter was the first one to open the Gospel to the Gentiles (Acts 10–11) where he broke the silence of the Jewish evangelism by preaching to Cornelius, a Roman centurion. That put him into a lot of trouble with the Jews.

FOURTHLY, you never hear of 13 apostles, or 13 gates of the city of the New Jerusalem (Revelation 21:14). There are no thirteens mentioned anywhere, concerning apostles, or tribes.

Besides, isn't thirteen an unlucky number? Who would want to be number thirteen? Ooooh!

No! Twelve is the correct number and Paul is number 12. Sorry Matthias. Blame it on Peter, and the other ten for not waiting like the Lord Jesus told them.

"And shewed me that great city, the holy Jerusalem, descending out of heaven from God . . . And (it) had a wall great and high, and had twelve gates, and at the gates twelve angels, and names written thereon which are the names of the twelve tribes of the children of Israel. And the wall of the city had twelve foundations, and in them the names of the twelve apostles of the Lamb" (Revelation 21:10–14).

"Verily I say unto you, That ye which have followed me, in the regeneration when the Son of man shall sit in the throne of His glory, ye also shall sit upon twelve thrones, judging the twelve tribes of Israel" (Matthew 19:28).

BEAM 28

RELIGION WON'T DO IT

ACTS 10

Cornelius was a religious man. Acts 10:2 says he was a devout man. This is unusual because Cornelius was also a man of war. He was a centurion, or a captain of a hundred-man unit of the Roman army. He no doubt had seen death many times, and most likely caused the death of some. But that is what soldiers do.

He was a religious man. He was reared in a society where there were many gods. Somewhere he heard of this God of the Hebrews. He began praying to this one God, instead of the many. He also prayed consistently to this one God. His life was a constant testimony of his religion. He brought his family together to hear the word of God. He did not send them to Sunday School, and then go home. Sunday school is for the children you know?

He was a religious man. He gave out of his own money "much alms to the people." He would give back some of what God had given him, to help those who were in need and had little. He was a religious man. He had a good report (Acts 10:22) from those who were not of his religious persuasion. You might think of this as giving to another denomination. He was not a Jewish proselyte. When the Jews heard Peter had eaten in Cornelius' house they were angry and rebuked Peter. So from this we know Cornelius was not a converted Jew. Yet he had a good report from all the nation of the Jews (Acts 10:22).

Yes, Cornelius was a religious man, a good man, a giving man, a praying man, a consistent man. Yet, he was a lost man. God sent Peter to Cornelius to tell him how he could be saved (Acts 11:14). There was one thing lacking, that Peter needed to tell him. Peter "opened his mouth" (Acts 10:34) and preached "Jesus of Nazareth" (Acts 10:38) Who was hanged on a tree, and raised up the third day (10: 39–40). Religion was not enough.

It is difficult today for someone who is a member of a church, who gives to the church, who may sing in the choir, or who may be on the board of deacons of the church, to believe that he may still be lost. But one thing is still needed, A SAVING FAITH IN Jesus Christ.

While Peter was speaking (10:.44) the Holy Ghost fell upon Cornelius and his family. Religious and lost. One thing, or Person, was lacking–the Lord Jesus Christ as a personal savior. A belief in Him Who alone is the Door, the Way, the Truth, and the Life. What a beautiful story! By hearing the Word, by believing the Word, by trusting in One who died to save the lost, a religious man, one that the world would call a "good man," was saved.

Is He lacking in your life? Without Him, life has no real meaning. Religion is not enough. We can join every religion, every church, every theory of religion and still be lost. There is only one Door to God. Don't call me narrow minded and bigoted. I didn't say it. The Lord Jesus did. He is the One who said He is the only Door. Take it up with Him. Better still, enter through the Door.

There is something else that should be noted. It would have been easier for God to have the angel simply tell Cornelius what he lacked. Why send 30 miles away to fetch Peter to tell him? God's method of preaching is to have sinners who have been saved by His grace, tell other sinners how they can be saved by grace. He depends on us for His feet, and His tongue. We are His mouthpiece. Use it for Him! The word "angel" means messenger so that is what we become, angels bringing the good message to all.

BEAM 29

IS THERE ANYTHING LEFT OUT HERE?

ROMANS 8:38–39

Paul asked the question in verse 35. "Who shall separate us from the love of Christ?" Then he goes through a list of everything one could possibly think of. None of these can separate us from the love of Christ. He names some of the troubles of life that some may fear would separate us. These include tribulation, distress, persecution, famine, nakedness (that is going without), peril, or sword? The answer is no, not one of them. Oh, we might feel like God has left us, or we have left Him, but that is only our feelings. Come to the Word. He goes on to say we are more than conquerors through Him that loved us. And if that is not enough he gives another list in verses 38 and 39. Look at this list. Is there anything left out?

Death: Death is the most sorrowful separation of all. For the Christian it is a change of residence. We move from here to heaven. "Whilst we are at home in the body, we are absent from the Lord. . . . We are confident, I say, and willing rather to be absent from the body, and to be present with the Lord" (2 Cor. 5:6,8).

Life: Being alive means we are subject to all kinds of temptations and trials. We may possibly fail and commit some awful sin. Nevertheless, He is true. "Him that cometh to Me I will in no wise cast out" (John 6:37).

Angels: Angels are subject to Him ""Thinkest thou that I cannot now pray to my Father, and He shall presently give me more than twelve legions of angels?" (Matthew 26:53). "Know ye not that we shall judge angels?" (1 Corinthians 6:3). The saints shall judge angels.

Principalities: These principalities are fallen angels who have followed their leader, Satan. Jesus is "the head of all principalities and power" (Colossians 2:10). Our Head is above all principalities, fallen or not, and we are with Him so we are also above all with Him.

Powers: Christ has been exalted "Far above all principality and power, and might, and dominion, and every name that is named, not only in this world, but also in that which is to come" (Ephesians 1:21).

That should cover it all. We are with Him so we are also over all with Him.

Things present: That says everything that could possible hinder us or try to deny us the love of Christ.

Things to come: This certainly would take in any form of temptation, Satanic power, tumors of the brain when we might not know who we are and could possible wonder Who He is, or even deny we know Him, like Peter did. No matter what, we still have His love.

Height: That would again include Satan and any of His angels.

Depth: Are there any fallen angels below that could some how harm us and separate us from His love? No they could not.

Nor any other creature: This would include any false cult, false teacher, false doctrine, false Christs. None of these either. But, as someone said to me years ago, "We can jump out of His hand." If we could, His promise is still true. "They shall never perish." I never thought of it then but suppose I were a finger in the body of Christ? Could the finger jump out of His hand? I think not. And if it could the promise is still true. "They shall never perish" (John 10:28).

I believe Paul has more than covered it all. It looks like he has repeated himself. But all of this is to make sure we understand that nothing, no one, nothing now or in the future, nothing can separate us from the love of God in Christ Jesus. Now can there be anything better? How can there be a salvation greater? How can there be a God with greater love than this? There just isn't any. This is that "so great salvation" spoken of in Hebrews 2:3. How could it be greater? It can't. Receive it and rejoice in it!

"How shall we escape, if we neglect so great salvation?" (Hebrews 2:3). We can't.

BEAM 30

LIVING IN TWO WORLDS

COLOSSIANS 1:2

In this verse Paul addressed those saints of God, the brethren who are "in Christ which are at Colosse." They are living in two different places or worlds. They are "in Christ." They are also "at Colosse." This is something every saint of God, and that means every believer, must do. But how do we do this? We are "at" some place. If it is not Colosse then substitute the place where you live. Let's say Columbus, Ohio. We are "at Columbus" and must learn to live there. This means we are subject to the laws of Columbus, or Springfield. Paul was a Roman citizen and had to live by certain rules of the Roman Empire. He sometimes used that citizenship to his advantage.

When Paul was giving his testimony before the people of Jerusalem he got to a point where the leaders of the people could stand it no longer and they had Paul bound with chains and were crying out for his death.

The chief captain commanded that Paul should be examined by scourging (Acts 22:24). That was a horrible way to "beat the truth" out of someone. The leather thongs had pieces of lead, or stones, imbedded in them to make the whipping more brutal. Paul did not mind suffering for the Lord. He suffered many times and in various ways. But here was a Roman centurion about to whip Paul. That is when Paul says to him "Is it lawful for you to scourge a man that is a Roman, and uncondemned?" (Acts 22:25). Paul knew, and the centurion knew, that it was not lawful. The Roman citizen must be given a trial first. You could get into a lot of trouble back in Rome if you did not do this. They became "afraid after they knew he was a Roman, and because he had bound him" (Acts 22:29). That is one of the problems of living in this world. You must abide by the law of Rome, or Santa Fe, unless they go against God's law.

But there is another world we must live in. That "we" means everyone who has trusted the Lord Jesus as his Savior. We live under the laws of Christ. We are citizens of another world. "Now therefore ye are no more strangers and foreigners, but fellow citizens with the saints, and of the household of God" (Ephesians 2:19). We must learn how to live in this world also. We must "put off concerning the former conversation the old man, which is corrupt . . . and that ye put on the new man, which after God is created in righteousness and true holiness" (Ephesians 4:22–24). That word "conversation" does not mean just our language. It is an old English word that means our manner of living, our behavior. We have to live in a new world, in Christ. In Philippians 3:20 Paul says "Our conversation (here it is again, our manner of living) is in heaven; from whence also we look for the Saviour, the Lord Jesus Christ." So we are living in two different worlds. One is here in Dallas and the other is in Christ. How do we do it?

One important thing must be kept in mind. Every Christian must live IN two different worlds, but it is certain that he cannot live FOR two different worlds. The Lord Jesus made that clear. He said "No man can serve two masters; for either he will hate the one and love the other; or else he will hold to the one and despise the other. Ye cannot serve God and mammon" (Matthew 6:24). You can't do it. One must come first. There cannot be two heads on one body. One must be first. You cannot have two firsts. Which will it be? You MUST live in two different worlds. We CANNOT live FOR two different worlds.

This world, and all it stands for, is going to pass away. There is to be a new heaven and a new earth. Why live for what is temporary? We must live in two worlds. Let's live for the right one. Let's live by the laws of the family. We are God's family now. Let's live like it. OK? Of course we cannot live in God's family until we are alive. We get that life by trusting the Lord Jesus. Have we?

"I am the way, the truth, and the life; no man cometh unto the Father but by Me" (John 14:6).

BEAM 31

JEHOVAH OR JAHWEH

GENESIS 4:1

There is a beautiful story in the name of God. Names in the Scripture teach us lessons. The names of people are not just given because they are a "junior" or they have a red face, or they have dark eyes. The names may have been given some time after birth because the names describe the characteristics of the child. The names of God are many, each giving some facet of His attributes. There are a number of combination names with the name Jehovah. Here are a few:

Jehovah-nissi	The Lord is my banner	Exodus 17:15
Jehovah-shalom	The Lord is peace	Judges 6:24
Jehovah-shammah	The Lord is there	Ezekiel 48:35
Jehovah-tsidkenu	The Lord is our-righteousness	Jeremiah 23:6
Jehovah-jireh	The Lord provides	Genesis 22:8, 14
Jehovah-Sabaoth	The Lord of Hosts, (that is armies)	1 Samuel 1:3

But what does the word Jehovah mean? Most commentators will go to Exodus 3:13, where Moses asks this God Who is sending him back to Egypt. "What is His name? What shall I say unto them?" (The children of Israel). God says "I am that I am and He said Thus shalt thou say unto the children of Israel, I AM hath sent me" (Exodus 3:14). Most teachers will say this is the first use of the word Jehovah, the I AM, the self-existing One.

However, this is not the first time the work "Jehovah" is used. It may not be seen due to a translation of the passage, but anyone looking at some marginal note, in the Scofield Bible for instance, will see otherwise. Genesis 4:1 says this in the King James, "I have gotten a man from the Lord." Actually Eve said "I have gotten a man, even Jehovah." This is the first use of the word. The meaning is not given. Here is another case of having to read in between lines. That does not mean reading something that is not written, but sometimes it means we have to put two and two together to make five, oops, I mean four.

What was it to Eve? What did she mean by using this word "Jehovah?" What was Eve looking for? God had made a promise to Eve after she and Adam sinned against the Lord. They had listened to Satan's lie, which he spoke using a serpent as a mouthpiece. This brought separation from God and death, not only for Adam and Eve, but for all of their descendants. Through sin death entered the world. "Wherefore by one man sin entered into the world, and death by sin; and so death passed upon all men, for that all have sinned" (Romans 5:12).

But God promised Eve a deliverer. In Genesis 3:14 God cursed the serpent above every beast of the field. Then He said to the serpent "I will put enmity between thee and the woman, and between thy seed and her seed; it (that is Messiah) shall bruise thy head, and thou halt bruise his heel" (Genesis 3:15). This is the first promise of the Messiah, the Deliverer, the Christ Who was to come. It would have been expected that when Eve had a son she would have thought "This is the promised One, this is the Deliverer that God promised us." Only that son turned out to be a murderer instead. Cain not only murdered, but he murdered his own brother.

This gives us some light on what the word "Jehovah" means. It means the Promised One, the Savior, the One Who would crush Satan's head, the Coming Redeemer. It took many centuries before that One came but the Old Testament saints, like Abraham, Isaac, Jacob, and David, looked forward to His coming. He came to a virgin and was born in a stable in Bethlehem. But He came. Do we rejoice in our Jehovah? We should.

BEAM 32

INVITATIONS–COME WITH US

NUMBERS 10:29

It was the second year since the children of Israel came out of Egypt. They spent nearly a year in building the Tabernacle, the Ark, the brazen altars, the Holiest of Holies, etc. The Shekinah Glory cloud was taken up from the Tabernacle and it was time to move on. They were on their way now to that promised land that God said He gave them, a land flowing with milk and honey. That means a very fruitful land for crops and herds. They are moving out. We are doing the same thing. We are moving to a much better promised land.

Hobab was a brother-in-law to Moses. Moses wants him to come along with them, so he gives this invitation. This is a lesson for all of us. Moses says "We are journeying unto a place of which the Lord said, I will give it you; come thou with us, and we will do thee good: for the Lord hath spoken good concerning Israel." This is a simple invitation, such as we have today. His was to the promised land. Ours is to a more wonderful promised land. What can we learn from this invitation?

First there is our RESPONSIBILTY. We are responsible to tell others the good news. We may not be able to change their minds and get them to come along, but we are responsible to tell the message that God has given us. It was a venture of faith for Moses and Israel to start out and move to another land, even one that had been promised to the fathers. It meant hardships and sacrifices along the way, just like we have today. No one said it would be easy. But it also meant there was a goal ahead, a purpose in life, a definite aim. We have this also. We are not a part of this world but are citizens of another and we are headed home. Ah, but there awaits us a glorious welcome. Here we have a temporary abiding place, a body that we inhabit for a little time and then we shed it for a permanent one that will never know sin, or suffering, or death.

Secondly, there was the SINCERITY. Moses did not say "go to this land that flows with milk and honey." He said "come with us," showing that he was going along also. We not only invite others to come to the promised land that God has in store for them but we also are going that way. We are traveling the same road. Whatever the trials and hardships we also are going along with those we invite. Jesus warned about the scribes and pharisees who "Say and do not" (Matthew 23:3). We are not to be like them.

Thirdly, notice the MOTIVE. "We will do thee good." This is what it is all about. All of God's promises to Israel and Moses would be Hobab's. God has given us precious promises. Peter tells us about the glory of the Lord Jesus Christ Who "hath called us to glory and virtue: whereby are given unto us exceeding great and precious promises: that by these ye might be partakers of the divine nature" (2 Peter 1:3–4). We, poor sinners, are to partake of the divine nature? Wow! And this is the good that we will do to anyone we invite to come along with us. Wow! What an invite!

Have we invited anyone to come with us? We will do them good. It is such wonderful good news we should be glad to tell everyone we can. Many years after World War II was ended there were some Japanese soldiers on a pacific isle that had to be told by a PA system that the war was over and a reconciliation had been made. They were still ready to fight in a war that was ended. We need to tell the good news. The penalty for sin has been paid. God invites one and all to come. He invites "whosoever will" let him come. Let's give out the invitation. We will do you good. Come along with us. We are traveling to the promised land. "Eye hath not seen, nor ear heard, neither have entered into the heart of man, the things which God hath prepared for them that love Him" (1 Corinthians 2:9).

BEAM 33

BUSY BUSY BUSY

1 KINGS 20:40

This story is about a "certain man of the sons of the prophets." It was a parable, or a story, told to a wicked king Ahab, who ruled over Israel and was himself ruled by an even more wicked wife, Jezebel.

Ahab joined forces with an oppressor of Israel, Benhadad king of Syria, contrary to God's purpose.

Ahab even made a treaty, or a covenant, with Benhadad.

God wanted to warn Ahab that it was wrong. This nameless prophet disguises himself with ashes on his face (verse 38). When the king comes by the prophet tells him a story. He says he was in a battle and a man brought a prisoner to the prophet. This man gave strict orders to the prophet that he was to keep this prisoner at all costs. He was to guard him with his life. He states that the man told him "if by any means he (the prisoner) be missing then shall thy life be for his life" (20:39). This was the penalty under Roman Law that came later.

If a Roman guard let a prisoner escape he forfeited his own life. So much for the tale that is sometimes told that the prisoners who guarded the tomb of Jesus fell asleep and "someone took His body."

In Matthew 28:11–13 we read that some of the guards came into the city to tell the chief priest that the body was gone. Of course they told them what really happened, that an angel rolled back the stone and this angel did shine like lightning and the guards became as dead men (Matthew 28:4). So the story is made up that his disciples came and stole away the body. Aaaah hah! And the priests gave large sums of money to the soldiers. Aaaah hah! The solders lives were forfeit, if Herod wished to pursue it. And how could anyone know what happened while they were sleeping?

So what is this story about? The prophet says he was busy, busy, busy, here and there and his prisoner escaped. What to do? Ahab says you know the penalty, it is from your very own mouth. Then this unnamed prophet removes the ashes from his face and pronounces the verdict. Since Ahab let the enemy escape, the one God had appointed to destruction, Ahab's life would be forfeited for Benhadad's.

Busy, busy, busy. We get so busy doing things here and there. I have to finish my college and then get a good job. I have time. I have to get a house, but I have time. I'm still young. I have to get money for the kid's college. I'll get to it. I have to pay off this mortgage so I can get started on my retirement savings. I'll get to it. Just give me some time. What's the hurry? Mom is sick. I have to take care of her. I'll get to it. Just give me some time.

The one vital, urgent thing, the crucial thing is neglected. That one thing is what life is all about. What have we done with Jesus? Have we gotten so busy, here and there, that we have never given any time nor thought about His claim upon us? We forfeit our true life, our eternal life, if we let Him get away. "And this is the record, that God hath given to us eternal life, and this life is in His Son" (1 John 5:11).

We cannot let Him get away while we are busy. This is the dressing room for the real world that is ahead. Are we busy? No one should be that busy. If so, we are too busy for our own good. First things come first.

"Keep thy heart with all diligence; for out of it are the issues of life" (Proverbs 4:23).

"There is a way which seemeth right unto a man, but the end thereof are the ways of death" (Proverbs 14:12).

BEAM 34

RIDICULE

NEHEMIAH 2:19

"They laughed us to scorn, and despised us" (Neh. 2:19). They also said "If a fox runs upon their wall, it will fall down" (Nehemiah 4:3, free translation).

How we hate to be laughed at. It is OK for a comedian. He welcomes people to laugh at him. That is how he earns his bread. But, Saints? Ministers? Disciples? No, no! Here was a handful of men who were building the walls of Jerusalem. Nehemiah had grieved because the walls of the city, "the place of his father's graves, was lying in waste and the gates of the city had been burned." Nebuchadnezzar had destroyed the city and the temple around 587 BC. It was now the middle of the fifth century BC, more than a hundred years later.

Walls were a city's protection against enemies and intruders. The gates regulated the traffic in and out. The Temple was the place of worship. All was destroyed by Nebuchadnezzar. It was a sorrowful man who grieved about this situation. It was not proper to be sad around the king of Persia. You were to express joy and gladness to be in the presence of such a great one, but Nehemiah could not hide his sorrow. Then the king, Artaxerxes, noticed the gloomy countenance of Nehemiah and Nehemiah was afraid (2:2). When the king hears why Nehemiah was mournful he gives him permission to go to Jerusalem and rebuild the walls of the city.

Then came the opposition. When you try to do something for the Lord, you can expect opposition. Satan is behind it. One of the ways to stop the work is by ridicule. We do not like to be laughed at. They made fun of these poor, weak, ignorant Jews and tried to stop the work. But Nehemiah had men spaced along the foundation of the wall and they marked off where each man would build. Because his enemies would not stop at laughter, he also had them keep a sword handy. We are told that they "with one of his hands wrought in the work, and with the other hand held a weapon" (Nehemiah 4:17).

Building and battling. That is what they were doing. Laughter could not stop them. "Sticks and stones," remember? So the wall was finished in 52 days (Nehemiah 6:15). Laughter, threats, lies, ridicule, none of this worked. The Lord's work went on and the wall was finished.

I like to think of this as building and battling, trowels and sword. This is a love story about what the Lord is doing now. He is building and battling. He said He would build His church upon the Rock, which is Christ, the Messiah, and the gates of hell shall not prevail against it (Matthew 16:18). He is building His church. He is also battling an enemy. And we are building with Him. Are we warring with Him?

Are we good soldiers? Can He count on us? Jude tells us that in the last days there should be mockers (Jude 18). In Luke 6:22–23 we read that we are blessed when men hate us and separate themselves from us and cast us out for the Lord's sake. We are told to rejoice and leap for joy.

Ridicule! Yes, no one likes to be a laughing stock, no one wants to look like a fool. But, we have the work to do, preaching the Word to those who are lost, and we have the Sword, which is the Word of God, to fend off all attacks from the enemy. His building will be finished. If we do not do the work, someone else will. Better for us to do the work and leap for joy when we are mocked and ridiculed.

"But God hath chosen the foolish things of the world to confound the wise; and God hath chosen the weak things of the world to confound the things which are mighty" (1 Corinthians 1:27).

BEAM 35

MOSES' MOM

EXODUS 2:8

BEING PAID TO NURSE YOUR OWN

Psalm 37:5 reads "Commit thy way unto the Lord; trust also in Him; and He shall bring it to pass."

Sometimes we try everything else first, second, third, etc. When nothing else works, we try what this passage exhorts us to do.

The new Pharaohs did not look favorably upon the Israelites. What Joseph had done to save that nation was not considered by the new Pharaohs. The word went out, "Kill them, kill all of them. No boy of Israel shall be spared. The girls, OK, but no boys." There would soon be such a lack of males that Israel could never have any kind of an army to battle against Egypt, even if they wanted to. The method of execution–cast them into the Nile. Let the alligators eat them.

What was a mother to do? To disobey Pharaoh meant execution of the Egyptian or the Israelite. But, how could a mother cast her son to the crocodiles? So Jochebed committed it unto the Lord, even before Psalm 37 was ever written. And what happened?

She made a little waterproof boat to put Moses in and had the little ark placed in the river. There is little doubt that she placed the baby where Pharaoh's daughter came to do her bathing, for cleansing. She may have known that Pharaoh's daughter was childless and might have pity on the little fellow. And, she had his young sister, Miriam, to watch what would happen. Jochebed might have been too fearful to watch for herself. God does not always do things the way we would like Him to do them. Remember Lazarus was sick and the Lord Jesus remained where he was two more days until Lazarus died (John 11:6).

So what happened by committing herself to the Lord's will? When Pharaoh's daughter saw the boat she became curious and sent a maid to see what it was all about. When she opened the boat Moses cried at just the right time. That was all it took to adopt this little fellow. Pharaoh's daughter knew it was a Hebrew child. Against her own father's will she adopted Moses, this Hebrew baby, right there and gave him his new name, Moses, "drawer out." It is hardly to be imagined that Pharaoh's daughter thought it was a coincidence that a little Hebrew girl just happened to be standing nearby, and offered to get a wet nurse for her to take care of this little fellow.

So Jochebed gets to keep her son alive. She gets to rear him, and gets paid for rearing her own son.

What a beautiful story this is. Why don't we commit our way unto the Lord and let Him work out the details? Only our will stands in the way. Let us put our will behind us and put God's will in front of us.

Let's see what God will do for us and to us. He wills good for us.

I do wonder if Pharaoh's daughter was a convert to the God of the Israelites. It looks like it. She would have to be quite dense to not know where Moses came from. So Moses is with his step mom in heaven now. Isn't that a happy ending?!

"Trust in the Lord with all thine heart; and lean not unto thine own understanding. In all thy ways acknowledge Him, and He shall direct thy paths" (Proverbs 3:5–6).

"What time I am afraid, I will trust in Thee" (Psalm 56:3).

"Every word of God is pure: He is a shield unto them that put their trust in Him" (Proverbs 30:5).

BEAM 36

SLEEPLESS IN SHUSHAN

ESTHER 6:1

Perhaps he ran out of Sominex. Or was it Sonata?

The king could not sleep one night and oh what a difference a day makes! There was a man, named Haman, who wanted to kill every Jew in the world. Here was a Hitler, before Hitler came.

All because a certain Jew, named Mordecai, did not bow and do reverence to Haman (Esther 3:2).

How proud man is. Of the six deadly sins that Solomon writes about in Proverbs (6:16–17), the number one is "a proud look." This pride was what gripped Haman until he could no longer rest. It was not enough that the king's servants reverenced him and his seat was above all the seats of the princes of the land. That was not enough for Haman. This one Hebrew would not bow. That was too much for his ego. He would kill every one of those Hebrews.

But the king could not sleep one night. He had his servants read him some boring records from the chronicles. He is almost asleep when he is read a passage about some man who saved his life from some would-be assassins. "Wait a minute," the king says, (free translation), "not so fast here. What did we do to reward this man?" the king asks. "Nothing Sire. It was turned over to a committee. They are still working on it." "Hah!" the king says. "No wonder nothing has been done yet. This has gone on long enough. We need to do something to honor this man" (6:3).

"So who would be the best man to do this job of honoring someone the king delights in? Haman, of course. He knows how to bestow honor on someone. I have bestowed honor on him, so he should know. Call Haman" (Esther 6:6). You may have already read the story. Haman thinks the king would give more honor to him. Who else would be more honorable? Certainly, he thinks, it is I. Man was he fooled.

Haman wanted to be honored above all men, next to the king, so he comes up with this idea. "Let that man be clothed with the royal robes, let the royal crown be put upon his head, let him ride upon the royal horse, and let him be led through the city by a noble prince in whom the king delights and let him proclaim to everyone, 'This is how the king honors someone he delights in.'" Was he fooled. "Pride goeth before destruction, and an haughty spirit before a fall" (Proverbs 16:18). And, what a fall! The king said, "Right, that sounds like a good idea. Go get Mordecai and honor him just like you said" (free translation). "Huh? You mean I am to lead Mordecai?" Some fall! Haman had a scaffold built to hang Mordecai on but he ends up being hanged on it himself. That's another story.

Where is the love story? By saving the king's life Mordecai saved his nation. The decree had gone out to all of the various provinces that on the 13th day of the 12th month to kill and destroy and take spoil of all Jews, young and old, women and little children, all in one day (Esther 3:13). Now the Jews could DEFEND themselves. It would have been a wholesale slaughter such as Hitler did. But Mordecai trusted the Lord and committed it into His hands. And Israel mourned, and fasted, and prayed. God worked it all for their good.

Because a king ran out of sleeping pills? All things do work together for good. It did for Mordecai and Esther. It does for us, also. "And we know that all things work together for good to them that love God, to them who are the called according to His purpose" (Romans 8:28).

This is only part of the beautiful story. You need to read about the Miss Universe Contest to hear the rest of the story.

BEAM 37

ALMOST IS NOT ENOUGH

ACTS 26:28

We may wonder if Agrippa ever got persuaded and became a Christian. Someday we'll find out. He certainly had an excellent witness and evangelist, the Apostle Paul. Paul was given the freedom to speak for himself and tell King Agrippa how he was saved and how he was converted from being a Christian hater to a Christian evangelist and apostle. Paul was happy to come before Agrippa to answer all the charges that were brought against him. He knew, also, that Agrippa was an "expert in all customs and questions which are among the Jews" (Acts 26:3). So Paul tells him how he, Paul, was a strict Pharisee and a persecutor of Christians. He tells Agrippa how he shut them up in prison, punished them oft in every synagogue, and compelled them to blaspheme (Acts 26:10–12).

Then he tells how he was met by the Lord Jesus while on the way to persecute more Christians. He tells how the Lord said to him "Saul, Saul, why persecutest thou me?" (26: 14). He tells Agrippa that this was the risen Savior that had been crucified and this Jesus made Paul a witness of His resurrection and that he was to be sent to the land of the Gentiles with the message of salvation, "to open their eyes and to turn them from darkness to light, and from the power of Satan unto God, that they may receive forgiveness of sins and inheritance among them which are sanctified by faith that is in Me (Christ)" (26:17–18).

Agrippa listened to this testimony from the Apostle Paul. Another listener was Festus, who cried out that Paul was crazy. "Too much learning has made Paul mad" (Acts 26:24). However, Agrippa did not say anything like that. Then Paul says that these things, the crucifixion and the resurrection, were not done in a corner (v. 26). We can all say amen to that statement. Whether we believe on the Lord Jesus or not, He came into this world and the world has never been the same since. Even infidels and atheists must date their legal documents by the years that are counted from His coming into this world.

Paul then gets personal. Many people listen to sermons that are general and then go home to live the same life they have for years. But if the sermon gets personal it can bring joy to some hearts who accept the Savior, or may bring anger to others who feel they do not need Him. Paul asks if Agrippa believes the prophets. They would be the ones that told about Jesus' coming and crucifixion and resurrection. Then Paul answers his own question. "I know that thou believest" (26:27). Then we have the statement from Agrippa that is difficult to translate. "With a little would you persuade me to be a Christian." Or is it "With a little more you would make me a Christian?" Or is it "Almost you persuade me to be a Christian."

It is not an easy statement to translate. It is certainly agreed by translators that Agrippa is not saying he is a believer. He could be saying "Almost you persuade me." Or he could be saying that "with that little persuasion you expect me to be a Christian?" What ever it was, he was not a believer. He may have thought he was too big a man to be persuaded by one sermon. "Me a Christian?" he might have thought.

"Do you realize who I am? I am King Agrippa. Me a Christian? Huh!"

It would be a pity and a tragedy for him to continue with this attitude. He needs a savior like all of us do. He was a BIG and IMPORTANT MAN. But there were no steps leading up to God's altar. The ground at the cross is level ground. We all come to Him as sinners. We may want to come as doctors, or lawyers, or college professors. But we must all appear before Him as lost sinners needing His mercy. Someone has said that close does not count, except in horseshoes. Close does not count in coming to a Savior. Almost is not enough. It only takes a step. That is all. "Believe on the Lord Jesus Christ and thou shalt be saved, and thy house" (Acts 16:31). "For by grace are ye saved through faith, and that not of yourselves, it is the gift of God" (Ephesians 2:8). Be fully persuaded like Paul, the Jesus hater, now turned Jesus preacher.

BEAM 38

AS IN THE DAYS OF NOAH

MATTHEW 24:37–41

A great many people delve into prophecy. There seems to be a hunger for knowing what's ahead. Even those who seldom attend any church service will attend special prophetic conferences. We want to know the future.

Here is a passage that fascinates thousands. And there are many interpretations of what it means. It is sometimes taught that it means the Rapture of 1 Thessalonians 4:13–17. I do not want to be too theological at this point. Well, just a little. I believe the context rules out the Rapture in Matthew 24:37–41. Verse 39 says the flood came, and took them all away. Not in any rapture but in a judgment. I believe the context certainly teaches that the coming of the Son of Man shall likewise take many away in judgment.

There is another aspect of this passage that is woefully overlooked. That is where the love story comes in.

Why do we do it? We think of Noah, because He says as it was in the days of Noah, but forget another wonderful character that also was a part of the Flood of Noah. At least he was a character that lived in the days before the flood of Noah.

Enoch! He was alive before the great judgment came along. But instead of going through the terrible judgment of the flood, and this was the greatest judgment the earth ever saw at that time, he was rescued, or raptured. A check on the theology tells us that Enoch had a son which he named Methuselah. This was because God had forewarned Enoch the judgment would come when that boy died. After this, not before, but after this, we read that Enoch walked with God, and was not (found dead) for God took him (Genesis 5:24). So we have two who are rescued from the terrible judgment, Enoch and Noah, and Noah's family of course.

The first love story is in the words of God as He spoke to Noah. He did not say "go into the ark," but He said "come into the ark" (Genesis 7:1). God would be with him in the ark. He also gives mankind 7 days to come into the ark with Noah and his family. Twice in that chapter He says it was 7 days after Noah entered the ark that the flood came (Genesis 7:4, 10). Noah is then saved THROUGH the awful judgment.

But as it was in the days of Noah, there was another one saved FROM that awful judgment. We must not forget Enoch. Enoch was raptured so that he never went through the judgment. Noah and his family were rescued but went through the judgment. This is a picture of the New Testament teaching about Israel and the Church. The Church is raptured BEFORE the great and terrible Tribulation judgment. Israel is rescued and saved THROUGH the great and terrible Tribulation Period.

What a beautiful story. God saves the Bride of the Lord Jesus Christ, as it was in the days of Noah, by rapturing it like He did Enoch. He saves His people Israel, as it was in the days of Noah, by keeping them through the Tribulation judgment.

Some teach, deceptively, that the word "rapture" is not in the Scriptures. Neither is the word "trinity." But "trinity" is taught. The English word "rapture" comes from the Latin, meaning "to be carried away by overwhelming emotion, an expression or manifestation of ecstasy or passion" (Webster New Collegiate Dictionary). The Greek word "harpazo" means "to snatch away or be caught up."

This is the word used of Philip in Acts 8:39 when he was "raptured' away from the Ethiopian eunuch. It is also used of Paul in 2 Corinthians 12:2, 4) when Paul tells that he was "caught up," that is raptured. It is wonderful to be saved from a terrible fire. Getting out of the house alive is something to be thankful for. It is even better to be out of the house before the fire starts. That is how the church is rescued, or raptured.

In the Scripture there are a couple of words translated "out of" or "away from." One is the word "ek" which gives us words like exhale, expire, or exit. We should not have any trouble understanding those words. Another word is "apo," which gives us words like apogee, away from the earth, or apostle, which means "one who is sent forth." If someone comes up to the door of your Sunday School class, looks in, and then goes away, he is going away from, "apo," the class. But he was never in the class.

If someone in the class gets up and leaves, he is going out of, "ek," exiting from the class. He was in the class. Paul says we are to wait for His Son from heaven, "even Jesus, which delivered us from (apo) the wrath to come" (1 Thessalonians 1:10). According to Paul, we have already been saved away from, without ever getting into, the coming wrath which shall be the Great Tribulation.

Israel will be saved "ek" out of the Great Tribulation, but she will go through it. The Church will be saved, or is saved already, "apo," away from the Great Tribulation, without being in it. It is great to be rescued out of a burning building, but I'd still rather not be in the building when the fire starts.

So, as it was in the days of Noah, if we are IN CHRIST we will not be IN the Great Tribulation. Are we IN HIM? It is by faith.

"For I am not ashamed of the gospel of Christ: for it is the power of God unto salvation to every one that believeth; to the Jew first, and also to the Greek. For therein is the righteousness of God revealed from faith to faith: as it is written, The just shall live by faith" (Romans 1:16–17).

BEAM 39

AND PETER

MARK 16:7

What a beautiful message this must have been for Peter. He did an awful thing. He did what one would think "proves" he was not a true believer. He denied he even knew the Lord Jesus. And he did this three times. Peter was afraid of what might happen to Peter when he saw what was happening to Jesus. Jesus was being brutally questioned and handled. It looked really bad for Jesus, and any of those who were a part of His gang. Why stick your neck out when it was not necessary? Why not wait and see what will happen?

In Matthew 26:69, when the little maid saw Peter warming himself, she believed he was one of Jesus' gang. She said "Thou also wast with Jesus of Galilee." Peter denied it and said he did not know what she was talking about. A little while later another maid says the same thing, "This is one of them." Again Peter denied it.

After a while a maid again says Peter was one of His followers because, she said, Peter's speech gave him away (Matthew 26:73). Maybe he had a Yankee dialect that she knew was not Southern drawl. He had to be one "of them Yankees." Then Peter did a terrible thing. He thought, "So you think it's my language, huh. Well you aint heard nothing yet. I'll show you. Listen to this language!" Then Peter began to cuss (Matthew 26:74).

There is another lesson here that may be missed in the overall lesson. They no longer bothered Peter after the cussing. That says that they knew enough about Jesus' disciples to know that they had a clean and pure language not punctuated with cussing and swearing. They left him alone. Is our language like that? Do people know that we would not use profanity and cussing and unseemly language? The words are a witness of our heart. "Out of the abundance of the heart the mouth speaketh" (Matthew 12:34). If our heart is clean our language should be also.

But Peter said he did not even know Jesus. What a terrible sin! It is one thing to fear for one's life, or to say you do not agree with Jesus, but to deny you ever knew Him is terrible. Then Peter remembers that the Lord already told him what he would do, deny Jesus three times, and Peter goes out so he can weep at his own weakness and failure. What right did he have to be called a disciple of Jesus, the One that he did not know? What right did he have to call himself a believer at all? What part did he have in the future plans of Jesus? What right did he have to think his sins were pardoned?

He surely must have thought that he had lost it all. How could he be called one of the twelve? There was no hope for Peter. We may feel the same way at times when we have failed miserably and acted shamefully. And it does happen to some of us.

Then, when all hope is gone, he hears this message. That is when an angel brings this resurrection message. "Go . . . tell His disciples and Peter . . . He goeth before you into Galilee" (Mark 16:7). Peter is named so that Peter will not say to himself "Yes, His disciples . . . but I am not one of them. Not after what I did. I have ruined my discipleship and ruined my life and ruined everything. He doesn't mean me. Not any longer." Peter may have thought this, if his name had been left out.

But He did mean Peter also. He said "Him that cometh unto Me I will in no wise cast out" (John 6:37). He is true to His word, even if Peter, and we, are not. He cannot lie. He cannot cast out one who comes to Him What a beautiful story. Have we come? We may fail, but He never fails.

BEAM 40

STUFF, AND LOTS OF IT

LUKE 12:15

Do you find it hard to throw out the "stuff" when you have to move? That's when you separate the chaff from the wheat, or the good stuff from the old stuff. We spend so much time, and money, gathering things. There are memories attached, of course, but sometimes we just have to give up something.

There are many people who are quite proud of the many "things" that they have surrounded themselves with. It is a mark of "class." Things stand for wealth, importance, taste (sometimes), respect, and honor.

And what happens when the head of the house dies? Death brings out the best in people. Death brings out the worst in people. There will be kind neighbors bringing food so the mourners will not have to cook. Others will just come and sit and share the sorrows of those left behind.

Then there are those who will fight over who gets the sofa or the TV set. And the car? Who is going to get that? Huh? Yep, the best and the worst. But what is this all about? Someone came to the Lord Jesus and said to Him "Master, speak to my brother, that he divide the inheritance with me" (Luke 12:13). Notice, he did not call Jesus Lord. He wanted possessions, and he wanted them now. Jesus came to seek and save the lost, not to be a court clerk. So He warns all of us.

Luke 12:15 states "Take heed and beware of covetousness: for a man's life consisteth not in the abundance of THINGS which he possesseth." He is saying simply that life is more than things that we have. I call it "stuff." Sometimes a room is rather "messed up," or not neat enough to the Lady of the House's standard. She might even say, "What is all this stuff?" That is what "things" are, "stuff." We are not going to take any of that "stuff" with us. We may have a difficult time deciding what "stuff" we will take when we move to the new home. We will have no trouble deciding what to take when we leave this world.

Someone has said that we never see a U-Haul going down the street behind a hearse. No! We do not take our bank accounts, nor our rings, nor our trusts, etc. We do take memories, so we should be careful what kind we are making now. Then why do we work so hard for, or covet so much, the "stuff" that we are going to leave behind? It must be that old covetous heart that has never been born again. It still has the old nature that is sinful and rebellious against God's will. We want, we want, we want, and many of us get, get, get. There is nothing wrong with wealth, or the common expression is money. Abraham was a wealthy man, and he was a good man also. Job was another wealthy man and there is hardly anyone who was so good from what we read in the Old Testament. And this wealthy man Job was a good man, so good that he became the target of Satan's lies, that Job only served God for what he could get out of Him. That was proved to be a lie of Satan

It is the love of money that is sinful. "For the love of money is the root of all evil" (1 Timothy 6:10). That is, the love of money, which is another way of saying "stuff" that we would buy with it, is the root of all kinds of evil. And then there are the thieves. Oh yes, sometimes they get the money that we are so covetous to store up. What fools we are. "Lay not up for yourselves treasures upon earth, where moth and rust doth corrupt, and thieves break through and steal. But lay up for yourselves treasures in heaven" (Matthew 6:19–20). We know how much we have in the bank. Do we wonder how much we have up there in heaven's bank? Some banks charge you for keeping your money. Heaven doesn't.

We can never imagine the wealth that our little treasure up in heaven will pay when we come up there to see it. How much are we sending up? Every little bit counts. This "stuff" is left behind. That treasure goes ahead and waits for us. What a beautiful story. Today we hear a lot about IRA's. That stands for Individual Retirement Account. We know how much we have in our IRA at the First National Bank. How much do we have in our heavenly IRA's? We need to put something up there, not just in the First National Bank down here.

Let's not fall for the trickery of treasures.

"There is that maketh himself rich, yet hath nothing: there is that maketh himself poor, yet hath great riches" (Proverbs 13:7).

The rich man said he had much "stuff" laid up for many years. But God said "Thou fool, this night thy soul shall be required of thee: then whose shall these things be, which thou hast provided? So is he that layeth up treasure for himself, and is not rich toward God" (Luke 12:19–21).

BEAM 41

JESUS DEFEATED . . .

LUKE 24:18

They said to Him "Art thou only a stranger in Jerusalem? You mean you have not heard all the things that have happened these last few days." They must have thought, "My, where have you been?" This is what happened on that resurrection day as two disciples of Jesus were walking along the road toward Emmaus. Jesus came alongside them, but their eyes were fixed so that they did not recognize Him. This was a temporary blindness, in part. They could see, but they could not quite recognize Him. This was so Jesus could have a talk with them and give them some Bible lessons.

They think he must have been a newcomer to Jerusalem. Someone who arrived after all of the commotion that happened some three days before. He did not know about the trials and the condemnation by the high priests and rulers. He did not know about how this prophet was crucified. Where had this stranger been? And they said "We trusted that it had been He which should have redeemed Israel: and beside all this, today is the third day since these things were done" (Luke 24:21). Hope is gone. They had defeated this Messiah. Death, that enemy that has conquered everyone else, has conquered again. Jesus defeated by death, like it defeats everyone else. You haven't heard all of this? Where have you been, stranger?

Then Jesus gave them a Bible study. I would have loved to have heard it. He began at Moses, that is at the beginning, and went through the Old Testament and pointed out how all of the Scriptures concerned Himself. What a study that must have been! When they got to the house they urged Him to come in and eat with them. Then it happened. He took bread and blessed it and broke it and gave it to them (verse 30). Then their eyes were opened and they saw it was Jesus and then He vanished from their sight.

Years ago I heard a story about the Winchester Cathedral. I have never been there but I was told that the tour guide tells visitors something about the wonderful history of that cathedral. Back in the days before there was any Morse code, messages were sent by flags, or semaphore. There was a tremendous battle raging in Europe. Much of Europe's freedom depended upon the outcome. A powerful dictator was trying to conquer all of the European nations and even some of the Asian nations, even Russia.

A ship came near the coast and started sending the message about the battle. The message began with "Wellington defeated." Then the fog came down and the ship could not be seen. But that message was relayed from hilltop to hilltop across Great Britain where they had no fog. The nation was plunged into dark gloom and despair. Wellington defeated! Now that dictator would get his desire and rule all of Europe. "Wellington defeated." After a few hours the sun warmed up enough to clear away the fog. Then the ship started to send the message. Again it started out with "Wellington defeated." Only now it continued with "the enemy." Everything changed. Now the message was relayed across Great Britain and there was rejoicing and great joy. Wellington had defeated the enemy, he had defeated Napoleon.

This may be somewhat like what these early followers of Jesus went through. "Jesus defeated" was the message. They thought He would deliver them. They thought He was the Messiah. But Jesus was defeated. They crucified Him. Death won the victory. That was how it looked, for three days. Now they see Him alive and the message is not "Jesus defeated" but "Jesus defeated the enemy." HE IS MESSIAH. No other religious leader ever came back from the dead and showed himself to the world. But this One did. He is alive. He is alive for evermore. Jesus defeated the enemy. He says all that come to Him will receive eternal life and be with Him forever. "Jesus defeated the enemy." Not only death but Satan, the liar, and all pain and sorrow and tears, and suffering, and death for us, has been defeated by Him. What a victory! What a Savior! And all of this comes to us by grace, through faith, without works, but as a free gift. But a gift is not any good unless we receive it. Have we received it? Have we received Him?

BEAM 42

OBEY THE LAW——EXCEPT

DANIEL 3:17

"These three Hebrew children that were brought to Babylon as captives from Jerusalem were getting to be a real pain. They wanted a special diet so they would not eat our food, and now they refuse to obey the King's command. What is it with these people?" This is something like the King's servants must have felt. These three Hebrew children did not want to disobey God's command and eat polluted food. However, after a trial period they were healthier looking than the rest of the king's prisoners.

But now they have really done it (the servants of Nebuchadnezzar thought). The King gave strict orders that when the orchestra played, everyone had to fall down and worship an image. This proud king erected an image that was over ninety feet tall, and made of gold. Think what that would cost in today's money. The orchestra was not the Big Band ensemble, not the Glenn Miller or Tommy Dorsey kind. It was made up of a cornet, flute, harp, sackbut, psaltery, dulcimer, and "all kinds of music" (Daniel 3:5), whatever that means. Six musical instruments is a wrong number in Scripture. Seven is the perfect or complete number. You can see something is wrong here already.

But falling down and worshiping an image would be worse than eating pork chops. "No," these three bold men said, "no way." But there is a fiery furnace waiting for those who refuse to obey the law of the King. So be it they said. Now we again come to the "If" God. Not that there is any doubt about God and His power and His grace, His wisdom, His righteousness. The "If" is not knowing His will. They say that IF God wants to, He can put out the fire. But IF not, we still won't worship any image no matter how hot the furnace is. That's the spirit. This brings us to how much are saints to obey the laws of the land.

We are told to obey the law. In Romans 13:1 we are told to "be subject unto the higher powers. For there is no power but of God, the powers that be are ordained of God." If we resist the power of the government we resist God. So then, is this a contradiction? Did these three Hebrew children do wrong in resisting the power of the government that God had put in place? Not so. We are to obey the law of the government, except when those laws are contrary to God's laws.

The apostles were told not to preach or teach in the name of Jesus (Acts 5:28). The answer given by Peter and the other apostles was, "We ought to obey God rather than men" (Acts 5:29). We are told to pay our taxes (Romans 13:6) even though they may seem outrageous, but if the government tells us we cannot pray to God, or worship Him, or wants us to commit some sin against Him, then the government must be disobeyed. We must put God first. If all else fails, we simply break the law. We must also be prepared to take the punishment of breaking the law. We cannot plead innocence when we know we have broken the law. Take the punishment. It is for His sake.

Oh, these three Hebrew children! They took the punishment. They willfully disobeyed the Law of Nebuchadnezzar and were cast into the fiery furnace. But they were unharmed. They did not know that God would intervene, but they did not care. They were not going to break God's command and worship an idol. But the men who threw them into the furnace were consumed by the heat. And there was a fourth Person seen with them in the furnace. Nebuchadnezzar says "Did we not cast three men bound into the midst of the fire? . . . Lo, I see four men loose, walking in the midst of the fire, . . . and the form of the fourth is like the Son of God" (Daniel 3:24–25).

That One could only be the One who would take our sins and die in our place. He was in the furnace with them. They cast in three, then there were four.

By the way, the fire did do one thing. It untied them. They were all tied up and bound and then when Nebuchadnezzar looks into the furnace he sees four men walking around. When the three came out they still had no singe on their clothes, and their hair was not burned off, and they did not have the smell of fire (Daniel 3:27).

What a miracle! But God does not always promise to do this. But IF He does not, we still should obey Him, like they did. We should.

"As for me and my house, we will serve the Lord" (Joshua 24:15). Do we?

"If ye be willing and obedient, ye shall eat the good of the land" (Isaiah 1:19).

BEAM 43

WHAT WE OUGHT TO BE

MATTHEW 5:13–16

What should we be like in this world? We are the living visible body of the Lord Jesus Who is the invisible head of the church. He represents us up there while we try to manifest His being down here. That is a great challenge, especially since we are the sinners who are trying to represent Him, who is the sinless Savior. He does give us some simple lessons and examples of what we should be like here on earth.

PRESERVATION: This is one of the examples He gives us in Matthew 5:13–16. We are to be the salt of the earth. Remember they did not have refrigerators in those days. Food was preserved by using salt. And they did not have the pure salt crystals or granulated salt that we use today. Much of the salt contained some rock or some other matter. It was of a rock variety and contained impurities. That made the outer layer lacking in flavor. But it was used as a preservative for food and was a valuable commodity. Part of the pay given to Roman soldiers was in the form of salt, which was called salarium. This gave us our word salary. But Jesus said if the salt has lost its flavor, it was good for nothing. It can be put back into the ground.

We are to be like that salt. We should be combating evil and sin and in a way preserving this earth. The time will come when the church is removed and the forces of evil will be let loose to totally corrupt this world, worse then it is. But while we are here we should be a preservative against evil.

ELEVATION: He says a city set on a hill cannot be hidden. It was strategic for cities to be built up high. It made for a better defense against enemies. We should not be ashamed of our faith. We do not shove it into somebody's face against his will but we should not be ashamed of it either. Peter writes in 1 Peter 3:15, "Be ready always to give an answer to every man that asketh you a reason of the hope that is in you with meekness and fear." I cannot add to that. It is clear enough. We don't push, but we are not ashamed either. We are ready to tell why we believe. A city on a hill.

ILLUMINATION: We are the light of the world. While He was here He was the Light. Now that He is gone, we are the light. You are to just let the light shine, that's all. It is letting Him Who is the Light shine out through us, the earthen vessels, so the world can see. The Light gives off rays and anyone who wants to see can come to this Light. Our light should point to His light.

This is what we should be like. Preserving this world against evil, living out in the open so that all can see, not hidden, and shining in the dark. It may not be much of a light but in a dark room a candle is easily seen. And even a small candle can be used in an emergency. It can also help us to find the light switch so we can turn on a brighter light. Shine for Him, even with our tiny little candles. It helps those who are in the dark to see the brighter Light.

Oh, there is one more facet of this threesome. Salt not only preserves but it does something else. It makes us thirsty. This is something we should all strive for, to make some poor lost sinner thirsty for the salvation that we have that gives us joy and peace and eternal life in Christ. Make someone thirsty for what you have. That is even better than preserving this earth. This earth will pass away, even if we preserve it temporarily. Souls are for eternity. Make some soul thirsty for what you have. And that soul lives forever. Be salty for the Savior!

BEAM 44

COLLECTING OUR PAYCHECKS

ROMANS 6:23

I once took on a new job with a company where I heard something that I had never heard before. I was a little surprised when I heard the boss telling another employee that I was a self-starter. I had not heard that term before. I wondered. Did he mean I did not need someone to tell me to start working. I thought that was what I came to work for, to "work." In some jobs in the past I was told to slow down by other employees. I was making them look bad. Sorry about that. I thought "we" came to work to "work." When payday came around I did not have to give thanks to my boss, or whoever handed out the checks, for my work. I was thankful if they brought it to me. Some places you had to go to the cashier or someone else and get your check. But I did not feel that I was receiving a gift from the company.

I felt that we had an agreement. I worked, they promised me so much per hour. That was it. I "worked" my hours all week, usually forty, and expected to be paid. I earned it. Once I received a "bonus" around Christmas time. That was something I did not count on. That was extra. But when I came to work, and I did my work, I was a self-starter. I did not have to feel like I was receiving a gift from the company. I earned it. I worked for it. They owed it to me.

Paul says in this verse that we all have earned something. We all have earned death, for our sins. He did not spell it out here but this death is more than just physical death. We all have earned eternal death, that is separation from God forever. The death most people are aware of is the physical death, the separation of the soul from the body. Many try to not think about this. We cover the grave with flowers so the grave, and what it stands for, is hidden as much as possible. We do not want to think about it. But there is a more terrible death than the physical. When God formed Adam out of the earth, and Eve out of Adam, He told them that if they ate of that tree of knowledge of good and evil, it was not an apple tree, in that day they would die. And they did. They did not die physically but they died that awful separation from God.

They had fellowship with Him in the Garden. Now they are dead to God. And all of Adam's race since then have been dead to God. This is spiritual death. If we die like this we are separated from God forever. That is the eternal death. Now Paul says we all have earned the first death. He says it's our wages; death and separation from God. But he says there is a gift from God that we can have. This is eternal life through Jesus Christ our Lord. This is something that we did not earn. We can never earn a gift. We can accept it, or reject it. If we receive it, or accept it, we have a gift for which we should always and forever be thankful.

If we do nothing, our pay day will come and it will mean eternal separation from God. Have we received Jesus Christ as Lord and Savior? Have we have received a gift that we can always be thankful for? Time is running out. We should not wait. Deathbed repentances are valid. They will save. But look at all the peace and joy that is lost. Look at all the blessings of the Lord that could be had. Why lose all of that joy and fellowship? The gift is ready. Why not receive Him now? Why wait? We would not leave a Christmas gift under the tree for months while we thought about opening it to see what is in it. Why wait?

"But not as the offence, so also is the free gift. For if through the offence of one many are dead, much more the grace of God, and the gift by grace, which is by one Man, Jesus Christ, hath abounded unto many. And not as it was by one that sinned, so is the gift: for the judgment was by one to condemnation, but the free gift is of many offences unto justification" (Romans 5:15–16).

"If ye believe not that I am He, ye shall die in your sins" (John 8:24).

"If ye continue in My word, then are ye My disciples indeed: And ye shall know the truth and the truth shall make you free" (John 8:31–32).

BEAM 45

HATED WITHOUT A CAUSE OR REASON

There is a beautiful story in the Greek word "dorean" and how it is used in the Scriptures. It is used nine times in the Bible. It is translated 'for naught" once, "in vain" once, "freely" six times, and once it is translated "without a cause."

In John 15:25 we read: "But this cometh to pass, that the word might be fulfilled that is written in their law, They hated me without a cause." This is mentioned in Psalm 69:4 where the Psalmist prophetically states "They that hate me without a cause are more than the hairs of my head." They had no reason to hate Him. What had He done to be hated? There was not a man that could bring any sin against Him. Even His enemies could not bring any sin against Him. It was pure hatred of the human natural man and his sinful heart. Jesus was the Light that came into the world and "Men loved darkness rather than light, because their deeds were evil" (John 3:19).

But this word "dorean" is also used in Roman 3:23–24. Here we read "For all have sinned and come short of the glory of God; being justified freely by His grace through the redemption that is in Christ Jesus." Think of that! Just as He was hated without a cause, for no reason, that is freely, so are we justified, made righteous before God, without any cause on our part, for no reason, on our part, freely God has justified us.

We have done nothing to deserve His blessings. Even a lesser punishment for our sins would be more than we could ask for or dream of. Yet He has declared that we are righteous before Him, that we are right with God and it is done "without a cause." If we can find one thing in Jesus that He should have been put to death for, then we could say that there is some one good thing in us that we should be saved for. Can you think of any? His enemies could not find any. That really says a lot. I am sure they could find a number of things about me that are not right. So they had to make up something about Him. They said He was perverting the nation and forbidding to give tribute to Caesar (Luke 23:2). This was a lie, of course, and they knew it.

When He declared He was the Son of God and would sit on the right hand of power and would come in clouds of heaven, they accused Him of blasphemy (Mark 14:62–64). Yet, what He said was true, because He was the Messiah. They had no legitimate cause for crucifixion even though they had watched Him minister for three years. He had done nothing wrong. They hated Him without a cause. And again, we come to how we are saved.

The one charge they made that was true was that He declared He was God. Yes, He did, but this was true and still is true. No sin could be attributed to Him. No wrongdoing of any kind was stated against Him. He had many enemies but they could not point to any sin, fault, flaw, or any bad thing. Oh, yes, He ate with sinners. I am glad He did. He was a friend of publicans and sinners. I am glad He was. But sin? What sin? None could deny His miracles. They were afraid of losing their jobs. It goes back to the god of money. They, the priests, would be put out of business.

"For by grace are ye saved" (Ephesians 2:8–9). We can do nothing but take it. That is what the faith is, the handle, that received the salvation that is "freely given, without a cause, for naught," to sinners that do not deserve it in any way. What is there about ungodly and unworthy sinners that God should come in human flesh and die on the cross for them? Nothing at all. To try to fathom this gracious and abounding love of a righteous and holy God for unholy sinners goes beyond our imagination. Some have said that God had a problem. God having a problem? Can He? Paul must have been aware of it. He says in Romans 3:26 "To declare, I say, at this time His righteousness: that He might be just, and the justifier of him which believeth in Jesus." That's the problem. How can a just God still be just, and spare the ungodly? By taking their place on the cross and paying for their sins Himself. The punishment of sin is carried out, so He is a Holy and Just God. The sinner is cleansed from his sin by believing on Christ Who took his sins and died for him. That makes God a Justifier. One does not contradict the other. Both needs are met in one Person, the person of Christ. Yes, without a cause, without any good thing in us, just like there was no bad thing in Him. Saved by grace, freely, through faith, the handle that accepts it. What a Savior!

BEAM 46

SEEING IS BELIEVING
OR IS IT BELIEVING IS SEEING?
JOHN 7:17

I do not know if "seeing is believing" is the state of Missouri's pledge of allegiance or not. I believe it is known as the "Show Me" State. Anyhow, they have gotten the reputation of wanting to see something first before they are fooled into believing something, sight unseen. When it comes to the Scriptures one might want to see first and then believe afterwards. But we can hardly go back nearly 2000 years to witness a resurrection of someone Who was killed and then rose up out of the grave and showed Himself alive on earth for forty days and nights before He ascended up to heaven.

Some, who do not believe, think Christians are a bunch of weirdoes who keep their heads in some old book and never have any fun. This last part may be because of some teaching, or misteaching, about the place of fun in the believer's life. Christians should be the happiest people in the world. They have their sins forgiven, to be remembered against them no more. Their sins are put behind God's back so that He does not see them anymore. He has promised to remember them against us no more. There is a wonderful eternity ahead for believers. They will receive a new and glorious body in which there will be no more pain (how does that grab you), no death, no sorrow, tears wiped away. No more locks on doors. There will be no more robbery, no thievery. And more than all of that, they will see the risen Savior in His glory for ever and ever. They could not look upon Him in His risen glory with the old eyes they had here on earth. So God will give them new eyes so they can behold His radiant glory.

And, like the hymn says, after ten thousand years there are no less days to sing God's praise then when they first began. They should be happy, more than any others.

But can a person believe before he sees? Is it fair to ask one to believe something without seeing something first? Well, we are told that we walk by faith and not sight. If it were completely by sight first, then we would hardly need any faith. We do not need faith to see it is raining, unless we are blind. Then we could feel it. But God is gracious. He provides any honest doubter with an opening. God provides any honest agnostic with a way out so that they are without excuse. He says to give Him a try.

In John 7:17 Jesus says this, "If any man will do His will, he shall know of the doctrine, whether it be of God, or whether I speak of myself." I might change the wording a bit to bring out the truth of what He is saying. He is saying that if any man is **willing to do His will** he shall know the truth, whether it is of God or not. How can God be more gracious and condescending and humble than that? He is saying "Give Me a chance." In other words, He is giving the TRUE agnostic, the TRUE doubter, no excuse whatever.

He is saying try Me. Try it My way. I guarantee that if you give Me a chance, if you will believe, then afterwards you will know. Then you will see. Believing is seeing. What excuse have we? Have we given God a chance? He invites us to test Him, if we are honest and have some troubling doubts about the whole thing. He says "If you are willing to do My will, you will then know."

So honest doubter, honest agnostic, honest Missourian, take Him at His word. Give God a chance.

You will be glad you did and you will find that believing is seeing.

"Thy word is true from the beginning; and every one of Thy righteous judgments endureth forever"

(Psalm 119:160).

BEAM 47

REMOVING THE MERCY SEAT

1 SAMUEL 6:19

1 Samuel 6:19 reads "because they looked into the ark of the Lord, even He smote of the people fifty thousand and threescore and ten and the people lamented because the Lord had smitten many of the people with a great slaughter." Why so many? Fifty thousand and 70 people! Why?

The ark had been captured by the Philistines and held by them for 7 months (1 Samuel 6:1). The ark became a curse to the Philistines. It was not supposed to be with them. They set it by their god, or idol, Dagon. In the morning Dagon had mysteriously fallen over. So they set Dagon up again. The next morning Dagon is fallen over again and his head and hands are broken off. Then the Philistines move the ark around from one city to another. They finally get wise and plan to send it back to Israel. They send it back by using two milk cattle that had born calves. They figure if the cows head toward Israel, leaving behind their calves, it must be the work of the God of Israel. They haul it by cart and put in some jewels of gold in the cart as a token of appeasement to this God of Israel. Sure enough, the cattle do not turn back when they hear their calves calling. So it must be of God.

The cart comes into the field at Beth-shemesh. The people of Beth-shemesh make the mistake of looking into the ark to see if everything that was supposed to be there was still there. Did the Philistines take some of it? No! It was all there. But why did so many of them die?

There was a proper way to handle the ark. It was to be handled only by the priests. It was to be carried on the shoulders of the priests when it had to be moved. Nobody was to look into the ark. Once a year the High Priest entered into the Holy of Holies and sprinkled blood upon the Mercy Seat. This was for the sins of the nation. Atonement means "covering," not at-one-ment. Their sins would be forgiven because the blood had been sprinkled on it, the blood of an innocent animal, for the sins of the guilty people. But what was it they did that was so wrong? They lifted the lid off the ark. That lid was the covering upon which the blood was sprinkled. Inside the ark were three things. There was some manna, a token of God's care over Israel during their wilderness journey. Then there was Aaron's rod that had budded, when there was a dispute over the leadership of Moses. Thirdly, there were the tables of the Law, the broken Law that they broke while Moses was up in the mountain getting more instructions about the Law from God.

Since they broke the Law, the only way they, or we, could approach a Holy God was by the sacrifice of an innocent animal whose blood was sprinkled upon the lid of he ark, the Mercy Seat. When the lid is removed God sees a broken Law and must judge the lawbreaker. He is a Holy and Righteous God Who cannot look upon sins without judging. When He sees the blood sprinkled upon the lid, the sins are forgiven. They have been covered by the shed blood of another. Uncover it and there is no refuge, no safety, no atonement for sinners. So God judged. John tells us that Jesus is the Lamb of God which taketh away the sins of the world (John 1:29). His blood takes away my sins and your sins and the sins of the world, if, if, that blood has been applied by faith to cleanse us from our sins. If we believe, then our sins are gone. The blood of animals could not PUT AWAY sins, the writer of Hebrews tells us (Hebrews 10:4). Sins in the Old Testament were FORGIVEN on an IOU basis. Forgiven, until the Lamb of God came. Then they were PUT AWAY by Him Who alone could put away our sins by His own blood sacrifice.

Has the blood been applied by faith? If so, we have the Mercy Seat separating us and our sins from a Holy and Just God. But He loves to forgive and forget. "When I see the blood, I will pass over you" (Exodus 12:13). Without that blood, there is no hope.

BEAM 48

THE RESURRECTION

"BUT EVERY MAN IN HIS OWN ORDER"

"For as in Adam all die, even so in Christ shall all be made alive. But every man in his own order: Christ the firstfruits; after-ward those that are Christ's at His coming. Then cometh the end, when He shall have delivered up the kingdom to God, even the Father" (1 Corinthians 15:22–24). Here are mentioned three parts to the resurrection. Let's get the order straight, if we can.

If one reads the Old Testament feasts days one will see a New Testament teaching about the resurrection. There is the feast of the first fruits. After that there is the harvest. Then there is the gleaning. If you read the Book of Ruth you will see the gleaning that goes on after the harvest. Each one of these is spelled out for us in the New Testament and each one points to a part of the resurrection of the saints.

After the Passover and the week of unleavened bread, which pointed to the death of Jesus on the cross, we are told that the children of Israel were to keep "the feast of harvest, the firstfruits of thy labours, which thou hast sown in the field" (Exodus 23:16). This feast points to the resurrection of the Lord Jesus.

There is a Scripture that seems to be overlooked when we read about the resurrection. We hear much about the resurrection of the Lord after three days and three nights but very little, if anything, about those other saints that were raised from the graves with Him. Oh, yes, there were saints who were raised from the dead when He was. Matthew tells us "And the graves were opened and many bodies of the saints which slept arose and came out of the graves after His resurrection, and went into the holy city, and appeared unto many" (Matthew 27:52–53). Most people have never heard of them.

Why do I not hear about these saints? The Word says "feast of the Firstfruits." That is a plural. It signified that this was only the beginning of the harvest. The greater part of the harvest would follow later in the season. The firstfruits was fulfilled when Jesus AND the other saints were raised from the dead. Remember, it was after His resurrection, for in everything He must have the pre-eminence. It is written like it happened when the veil of the temple was torn, but the quake only opened the graves. Later, after His resurrection, there were some saints that were raised from the dead. Jesus and these saints make a plural and are the firstfruits. And these risen saints were seen by many.

Then what about the harvest? After the firstfruits there is the "feast of ingathering, which is in the end of the year, when thou hast gathered in thy labours out of the field" (Exodus 23:16).

This would point to the great resurrection of the saints at the appearing of the Lord Jesus FOR His church. This comes when the millions and millions of saints are raised from the dead when the Lord returns. This is what is called the Rapture. Those who are alive at His appearing will be changed, in a moment, in a twinkling of an eye, Paul says (1 Corinthians 15:51–52). But before the living saints are changed into their new and glorious bodies there is something else that happens. All of the dead saints are raised from the dead, first, in their new and glorious bodies (1 Thessalonians 4:16). We, Paul says, shall not precede them. They come first. They died first. They are raised first. Then, if we happen to be alive at that particular moment, we will never see death but will be changed in a moment into glorious bodies. Alive, or dead, they all will have new bodies and will live in them forever with Him.

So what about that third part of the harvest? That would be the gleaning. The book of Ruth tells us what that is all about. The harvesters miss some grain and the gleaners went behind them and picked up the little bits that were missed, or dropped. God's harvesters are not careless like human harvesters. They do not miss anything. (You cannot press every part of a type, or a parable.) After Jesus comes back WITH His church to rule and reign over the earth there will still be some deaths that occur during His millennial kingdom. Not many, and not at a young age. We are living longer each generation. We will live even longer when the Prince of Peace reigns over the earth. But there will be some deaths. Isaiah says a man dying at 120 years of age will be like a child dying (Isaiah 65:20). So those who die after the Great Resurrection Harvest of the saints at His second coming will be raised later. This would be the gleaning, the gathering of those saints who die during the millennium.

This is the order of the resurrection. It has three parts. It is about

His church, which is His bride. Anyone can be a part of His church and therefore be in some part of His resurrection of the saints. First we must be one of His. That is what a saint is. The word "saint" means one who has been set aside for a particular use, God's use. Those who come to Him are set apart from the world and become His very own. Are you a saint? You can be. Just come to Him.

"And I give unto them eternal life; and they shall never perish, neither shall any man pluck them out of My hand" (John 10:28).

BEAM 49

BEHAVE YOURSELF

1 TIMOTHY 3:15

We ought to behave. We tell the children, or try to tell them, to behave. "Don't do that!" "Now, Freddie, stop that." "Gertrude, behave. That's not nice." But how do we behave? What do we do to behave? Paul gave a list of do's and don'ts in 1 Timothy. He says an overseer, or bishop, must be blameless, vigilant, sober, and not given to excess. That covers a lot of territory. He also is to rule his own house well, or he is not suited to rule in God's house, the church (1 Timothy 3:5). We should not be double tongued. That would be a physical impossibility, but you know what that means. The American Indians know how we spoke with two tongues. Sometimes we say speaking out of both sides of our mouth.

We are to have a good report of those who are not Christians. That's another tough one. We can be falsely accused by those who hate us. But before the Lord, we are to be honest and faithful to our words. Even when we deal with ungodly people we are to maintain our honesty. That may be one way of witnessing to them. Our word should be as good as our signature. If we are plumbers, we should be good plumbers. If we are carpenters, we should be good ones. Auto mechanics, the same also.

These are simple rules of decency that should characterize us. Not given to alcohol, not greedy for money. That would surely separate the sheep from the goats. We should be honest, law abiding, truthful people. But notice what all this is for. It is how we ought to behave ourselves in the house of God, "which is the church of the living God." Then Paul tells us what this is all about. It is for the church, the true church, which is the pillar and ground of the truth. And what are pillars for?

Baltimore is known as the "Monumental City." There are monuments all around the city. You do not go very far before you come to another monument. There is a Washington Monument in Baltimore too. But wherever you go to see these monuments you do not see them sitting on the ground. They are always set up on pillars. And what are pillars for? They hold up the monument so all can see it better. The church is to hold Him up so the world can see Him better, Who is the Way, the Truth, and the Life.

We can't do that if we do not behave. It would be easier if the Lord spoke audibly from heaven and said to us "Don't do that." But He leaves us the Word and in that Word he tells us to behave. What we do is a reflection on Him. He is in heaven representing us. We are here on earth representing Him. What kind of a job are we doing? Suppose He did the same kind of job for us in heaven? So behave yourself. We are to hold Him up before the world. We can't do that if we don't behave. Do it for His sake. Behave yourself. Let's lift Him up so the world can get a better look at Him. We should get out of the way. They don't need to see us.

"Lift up your heads, O ye gates; even lift up, ye everlasting doors; and the King of glory shall come in. Who is this King of glory? The Lord of hosts, He is the King of glory" (Psalm 24:9–10).

"Praise the Lord from the earth, ye dragons, and all deeps: fire, and hail . . . beasts, and all cattle; . . . kings of the earth, and all people; princes, and all judges of the earth: both young men, and maidens; old men and children: Let them praise the name of the Lord " (Psalm 148:7–13).

BEAM 50

REDEEMED

When I was a young boy, there was a place around the block that had three balls hanging up out in front of the store. They were black, or they looked dirty like they were black, and were the size of small basketballs. Old timers would recognize this place as a Pawn Shop. I would gaze into the windows of this store and wonder what it cost to buy some of the things in the window. There would be some musical instruments, usually a guitar, and there would be lots of jewelry. It was the place to hock something when you needed some money quickly. You might get twenty dollars for your guitar and more, I am sure, for a real diamond ring. When you wanted your guitar back you had to pay, perhaps, twenty two dollars, to get it back. The shop owner had to make a little money. I wondered how much that guitar would cost, even though I could not play one.

This was called redeeming your goods. And it might be held for perhaps 60 days for you to redeem it. If you did not come back with some money, then the Pawn Shop had the right to sell off your property.

That is what redemption is. It is buying back something by paying the price. That is what the Lord Jesus did for us.

There are three words that we should get a hold of to appreciate what He did for us. The Greeks have a word for the market place. It is the word "agora." When Paul was driven out of Thessalonica he then went on to Berea (Acts 17:10). He was accused of turning "the world upside down" (Acts 17:6). I wonder if anyone says that about us. He went to Berea where the Bereans checked out every thing Paul said to see if it were Scriptural or not. They were called "more noble" than those of Thessalonica. Then Paul came to Athens, the Greek city. We read that Paul disputed daily with the Jews in the synagogue and with the devout persons, we can assume were Greeks, in the "agora," the market (Acts 17:17).

The verbal form of the word is "agoradzo." This word means to buy at the market place, the agora. In Revelation 5:9 the saints sing to the Lamb of God, Jesus Christ that he "has redeemed us to God by Thy blood out of every kindred, and tongue, and people, and nation." He, Jesus, redeemed them buy paying the price for their sins.

Not only does He redeem us AT THE MARKET, but He also redeems us OUT OF THE MARKET. That is the word "exagoradzo." You can recognize the prefix "ex," which gives us our word exit, out of, or the way out. He not only paid the price for our sins, but He bought us out of the market. But there is another word that also should be noted. That word is "lutrao." It is the word for SETTING THE SLAVE FREE. Manumission is what we call it today. Jesus paid the price to buy back the sinful goods that were in hock.

Peter tells us in 1 Peter 1:18–19, "Forasmuch as ye know that ye were not redeemed with corruptible things, such as silver and gold . . . but with the precious blood of Christ."

Silver and gold are corruptible things he says; the blood of Christ is precious. As a child I had nothing to pay for a guitar. As an adult I have had nothing to pay for my sins. If I had silver and gold they would be corrupt. You cannot redeem from sins with money. It takes the blood of the Sinless Savior to do it. No one has the price it takes to redeem. Only Jesus had incorruptible blood that could be placed on God's altar so we could be redeemed. He paid the price, willingly and gladly.

He deserves our love and devotion for buying us out of the market of sin, and setting us free to serve God in truth and love. What a wonderful Savior we have. Is He yours?

"The Lord hath appeared of old unto me, saying, Yea, I have loved thee with an everlasting love; therefore with lovingkindness have I drawn thee" (Jeremiah 31:3).

BEAM 51

WHY DID HE LIVE SO LONG?

Methuselah, that is.

Many people know who was the oldest living person, as far as the records are concerned. Some have even written songs about him. But why did this man live so long? And why would it be something that would be noted in the records? It was not because of his diet and/or exercise. There is a reason, and a love story.

We read that Enoch live sixty and five years and begat Methuselah (Genesis 5:21). Nothing is said about walking with God in this verse. Then we read that he walked with God. There must be a reason for the change. And there is.

There must have been a revelation from God to Enoch. "Methuselah" means "He dies and it (the judgment?) is sent" (Fausset's Bible Dictionary). Others translate it "when he is gone, it will come."

Now we read that:

Gen. 5:25	Methuselah begat Lamech when he was	187 years old
Gen. 5:28	Lamech begat Noah when he was	182 years old
Gen. 7:6	When the flood came Noah was	600 years old
Gen. 5:27	All the days of Methuselah were	969 years

So when Methuselah died the flood came, as God told Enoch it would.

What is all this about? So what? Methuselah is the oldest living human according to the Scripture. So what? What does it mean to me? It is connected with the "when once the longsuffering of God waited in the days of Noah" (1 Peter 3:20). Again in 2 Peter 3:9, "The Lord is not slack concerning His promise, as some men count slackness; but is longsuffering to us-ward not willing that any should perish but that all should come to repentance."

Why did he live so long? Why did God wait so long? Because He is longsuffering with sinners. He waited, He waited, He waited, and He waited. That is why Methuselah lived so long. But—the time ran out and the flood came. God waited, but man did not turn from sin.

God is doing the same thing today. But the time will run out and the fire judgment will come. But God's love is still longsuffering toward us now. He is still waiting now. Are you listening? Is God waiting for you? God still loves us and wants us to hear Him. There is an end to God's longsuffering. Even in Noah's day the time ran out. We should not wait. We should not tempt God. Go to Him now before the time runs out.

"Harden not your hearts, as in the day of provocation, in the day of temptation in the wilderness" (Hebrews 3:8).

"Now is the accepted time; behold, now is the day of salvation" (2 Corinthians 6:2).

"Seek ye the Lord while He may be found, call ye upon Him while He is near" (Isaiah 55:6).

BEAM 52

WILY DELILAH

THE LORD WAS DEPARTED FROM HIM

JUDGES 16:20

This was said of Samson. He "wist not," which is an archaic expression for "to know." Samson did not know that the Lord had departed from him. There is another Scripture similar to this one where we read that "the Spirit of the Lord departed from Saul" (1 Samuel 16:14). Because of Saul's disobedience the Spirit of the Lord left him. Samuel then anointed David as the chosen king, the one that God had chosen

Here also, because of Samson's disobedience, the Lord left him. Samson means "distinguished, strong," and strong he was. Whether a person reads the Scriptures or not, he has heard of Samson. The word means mighty strong like no one else ever was. We hear the word Goliath (an exile or soothsayer) and we think of a tall giant of a man. He could make the tallest basketball stars look like midgets. Well, shorties anyway. Goliath was six cubits and a span which made him about 10 ½ feet tall.

Samson was stronger than any Mr. Universe contest winner. One day while Samson was a youth, a young lion jumped out at him and roared and Samson tore him in pieces like the lion was a kid, a young goat that is, and Samson had nothing in his hands to be used as a weapon. Samson lost a bet he made with thirty Philistines he invited to a party. They cheated, so Samson went out and slew thirty of their men and took their clothes and paid off the bet. The Philistines were his enemies. They wanted to bind Samson so they persuaded his people, the men of Judah, to bind Samson and hand him over for all the trouble he was causing the Philistines. Samson lets the men of Judah bind him but when he is handed over to the enemy the ropes that were used to tie him were broken like so much flax, or cotton. He finds a jawbone of a donkey and picks it up and, using it for a weapon, he kills 1000 Philistines.

There was no one even close to being a competitor of Samson. The Philistine army could not take him. His was not super duper human strength. This was not something he built up by eating Wheaties and doing his daily physical workouts. This was super strength that came from the Lord. The Lord told Samson's parents that this baby they were about to have should be a Nazarite from before birth. His father, Manoah, was told that the child's mother should not eat anything from the vine, nor come near any dead thing. And the child should never have his hair cut. He was to be a deliverer of Israel (Judges 13:4–5). His parents obeyed the Lord. He was a Nazarite from before his birth.

However, Samson did not cherish his special relationship with God. He loved women. He loved the women of the Philistines. He also loved harlots. He loved the wrong women and did not control his appetite. One day he met THE wrong woman. This was wily Delilah. The chief men of the Philistines made a deal with Delilah, somewhat like the priests did with Judas Iscariot. "Find out Samson's secret," they said, "and we will pay you 1100 pieces of silver." That is far more than the 30 pieces that Judas sold Jesus for. So wily Delilah starts her attack on Superman Samson. She nags, and she nags, and she nags. Samson tells her some lies at first, hoping that would shut her up. As soon as Delilah finds out he has lied to her, she starts her nagging again. She nagged him so much "that his soul was vexed unto death" (Judges16:16).

Samson, who could kill lions and Philistines could not stand her nagging, nagging, nagging. It was driving him nuts. Samson finally broke down and told her the truth. You can see what nagging can do. He told her it was his Nazarite vow that made him strong. If he shaved, he would not have any more strength than any other man. BIG mistake. She had him sleep on her knees. She called for a barber. After the haircut Samson knew not that the Lord had departed from him. What a great deliverer he might have made if he had obeyed the Lord. Many a man has fallen because of a wrong woman. We should learn something from Samson.

So the Philistines come upon Samson. He shakes himself like before but he is now a wimp. They put out his eyes first, then they put him in the mill to grind corn. There is a somewhat beautiful ending. Somewhat. His hair starts to grow again and with the hair, his strength. God is still gracious to the fallen strong man. He is called into a party the Philistines are having in the house of their god Dagon (Judges

16:25). They want to have fun with this crippled weakling, Samson, whom they once feared. He is placed between the two pillars that hold up the roof. The Philistines want to make fun of Samson.

Samson makes a last request of God to die with his enemies (16:28). Too bad he did not realize this sooner. But God is gracious. God hears his prayer and gives him strength to push the pillars apart, the roof comes crashing down on everyone, including Samson. At his death Samson kills more Philistines than he killed all his life. This was in revenge for putting out his eyes.

But does God leave us today? Does God take away His Spirit from the true believer? Even when that true believer sins? Not at all. God is still faithful even when we fail. In the Old Testament He might take away His Spirit and maybe a Samson would not know it, or a Saul might not. But for the church it is a different promise. We are told that in John 14:16–17, "I will pray the Father and He shall give you another Comforter that He may abide with you for ever, even the Spirit of truth whom the world cannot receive."

Not only has He been given to us to abide with us forever, but He Himself is the earnest, that is the down payment, of our inheritance (Ephesians 1:13–14). He, the Holy Spirit, is the guarantee that God is true and will never take Him away from us. He is the down payment of what lies ahead as we come to the inheritance the Lord has promised. No, we will never have the Holy Spirit removed from us as long as God is true. Is God true? And how long is God True? Forever? Then that is how long the Holy Spirit will abide with us and be in us.

How loving and longsuffering our God is. We may fail, but He never fails!

BEAM 53

THE DEATH OF A CHILD

2 SAMUEL 12:23

We are told that "broad is the way, that leadeth to destruction, and many there be which go in thereat" (Matthew 7:13). How true that is. But it almost sounds like God is losing the battle with Satan. More are going to destruction than are going to paradise or heaven. Here we have a case that changes all of that.

What of children? Little ones that have not done wrong things. Some, who are little older, may have gotten sassy and shown their own willfulness, but does that send them the wrong way? Hardly. Yes, all born of Adam are sinners, even little ones who have not done what the world would call sinful things. David's son is an example. All death is the result of sin and the penalty of sin. "Wherefore, as by one man sin entered the world, and death by sin, and so death passed upon all men" (Romans 5:12). So little ones die because of sin, even though it is not some certain wrong that they have done. It is because of what Adam did. We are of Adam's race, so all die because of Adam's sin.

So is there any hope? Of course. God must somehow regenerate the little ones at the moment of death because the little ones are taken to be with the saints awaiting the arrival of their parents, if their parents are believers and are saved by God's grace, just as the little ones are saved by grace.

David committed an awful sin. He raped a beautiful woman who was married to another. This woman, Bathsheba, was the granddaughter of one of David's close friends, Ahithophel. Then he had Bathsheba's husband, Uriah the Hittite, murdered. Here was a foreigner who loved Israel and David and fought for them. There is nothing in the Scripture that speaks against Bathsheba. She was taken by soldiers and brought to David's palace so he could rape her (2 Samuel 11:3–4). Ahithophel becomes an enemy of David after this. We would hardly expect him to come to David's palace on Sundays to eat fried chicken with him after this rape of his granddaughter. David's close friend now seeks revenge on David.

David tried to cover it up, but there are no secret sins with God.

Whatever we think is secret here is headline news in heaven. God sends the prophet Nathan to enlighten David. He gives David a parable about a rich man who had everything and a poor neighbor who had nothing, except one little lamb. When a traveler came for a visit to the rich man, the rich man would not take one of his flock, but took the poor man's lamb for this stranger. David gets angry. He pronounces his own judgment. He says the rich man shall die and he shall restore fourfold for his sin. Then Nathan says, "You are the man" (2 Samuel 12:7).

Wow! That's a different story. So David fasts and prays. But the little lad dies. The servants wonder why, after the child is dead, David would now wash, change his clothes, and then ask for food. David then tells them. He says that while the child was alive he had hope that God might hear his prayer. But now that the child is dead he says "I shall go to him, but he shall not return to me" (12:23). The little one awaits for David. God in His grace gives eternal life to the little one, and to all other little ones who die as he did. David pronounced his own judgment. He said the rich man should pay fourfold. This is what David payed.

1. The child died.
2. Another son of David rapes his half-sister
3. The brother of the sister who was raped kills the rapist.
4. Another son of David, Absalom, dies in rebellion against his own father, David.

Ah! The wages of sin. We all have earned the wages of sin, which is death, but the gift of God is eternal life (Romans 6:23). You cannot bring your dead little one back, but you can go to him by God's grace.

The least the lesson teaches is that little ones who die go to be with the Lord. Thank you, Lord!

BEAM 54

FOOLING GOD

GREEDY GEHAZI

2 KINGS 5:20–27

To get a lesson from this passage one must first read verses 1–19 about Naaman and his cleansing from leprosy. Naaman was a leper. A servant girl he captured in one of his raids against Israel told him he could be cleansed if he went to the prophet in Israel. He brings a caravan of gifts to honor this prophet, if he could be cleansed. This sickness is an outward picture of the inward destruction of sin. Like sin, it brings one down to a certain and horrible death. There is no cure, unless God intervenes. God does in this case, because God is giving us an Old Testament picture of the death of Christ in the New Testament. His death saves us from the certain and horrible consequences of sin. Naaman returns from the Jordan, where Elisha sent him, and wants to pay Elisha for what he has done. This cleansing is a miracle that only God could do.

But God is showing us in the Old Testament what salvation through the cross is like. It is a free gift. It only requires faith in what the prophet said. In the New Testament, it is faith in Jesus. In Naaman's case, it was faith in what Elisha said, "go wash in Jordan seven times." That is it. Nothing more. If Elisha took a gift it would be giving us the wrong picture. It would look like we must pay something for this "free" salvation, however small the payment might be. God did not want us to think that, so Elisha refused any gift.

But greedy Gehazi, Elisha's servant, cannot let it be. He saw the treasures that Naaman brought with him and the willingness of Naaman to give it to Elisha. He lusts after the wealth that he sees getting away from him. He devises a plot to get some of that treasure. He says, "I will run after him, and take somewhat of him" (2 Kings 5:20). I am sure Elisha paid Gehazi an appropriate salary. Gehazi was not in any real need. But like sinful men that we are, Gehazi wanted more. There is never enough. If one is a millionaire, then that millionaire wants two million. If he gets two, he wants three. There is never enough for greed.

Gehazi runs after Naaman and tells him a lie about some unexpected guests that had just dropped in on Elisha. Could Naaman spare some money and changes of garments for these guests? Of course. Naaman gives him more than he asks for. But Gehazi cannot let Elisha see the money so he hides it and pretends nothing happened. This man had a mental problem. It was a sin problem but that is what sin does to us. He saw Elisha doing miracles for the Lord even before Naaman came along. Still he thinks he can fool Elisha and fool God. No one will ever know? God cannot see where Gehazi hid the money? There are secret sins we commit and we think no one will ever know. Maybe our friends won't, or our wives won't, but there are no secrets from God.

When Gehazi comes back to Elisha he is asked where he has been. Of course he must lie to cover up. He says "Thy servant went no wither" (5:25). Sin so blinds us we think we can get away with it, that God will not know. Jesus said "This is the condemnation, that light is come into the world and men loved darkness rather than light, because their deeds were evil" (John 3:19). The same God who made the light also made the darkness. He sees in the dark just as well as He sees in the Light. We cannot have any secret sin from Him. And Elisha knows Gehazi is lying through his teeth. The sad part of this whole story is that Elisha said his heart went out to Gehazi when he did this deed. He regretted what Gehazi did, but the punishment could not be avoided.

He lusted for what Naaman had so he got what Naaman had, his leprosy. It is terrible to think that he would have leprosy without a cure, and not only he, but his heirs. Elisha says "The leprosy therefore of Naaman shall cleave unto thee, and unto thy seed forever" (2 Kings 5:27). What a terrible price to pay for lusting. Greed was the downfall of Gehazi. Sin has its reward. We may not see it in its terribleness on this side of the grave but it is horrible in its end.

We can avoid the terrible penalty of sin. There is one way and only one way. Jesus is the Way. "The blood of Jesus Christ His Son cleanseth us from all sin" (1 John 1:7). Even a chief of sinners, as Paul said he was, can have a new life and pardon from all sins, by the blood of Christ. It is by grace through faith to every one who believes. It's free, for nothing, but faith!

BEAM 55

WHAT IS MAN ANYWAY?

PSALM 8:4

What is man that God should even bother with him? He is alive for a little while and then loses the battle with death, like every other "living" thing has. He may have lots of science and take many precautions to keep alive, but they last for a short time and then man is gone. Seventy or eighty years may seem like a long time. But Abraham lived 175 years, Sarah 127 years, Isaac 180 years, Israel or Jacob 147 years. This was after the Flood.

What is that compared to the length of time man lived before the flood? Adam live 930 years, Seth lived 912 years, etc, etc. No use mentioning Methuselah, who lived longer than anyone recorded in Scripture, 969 years. OK, I mentioned him. But he is a special case. But what is 900 plus years when we read that "A thousand years in Thy sight are but as yesterday when it is past, and as a watch in the night" (Psalm 90:4). Peter says it like this, "One day is with the Lord as a thousand years, and a thousand years as one day" (2 Peter 3:8).

That surely means that God is able to do in an instant what man might need a thousand years to do, if he can do it at all. And also, that God is able to not be in any hurry because years do not mean much to Him. He does not have to hurry. God is in the eternal state. That does not mean that there are no days with God. We just read Peter's comment about the days and how God relates to them. But God is not confined in the bubble that we call time. He was in the eternal state when He decided to create time and make man. He made time so He is aware of what time it is. And His clock is never wrong.

But what is man? A little puny creature that can be knocked over and even killed by some little thing that is so small you need a magnifying glass to see it. Sometimes it is too small even for the microscope. Pasteur did the world a great service when he discovered how these little micro-organisms can kill cattle and people. But the little things can still kill. And man has gotten so smart he has found ways to split an atom and make weapons that can destroy millions. But man has not been able to control man's appetite for the power that can kill multitudes. Every now and then a new dictator arises. If it is not Nebuchadnezzar, it is a Caesar, or a Bonaparte, or a Hitler. Man loves to have power over men.

Then there is wealth. Man loves to heap up the wealth of the world. Wealth means power. The more wealth the more power. Paul certainly knew what he was talking about when he said "The love of money (not money itself) is the root of all (kinds of) evil" (1 Timothy 6:10). So what does man heap up to give him comfort, fame, power, inheritance (which he leaves behind)? Millions, or these days it is billions. And then he leaves it all. Sometimes he does not even get to keep it till he leaves. He gets sued.

God owns all the cattle on a thousand hills (Psalm 50:10), all the gold, the silver, the oil, the radium, everything. He created it. Why should He bother with puny little, and ignorant, man. He made man and made man to rule over this creation He made. One day the Son of Man, the Lord Jesus, will rule over all of creation. Because He loves this puny little frail, ignorant creation, called man. He sent His Son into the world to buy back man, who was lost in sin. I cannot understand that. I can rejoice in it. Who can understand the love of God? We see it demonstrated on the cross when God the Son died for man the creature's sins. Understand it? No! But rejoice in it? Yes! "What is man that thou art mindful of him? And the son of man that Thou visitest him?" (Psalm 8:4). I cannot understand it. But I do know that God loves His creation and gave His most precious gift, His only begotten Son, to buy back puny little man. What a beautiful story! "For Thou hast made him a little lower than the angels, and hast crowned him with glory and honor" (Psalm 8:5).

BEAM 56

TASTING DEATH FOR EVERY MAN

HEBREWS 2:9

Some may think that there is some kind of a contradiction here. Did He only taste of death? Didn't He really die? Early church disputes argued about whether He really died on the cross or swooned only to be revived later. Some so-called Greek scholars have even tried to make the word mean somewhat more than what the translators gave to the word. A whole lot more in fact. The word "geuo" is translated "taste," and it means just that. When that certain man in Luke 14:16 ff. made a great supper and invited many to come, they all began to make excuses. One says he bought some land and had to go look at it. Imagine buying some property before he looked at it?

Another said he bought some oxen and he had to "prove" them. And another said he got married. He could not come. Imagine a wife who does not want to go to a banquet? Hard to imagine? It sure is.

Then the host said that those who were bidden "shall not taste of my supper" (Luke 14:24). Here is the word "geuo." He was not saying they would not get dessert, or the opening salads or appetizers. He was saying they would not get to taste even one morsel. Not a taste. That is what the word means. So how does this word "taste" fit in with the events of the cross? He did die. He did not swoon. So how do we understand this passage?

We should get away from the thought of physical death. Sure He died. He did not taste of physical death, He died. But there is another death given in the Scriptures. Adam died in the same day he ate of the tree of knowledge of good and evil (not an apple tree, please!). Death means a separation. Physical death is the separation of soul from the body. Spiritual death is the separation of a sinner from God. If grace does not intervene, there follows the eternal death of separation from God for all eternity. Now look at the passage. He tasted of the eternal death that is due every man. He tasted of the eternal separation, which is ours, if we do not take the One who can save us as our Redeemer. He tasted hell for us.

When He was on the cross He spoke of God as His Father.

"Father, forgive them for they know not what they do" (Luke 23:34). In the midst of His ordeal, after three hours of suffering, He cries out "My God, My God, why hast Thou forsaken Me?" (Matthew 27:46). Somehow, that I cannot understand, and perhaps no one can, God the Son was able to experience the eternal suffering of hell by being separated from God the Father. Then after three more hours He is again in fellowship with His Father. He says "Father, into Thy hands I commend My Spirit" (Luke 23:46). He is again the only begotten Son of the Father in Whom the Father delights. But He tasted eternal death on the cross. Only "tasted" for us the horrible separation of being cast away from the Father.

Let's see now. Mathematically speaking, that is. Since one day with the Lord is as a thousand years, as Peter tells us (2 Peter 3:8) one hour would be equal to 41.666 years times 3 would be 124.999 years. Round it off to 125 years. That may not be theological enough for some Bible students but it does come out to a long time, those three hours.

But He did this so that we may never be separated from the Father. What a beautiful story of God's grace that the true, real sinners should be spared that awful experience of eternal hell by His tasting. He tasted death for every man. There is no need for us to be separated from God the Father for even a moment because He, the Son, was separated from the Father for us. What love! And He did this for sinners, even for those who will not believe on Him. Don't be one of them.

BEAM 57

COURTSHIP OF REBEKAH

"WILL YOU GO WITH THIS MAN?" (Genesis 24:58)

We have all heard of "Love at first sight." Here is love before the first sight. A stranger had come to her father's house and told them all about his master's son, Isaac, who was seeking a bride. She was told how his master had given all to his one beloved son (verse 36), and how his master had sent him to fetch a bride for his son. It certainly looked like a good chance to become rich, if it were true. But who knows?

The servant did give some tokens of his master's wealth. He gave her jewels of silver and gold and clothes (verse 53) to verify what he had said about his master. All of the master's wealth would one day be Isaac's and what would be Isaac's would belong to the wife of Isaac. Would she believe him? Would she go? The answer was "Yes," sight unseen. This was not because of any wealth. She was given some tokens of the Master's son just like we give engagement rings, but they did not persuade her. They did catch the eyes of her brother, Laban, who lusted after them

Camel riding in the heat may not be a pleasure trip, even in those days, but they started off on their journey of over 300 miles. What do you suppose they talked about? I imagine it was the miraculous birth of the master's son, Isaac, when His father Abraham was 100 years old and his mother was 90 years old.

This would be a type of the miracle of the birth of Jesus.

Not only did he have a miraculous birth, but there was a miraculous "back from the dead" experience. He was offered to God by Abraham as a living sacrifice and God restored him to Abraham. This would be a type of the death and resurrection of Jesus.

All of these things point to the bringing home of the bride of Christ, the church, in the New Testament.

God's purpose is to call out a bride for His Son. The Greek word "ekklesiah" means "called out ones," and gives us our word church. The church, that is each individual sinner, is asked to trust this Son of the Father and to come along with the Holy Spirit to meet Him some day.

All things have been given to the Son. All judgment (John 5:22), all power (Matthew 28:18), all honor (Ephesians 1:20–23), and all glory (Philippians 2:9–11). And, the Holy Spirit is the earnest, down payment, of what will be our inheritance (Ephesians 1:14). He is the token of what will come to us later. What that is cannot be imagined, yet (1Cor. 2:9).

The question today is still, "Will you go with this man?" God so loved the world that He gave His Son for sinners. What a beautiful story it is. Will you go with this servant, who today is the Holy Spirit? Will you go with Him to meet the Father's Son? What a love this is!

Addendum

Just a little bit of theology, if you do not mind.

It has always been a blessing to see how these two meet. Not in His home, which would mean the church goes right to heaven. Not in her home, which would mean He comes down to this earth, the church's home. No. Neither one. They meet somewhere in between her home and his home in a field (verse 66). This fits exactly with 1Thessalonians 4:17, where we are told the church meets the Lord Jesus, not on earth, nor in heaven, but somewhere in between, in the air. What a beautiful message this is for us today!

BEAM 58

JOSHING JOSHUA

(OR PRAY EVEN FOR LITTLE THINGS)

JOSHUA 9:14

It seemed like such a little thing. If it had been something like crossing the Jordan on dry ground, or winning the battle of Jericho, or even the town of Ai, it would have been different. But this? It is only a peace treaty with a few strangers who live far, far away. These were Gibeonites who came a great distance to make a peace pact with this new nation of Israel. They told Joshua that they had heard about how the Lord God of Israel had brought Israel out of Egypt. They had heard about all that He did. How He opened up the Red Sea, won the battle of Jericho. They wanted no trouble with Israel. They wanted peace.

They even showed Joshua the evidence of their long arduous trip. They showed Joshua their shoes. They said "Look at them. They were new when we left home, but look at them now. They are worn out from such a long journey." They said again, "We brought some food also but you don't want to eat this stuff. Look at this bread. It has turned green. You don't want to eat this. It just took too long to get here." So Joshua asks them again. "Where did you say you came from?" "Oh," they say, "we came from Slobovia. Actually it is Lower Slobovia. Way, way, far over those mountains. A long way off."

So Joshua says "Well I guess it wouldn't hurt. Ok, let's sign this treaty so I can get on with my other more important business." So they sign a peace pact. Then everything changes. The Gibeonites say "Ha, Ha! We fooled you. We live just over on the other side of that hill. Ha Ha!" Then Joshua says, "Kill them. Kill all of them. Run them through with your swords. They lied to us." No, no. He did not say that.

We read in Joshua 9:4 that the Gibeonites "did work wilily." They were a clever bunch. But we also read that Joshua and his men "took not counsel at the mouth of the Lord" (Joshua 9:14). They did not pray about it. It was a little thing. But Joshua made a peace pact using the name of the Lord. They swore under an oath, in the name of Jehovah. They were to destroy all the inhabitants of the land of Canaan. But they were also to keep an oath made using the name of

Jehovah. So Joshua spared them, even though they made a fool of him. They were to be hewers of wood and drawers of water for Israel (verse 27). What is the lesson? One is that our word should be true and faithful, even if we have been tricked. People should be able to believe that what we have said we will do, we will do.

Another lesson is that there is nothing too small for us to take to the Lord in prayer. Joshua did not ask of the Lord. So he was fooled. But he learned a lesson. Pray. Pray about anything. God is not so busy He does not want to be bothered with "little things." "Ask and it shall be given unto you, seek and ye shall find, knock and it shall be opened unto you" (Matthew 7:7). Nothing is too little for prayer.

P.S. Years after this, King David is on the throne and there is a famine in the land for three years. David enquires of the Lord. God tells him it is because of what Saul did to the Gibeonites. Saul killed some of them. He saw his ratings go up in the polls, so he thought, "I'll kill some more. I'll really be popular then." But God did not forget the vow that Joshua made. God lets the Gibeonites make the judgment. They ask for seven of Saul's sons to be hanged. And they are (2 Samuel 21:1–6). What a terrible mistake Saul made.

So pray about anything and everything. Even little things. God hears those little things.

"Be careful (that is anxious, don't worry) for nothing; but in everything by prayer and supplication with thanksgiving let your requests be made known unto God" (Philippians 4:6).

BEAM 59

WISHING TO DIE?

IS SUICIDE PERMISSIBLE?

In these days we hear a lot about suicide and whether it is right for someone to help us die. Suffering may lead some to want to die rather than live, depending on how terrible the suffering is. But is suicide permissible?

There are two men in the Scripture that wanted to take their own lives. We have Elijah, that great man of God who prayed on Mt. Carmel and God sent down fire in answer to his prayer. After such a tremendous victory over the false prophets of Baal, he falls apart when he hears that Jezebel is going to kill him. She puts fear into Elijah so that he goes a day's journey into the wilderness. There he sits down under a Juniper tree and "he requested for himself that he might die, and said, It is enough now O Lord, take away my life for I am not better than my fathers" (1 Kings 19:4). He asks God to kill him.

The other would-be suicide is Jonah. He prayed while in that fish and God heard him and rescued him from the fish's belly. He then preaches in Nineveh and has the greatest revival the world has ever seen. Even the animals are clothed in sackcloth and not allowed to eat. Everyone is fasting and in prayer that the Lord may turn from His anger and not destroy the city. There were 120,000 children that did not know their right hand from their left (Jonah 4:11). How many thousands of adults? They were all fasting and praying. Since they turned from their sins, God turned from the judgment.

After God turns from His anger and judgment and spares Nineveh, Jonah gets angry with God because He spared Nineveh. Jonah goes outside of the city and asks God to kill him. But God had other plans. He had other plans with Elijah also. The point is that these two men wanted to die. They could have cut their wrists and bled to death, or they could have hanged themselves. They could have taken poison, they could have jumped off some cliff. There are many ways of committing suicide. They never tried one. They asked God to take their lives. This must say something about the sacredness of life.

We might not fully understand what it meant when God said

"Let us make man in our image, after our likeness" (Genesis 1:26). We may argue about it. One thing is sure. When these men of God longed to die, and they were suffering, they did not think it right or permissible to take their own lives. They wanted to die. But to die at their own hands, uh, uh. They asked God to do it for them. Even though we may be suffering, we are not permitted to take that life that God has given us. And surely we cannot ask man to help us.

It would be all right to pray for an early death, some kind of death to take us out of this world. After all, we have a better place waiting for us. Why struggle here with ungodliness and suffering and wickedness.

But this life He has given is sacred. We are made in God's image and we do not destroy what God has made.

The same God who had other plans for Elijah and Jonah had other plans for Paul. He did not wish to die but he did suffer and wished to be healed. But here again, God did not grant Paul's wish anymore than He granted Elijah's or Jonah's. But He said to Paul "My grace is sufficient for thee: for My strength is made perfect in weakness" (2 Corinthians 12:9). He will provide. And in His good time He will take us out of this world of wickedness, sin, and suffering, and take us home. What a gracious God! There is a better alternative to suicide, or death, and that is life, eternal life through Jesus the Savior. Then death brings us a better life with God and the angels for ever and ever. Suicide? No. Let His strength be perfected in our weaknesses.

BEAM 60

FISH

ARE YOU ONE OF THOSE, YOU KNOW?

Did you ever wonder how a fish got to be a Symbol of Christianity? Remember that those followers of Christ were outlawed, hunted, and put to death for their religion. Some unlearned unbelievers accused them of being cannibals. They heard some kind of a rumor that these "Christians" got together sometimes and ate some body. Sure, they heard about the communion. "Take, eat, this is My body which is broken for you." They heard right, but the meaning applied to it was entirely wrong.

It was dangerous in those early days of the church. Christianity was not declared a legal religion by Roman emperors until AD 313, when Emperor Constantine pronounced it a legal religion in the Edict of Milan. Before that you could be burned at the stake or fed to lions, or given various other means of torture and death. Nero regrets greatly that he did not become a believer and make Christianity legal. So does Pilate, who washed his hands, but did not remove his guilt. He could have had all of his sins washed away.

Someone may have had a suspicion that someone else he met might be a believer in this "new and forbidden" religion called Christianity. But to say "I am one also" might put your head on the chopping block. Some clever person thought there might be a secret code that would let the other fellow know that you are a believer. If he were not, then he might find it amusing, but not understand it. One would write a curved line in the sand, something like an arc. If this other fellow were a believer, then he might draw another arc, crossing your arc so that it would look like a fish.

But why a fish? There would be certain words that would spell out another word, if the first letters were taken by themselves, an anagram. The first word would be the word for Jesus. In the original, having no letter J, the word would be "Iasous." The second letter would be taken from the word for Christ, or Messiah. That would be "Christos." The third would be the first letter from the word for God "Theos." The fourth would be the word "Uios" which is the word for son. The last letter would be the word "Soter," which means "savior," and the first letter would be the letter S.

Putting these five first letters together we have I X (T H) U S. We have a combination of letters in the letter X for Christos, or Messiah. We have a combination also in the letter for the word Theos, meaning God. We recognize it when we see the word "theology." And guess what the word Ichthus means?

If there are any ichthyologists in the crowd they know. Back to the beginning. It means FISH.

Put it all together and you have in a code "Jesus Christ God (or God's) Son (and) Savior." A neat way of letting someone know that you also are a believer. If he does not know what you are doing, making half a fish in the sand, so what? He is not in on it. If he draws the other half of the fish, makes an arc that completes yours, then he is a fellow believer.

So what? If we have that fish on the back of our car we better drive like a Christian ought to drive. And we ought to behave ourselves like a Christian ought to behave. And if we do, we are letting the world know that we also are believers, and followers of the Lord Jesus. Are you a fish? Better become one then. Men go fishing for fish. These fish go fishing for men. What a difference!

You don't have to keep it a secret now, unless you are ashamed of Jesus. How could you be ashamed of Him? Are you one of them? I am one of them, too. We should let the world know. Let's tell them.

BEAM 61

SABBATH DAY: OK, WHICH ONE?

LEVITICUS 23:5

There is quite a confusion about the Sabbath day. Which leads to more confusion about the Passover Day.

The word "Sabbath" means to desist or cease. In Genesis 2:2 we are told that God ended His work of creation, or re-creation, and rested on the seventh day. God was not tired. The rest was for man's sake. Later, God would give man that one day in seven for rest. So there was always a weekly Sabbath.

But every Holy Day that the Lord gave in the Mosaic Law also was a Sabbath, a day when you ceased from your ordinary labors. The confusion comes from not knowing the Old Testament way of counting months. They were lunar. The word "chodesh," which is translated "month" about 220 times, is also translated "new moon" about 20 times. The month started with a new moon. That means the Passover was counted from the new moon and was held on the 14th day of the month. That made it a full moon day, or night, which made it easier for travelers to go up to Jerusalem, as all men were required to do.

That also made it possible for the Passover to be on a Wednesday, or Sunday, or Thursday. It could be any day of the week. It does not take much of a brain to see that there could be TWO SABBATHS in the same week, the regular Sabbath and the Passover Sabbath. The same is true of the other Holy Days. The Day of Atonement was on the 10th day of the seventh month (Leviticus 23:27) and it too, we read, "shall be unto you a Sabbath of rest, and ye shall afflict your souls: in the ninth day of the month at even, from even unto even, shall ye celebrate your Sabbath" (Leviticus 23:32).

Likewise the Day of Pentecost and the Feast of Tabernacles were Sabbaths. "On the first day shall be an holy convocation: ye shall do no servile work therein" (Leviticus 23:21, 34–35). So what is the point of all of this? We must remember that Christ is our Passover Lamb that was sacrificed for us (1 Corinthians 5:7). So there were two Sabbaths in the last week of the Lord's ministry before His crucifixion. There was the Passover Sabbath the day after His crucifixion. They wanted to get the execution over with and get His body down from the cross because that day was approaching. John 19:31 tells us that "because it was the preparation, that the bodies should not remain upon the cross on the Sabbath day, (for that Sabbath day was an high day), (the Jews) besought Pilate that their legs might be broken, and that they might be taken away." Breaking the legs of the crucified victims made them die faster. Their chest would have no support and it would collapse and bring on death quicker. It states clearly, "It was a high day."

But Jesus was already dead. He paid the necessary price by being separated from the Father for three hours, tasting the eternal death of every man who is separated from God eternally, when He cried out "My God, My God why hast thou forsaken Me?" That would make the next day a Sabbath, a High Day, the Passover Day, which could be any day of the week. You could not buy spices or myrrh which would be needed to adequately prepare a body for burial. So the women had to wait a day because the stores were closed. Then there was a regular day in which they could buy. After that came the regular weekly Sabbath. Then we read that on the first day of the week, "They came unto the sepulchre bringing the spices which they had prepared, and certain others with them" (Luke 24:1). That means that it was not a Friday when He was crucified, but that is another story. And it means that Pentecost did not fall on a Sunday. It could have been any day in the week. So when we say the Sabbath Day, we need to spell out which one.

A thought, if anyone cares. The Passover Lamb was taken on the 10th day of the month. It was kept for four days and then slaughtered on the 14th day of the month. The 10th would be His entrance into the city. What does that say about the Day of Crucifixion? That's to be continued in another episode.

BEAM 62

THE TWO WITNESSES

REVELATION 11:6–9

It was not long ago when skeptics laughed at this passage. They said "How could the world see two dead people in Jerusalem for three days? Could they make movies of them? And if they did, how long would it take for the world to get copies of the movies? By that time three days would be long gone." My how things have changed! Now we can see the trucks rolling along the roads in Iraq, or the rocks being thrown in Jerusalem. What a fantastic job these techs are doing these days. We have the satellites spinning around this globe and they give us instant pictures of fires, gunfights, earthquakes, whatever. But the skeptic will think of something else to find fault with.

But who are these two witnesses that will be on earth during the Great Tribulation, that will tell the world about the Antichrist and the False Prophet, who will be deceiving multitudes of people? They are able to shut up the heavens so that it does not rain during their prophecy (11:6). They will have power to turn water into blood, and smite the earth with plagues. Does this sound familiar? It should. There were two people in the Old Testament that did this very thing, Moses and Elijah. There may be some disagreement over these two, but I believe the evidence is quite clear.

Elijah shut up the heavens for three and a half years (James 5:17). Wow! What a drought. Like the Sahara? Then Elijah prayed and the rain came. And Moses? He struck the waters and they turned to blood (Exodus 7:20). And he did a lot of other things, like bringing plagues upon Egypt until Pharaoh let the people of Israel go. So what is the problem here? Some take it that these two witnesses are Enoch and Elijah because Enoch and Elijah did not die. So what?

There will be millions of people that will not die when the Lord comes back FOR His church at the Rapture. Paul says "We shall not all sleep (that is die), but we shall all be changed, in a moment, in the twinkling of an eye . . . we shall be changed" (1 Corinthians 15:51–52). That means the dead are raised in new eternal bodies and we who are alive, when He comes, will be given new glorified bodies, without dying. After all, no matter when He comes there will be believers alive and they will not go through the portal of death. They will simply be given their new heavenly bodies right then.

Now look at Moses. It is said that he died and was buried by God. That means he would be dying twice.

Again, I say so what? There have been other people who have died twice. Lazarus was raised from the dead after he had been dead four days (John 11:39). There is no reason to believe he did not die again later. And how about Jairus' daughter? She died once (Mark 5:35, 41) but surely she died again.

The same could be said of the widow's son (Luke 7:12–15). And there is a group of resurrection saints that seems to be overlooked by many Bible teachers. When Jesus rose up from the grave, and the veil of the temple was torn in two from the top to the bottom, we read that the earth did quake and the rock rent, "and the graves were opened and many bodies of the saints which slept arose . . . and appeared to many" (Matthew 27:51–53). Please–it was after His resurrection, for He must have the pre-eminence. We are told that He is the firstfruits from the dead (1 Corinthians 15::23). Firstfruits is a plural which points us back to the Old Testament Feast of the Firstfruits. Certainly these saints died again. So these two Witnesses look like Moses and Elijah from the things they did. After the world rejoices over the death of these two, they also are raised again from the dead. Then they are taken back up to heaven again. They did their work and it was over. We also are to be His witnesses, while here. We have a work to do also. How are we doing it? No, we do not bring plagues upon the people, but rather a blessing. Let our light shine. Talk Jesus. Give a reason for believing what we believe. One day we also will be caught up, ether before death or after. But does it matter? So long as we are with Him. Let's talk Jesus. Be a witness!

BEAM 63

CAREFUL WHAT YOU PRAY FOR YOU MIGHT GET IT

2 KINGS 20:5

Hezekiah was a good king. This was in a time when good kings were few and far between, years that is.

When it came to his time to die, God told him to set his house in order. God did this with a number of people. It is a beautiful story in many ways because we read that someone, like Abraham, was told he would "go to thy fathers in peace" (Genesis 15:15). His father was buried many miles from where Abraham was buried so the Lord is talking about another place. Not the graveyard but a place where the saved are gathered. We read that "Isaac gave up the ghost, and died, and was gathered unto his people" (Genesis 35:29). So it is not the body that God is talking about, but the soul.

When Jacob was about to die we are again told that "he gathered up his feet into the bed, and yielded up the ghost, and was gathered unto his people (Genesis 49:33). This was quite common. God would warn someone that he was about to die and he could put his house in order and gather his feet into his bed, give up the ghost, die, and be gathered unto his people, even when their bodies might be buried miles apart.

Here in 2 Kings 20:1 the Lord tells Hezekiah that he is about to die. But Hezekiah does not want to die yet, so he prays unto the Lord to spare him a bit longer. And he cries. The Lord hears his prayer and sees his tears and says He will add 15 years more to Hezekiah's life. So Hezekiah had his prayer answered.

Then what? Three years later a son is born to Hezekiah, a son named Manasseh. We read in 2 Kings 21:1 that Manasseh was 12 years old when he began to reign.

Up till now it all sounds good for Hezekiah. He had a son who would reign when Hezekiah's fifteen years were up. Good! Or was it? This young boy, Manasseh, reigned 55 years. But his reign was so full of wickedness and evil he made the heathen look good. This is what we read, we are not exaggerating. In 2 Chronicles 33:9 it states

"Manasseh made Judah and the inhabitants of Jerusalem to err, and to do worse than the heathen whom the Lord destroyed before the children of Israel." If Hezekiah could have foreseen what the future would bring I am sure he would not have prayed for longer life.

Manasseh built up the altars his father had torn down. He built up altars to Baal, made the groves again a place of worship. This was for Asherah the mother-goddess of the Canaanites. He worshiped all the host of heaven. More idolatry that was forbidden. He made his son to pass through the fire, observed times, used enchantments, dealt with familiar spirits etc., etc. He even put an idol in the house of the Lord. He seemed to go out of his way to commit evil. If it were possible, as we say, Hezekiah would have turned over in his grave. Why anyone would do that I do not know. A dead body is not tired of lying in one position, is it? Anyhow, Hezekiah would have taken back his prayer. We may get what we ask for in prayer, so we need to always accept God's will in all that we ask. He knows what is best for us.

There is a beautiful and gracious ending to this story. Manasseh was so wicked that God judged the nation and had the nation of Assyria defeat Israel and carry off to Babylon multitudes of Israelites. And Manasseh himself was carried off a prisoner of Assyria. Where does the beauty of all this appear? Over in Babylon Manasseh comes to his senses and turns to God in prayer and repentance. God hears his prayer and is gracious even to this wicked king. This is a good example of what grace is. After reigning for 55 years, and doing more wickedness than the heathen, when Manasseh turns to God, God hears and is gracious to save a wretch like Manasseh, (and me). He is brought back to Jerusalem again to reign for a little while (2 Chronicles 33:13). And Manasseh slept with his fathers, and was buried in the garden of his own house (33:20). That's what grace is all about. What a beautiful ending to a wretched life. Getting what we don't deserve. That's grace. Watch what you pray for. You might get it!

BEAM 64

MIRIAM THE LEPER

NUMBERS 12:10

Why not Aaron? He also spoke against Moses. Here we have in-law trouble and a somewhat family feud.

Miriam was the one who watched the little baby Moses when he was placed in an ark of bulrushes and put in the river. This was because Pharaoh had decreed that all Hebrew children who were males should be killed. Moses' mother trusted in the Lord to thwart this decree. She sent Miriam to see what happened after this little floating baby crib was set afloat, (Exodus 2:4). So she was a little older than Moses. So was Aaron.

But there arose some jealousy. After all they were older than Moses. Aaron was the first High Priest over the people of Israel. He should be given some honor for his position. So we read in Numbers 12:1–2 that they spoke against Moses, He married an Egyptian woman. What do you think of that? And they said God hadn't spoken only to Moses. Hasn't God also spoken by us? And God heard it. Of course God hears everything we say. We can whisper but it does not come across to God as a whisper. It's more like a PA system blasting it. This made the Lord angry. He called the three to the tabernacle and there He appeared in His Shekinah glory form and spoke to them.

He said that He may speak to a prophet in a vision or in a dream. But, God says, Moses is different. God says "With him I speak mouth to mouth, even apparently, and not in dark speeches" (Numbers 12:8). This is what the Lord said. That He spoke to Moses plainly in verbal speech, mouth to mouth, like one person would speak to another. Strange how I hear so many of today's preachers and evangelists saying God spoke to them. They say it was audibly, just "like I am speaking to you." Wow! Moses was singled out to be unlike anyone else yet today it sounds like it is a common thing for God to just speak audibly to many preachers.

The anger of the Lord was kindled against Miriam and Aaron and when the cloud departed from them Miriam was a leper. But why not Aaron? He also spoke against Moses. Why wasn't he smitten with leprosy? Ah, this is a beautiful story. Aaron was the High Priest. As High Priest He was an Old Testament picture of the New Testament High Priest, Jesus. The writer of Hebrew says, "Seeing then that we have a great High Priest, that is passed into the heavens, Jesus the Son of God, let us hold fast our profession" (Hebrews 4:14).

Here again, like in so many other places in the Old Testament, we see New Testament truth being pictured for us. Aaron did the same thing that Miriam did. However, he represented Jesus the High Priest of the New Testament. God could not allow anything to be done that would take away from the picture of the perfect holiness, the perfect sinlessness of His Son. He was without sin. Even His enemies could not condemn Him for any sin. He alone was the perfect man that God had on earth. So, even though Aaron deserved it, just as much as Miriam did, he was spared. Nothing in the Old Testament could in any way appear to show some imperfection in Jesus. Yes, it is only a picture of Him, like the Rock at Horeb, but it must be kept pure and without fault. So Miriam becomes a leper for her backtalk, but not Aaron.

And oh yes, Miriam is cleansed of her leprosy after a seven day spell. This would get her to keep her mouth shut, I am sure. But Miriam earns our sympathy. We feel the same way sometimes about our brother. Who does he think he is anyway? I changed his diapers when he was a baby. Look at him now. Some big shot. Yes, we do the same thing. But God was merciful to both Aaron and Miriam. It took seven days, but I am sure she was a much better sister to Moses after that. And much better witness of God's grace. After all, how do you get cleansed from leprosy? What is the cure? Man has none. But God was gracious to her. He is gracious to us also. There is a far worse sickness than leprosy. It is the sin-leprosy that has every one in its grip. Jesus' death on the cross breaks that grip, and sets the leper free. What a wonderful gracious God to do this for undeserving sinners. But that is the kind of God He is. A gracious God.

BEAM 65

THE SHORTEST PRAYER

MATTHEW 14:30

There are many different views on prayer. There are occasions when we fall flat on our faces. This is called lying prostrate. When sinners meet the Holy and Righteous God, the Creator of all the earth, the Omnipotent and Omniscient God, they are certain to fall on their faces in worship. How could they be allowed to come into the presence of this Perfect and Omnipresent and Longsuffering and Merciful God without falling on their faces? Some people talk like they will just walk up and wrap their arms around Jesus, but I believe they are mistaken. Even John, who ate next to Jesus, and could say that his head was on the bosom of the Master, fell at His feet like a dead man (Revelation 1:17).

They ate Roman style, lying on the floor on some kind of mattress and reaching into the middle of the circle to take food. (Sorry about that DaVinci. They did not eat at the table as we do today.) This would put Judas on the left of Jesus, where the Savior could reach a sop and hand it to Judas. This, by the way, was an act of courtesy. An act that honored a guest. A sop was a morsel, such as bread, that was dipped in a gravy or sauce and given to the guest of honor. John being on the right hand of the Savior was almost lying on Jesus' bosom. But when He sees the risen Savior in His glory, he falls down as a dead man.

But it is perfectly all right to pray standing up. Jesus said, "When ye stand praying, forgive" (Mark 11:25).

Solomon stood before the altar of the Lord in the presence of the congregation of Israel and prayed (1 King 8:22).

Praying with eyes open is permissible. Before Jesus fed the multitude He "took the five loaves, and the two fishes, and looking up to heaven, He blessed, and brake, and gave the loaves to His disciples" (Matthew 14:19). This may not be the usual practice. We may want to shut out the world while we focus our attention on God and what we are praying. But it is all right. He did not have to shut out anything.

Kneeling in prayer is standard. Peter put them all out and kneeled down and prayed before he raised Tabitha from the dead (Acts 9:40). Yes, Peter also raised one from the dead. This was after Pentecost when Peter was filled with the Holy Spirit.

Long prayers are best done in private. We are not to draw attention to ourselves. We are warned about making public prayers to be seen of men. We are told we do not have to keep making repetition in our prayers. God can hear us. We are not to ring a bell so people will know we are a praying person.

But what is a prayer anyway? It is simply talking to God. We bring our needs to Him. We make requests to Him. We intercede for others to Him. And we should not forget to give thanks and praise for Who He is and what He has done. But here is the shortest prayer. Peter cries out, "Lord, save me" (Matthew 14:30). Peter certainly was not thinking about saving him from his sins and giving him eternal life. He was not thinking about granting him wisdom so he could make the right decisions. He was not thinking about guidance. He wanted to be saved from drowning, that's all. He had little time to think of the proper address, or the proper position. He just wanted to stay alive and not drown. A prayer can be as simple as that. Oh yes, this happened when Peter took his eyes off the Lord and put them on the boisterous wind and waves. He actually walked on water, for a while. Then he took his eyes off the Lord. But the Lord is kind. He saved (rescued) Peter. The shortest prayer that I know of is "Lord save me." But He is always ready to hear us say "Lord save me from my sins. Give me eternal life and make me your servant." And oh yes, "help me to never take my eyes off You."

BEAM 66

SAW JESUS ONLY

HE IS ALL THEY NEEDED

MARK 9:8

He was all they needed. This was the time when Jesus took three of His apostles, James, John, and Peter, up into a high mountain (Mark 9:2). These three were given privileges of going with Him on other occasions when the remaining 9 apostles were not. This mount is called the mount of transfiguration. This is where, for a brief time in His ministry, the Lord Jesus lifted the veil that covered His glory and allowed some of it to be seen. All of it would be too much. After Paul saw some of that glory, he was blind (Acts 9:9). The glory is just too much for our eyes until we get new eyes in a new glorified body.

These three see glory coming from the Master that looked like lightning flashing. Not only from His body but also from His clothes. We read that "His face did shine as the sun, and His raiment was white as the light" (Matthew 17:2). Peter gets the bright idea of building three tabernacles there on top of the mountain; one for Jesus (he did put Him first), one for Moses and one for Elijah. But Mark tells us that Peter did not know what he was talking about. He didn't know what to say, so he said something (Mark 9:6). Good ole Peter. We sure need him and love him. We do the same thing. We speak when we don't know what to say.

Then a cloud overshadowed them and a voice from heaven spoke saying "This is my beloved Son: hear Him. And suddenly, when they looked round about, they saw no man any more, save Jesus only" (Mark 9:8). They had just seen two great men of God from the past: Moses and Elijah. How they recognized them I do not know. This was before the days of artists painting heads of Christ, or Last Suppers, etc. That art is out of the imagination of the artist's mind. But these three recognized Moses and Elijah. Perhaps this tells us something about the "perfect knowledge" we shall have later when the veil is moved away from our old natural bodies and we shall know as we are known by God.

So here is Moses, who has now gotten into that land that he was denied entrance to before he died. (That is another story.) And here is Elijah, that fearless prophet who prayed and fire came down from heaven. They may be there representing the whole Old Testament. One, Moses, represents the Law while the other, Elijah, represents the Prophets. And all of the Old Testament, Law and Prophets speak of Him, the Son, and coming Lamb of God. Jesus taught this when He gave the two disciples who were on their way to Emmaus a Bible lesson from the Old Testament (Luke 24:27). What good would it do to build another tabernacle for these two, or even for Jesus? The Old Testament sacrificial system would be done away with at His death. The veil of the temple would be torn from top to bottom, signifying the end of animal sacrifices, after the Lamb of God has died for sinners.

All we need is Jesus. God the Father removed Moses and Elijah and spoke from heaven saying Jesus was His beloved Son. Hear Him. He is all you need. The Father removed those heavenly visitors to make it clear, even to Peter, that Jesus is all you need. Hear Him. See Him now and see Him later in His glory, when our eyes can take it. Have we seen Him? Have we believed Him? He is all that we need. But, we do need Him. Without Him we can do nothing. Without Him we have no hope. Without Him we have no forgiveness. Without Him we are lost. Hear Him. He is all we need. But we do need Him. Have you heard Him?

"Verily, verily, I say unto you, I am the door of the sheep. All that ever came before Me are thieves and robbers: but the sheep did not hear them. I am the door: by Me if any man enter in, he shall be saved, and go in and out, and find pasture" (John 10:7–8).

BEAM 67

THE SHOULDER WORK OF GOD

LUKE 15:5

This may come as a disagreement with other Bible teachers but we are brothers still, not identical twins, but brothers. The Lord "spake this parable unto them, saying" (Luke 15:3). Notice He did not speak these parables to them. He spoke A PARABLE unto them. Not much of a difference but it may count for a lot in the interpretation. So there is one parable and it is about a lost sheep, a lost coin, and a lost son. But not three parables.

We can say from the Scriptures that a sheep represents a believer. One day He will come back and He will gather all nations before Him "and He shall separate them one from another, as a shepherd divideth His sheep from the goats" (Matthew 25:32). In John 10:3 we read "He calleth His own sheep by name," and "I am the good shepherd: the good shepherd giveth His life for the sheep" (John 10:11). So it should not be difficult to see that sheep represent His flock, the believers who have come to Him.

The next part of this one parable is the part about the coin. A coin is of value to the owner. It also bears an image of the King. This coin is lost inside the house. When the lady of the house finds it she rejoices over the finding. It is not like it was lost outside on the streets. It is not outside of the house, but still inside the house, out of place.

Next, there is the third part of this one parable. This is the familiar part about the prodigal son. He wants his money now so he can have a good time now. He goes off to have fun. When the money runs out he loses his so-called friends. Then he takes whatever job he can get and ends up caring for hogs. This was contrary to the Law of Moses and the custom of Israel. That was not bad enough, but he gets so hungry he is ready to eat the hog's food. No money, no friends, no food. Then he comes to himself. That is what we all need to do. He realizes the folly of what he has done. His father's servants eat better than he does. But he wonders if his father would have him if he came back.

His father is more than willing to take him back. If the father of this part of this one parable represents God, it is the only place where God is in a hurry. The father rushes out to meet his son, when he is a great way off, and falls on his neck and kisses him and welcomes him back. I know that the father says his son was dead but is now alive, but that is not to be taken physically, but spiritually. He was dead to his father's fellowship. But even in that far off country he was still a son and not a hog. The sheep that was lost was not a goat but still a sheep. The coin did not turn into a wooden nickel. All of these tell the same story, in different view points.

And the main point is? The love of God the Father for that child who has gone astray, who is sometimes called a backslider. I know this parable is used as three parables and used to show God's love for the lost. However, the sheep was still a sheep, the coin was still in the house, and the son was still a son even in that far off land. I will always be my biological father's son. I can embarrass him, or disobey him, but I am, and always will be, his son. He may disown me, he may disinherit me, but I am still his son. I will always be God's son if I have believed on His Son. I may lose my inheritance, but I am still His son because He has given me Eternal Life, in the Family of God. That He does not take back.

But what does this say about God's shoulder work.

First we read about His finger work of God. CREATION!

"When I consider Thy heavens, the work of Thy fingers, the moon and the stars, which Thou hast ordained; what is man that Thou are mindful of him?" (Psalm 8:3–4).

Secondly there is the arm work of God. SALVATION!

"Who hath believed our report? And to whom is the arm of the Lord revealed? For He shall grow up before Him as a tender plant, and as a root out of dry ground, He hath no form nor comeliness; and when we see Him, there is no beauty that we should desire Him" (Isaiah 53:1–2).

Thirdly, I believe we have the shoulder work of God. RESTORATION!

"And when He hath found it (the lost sheep), He layeth it on His shoulders, rejoicing" (Luke 15:5)

I believe that the shoulder is stronger than the arm, which is stronger than the fingers.

If I am correct, then the strongest part of this whole teaching is that GOD WILL NEVER LOSE ONE OF HIS OWN. That sheep may wander away. He is lost to His father's will and fellowship, but he will always be a sheep. He has said "I give unto them eternal life, and they shall never perish" (John 10:28).

What a loving God He is. After all He has done for us, for us to go astray from Him you would think that He would leave us to our own tragedy. But He doesn't. He will never lose one sheep. He will never lose a son, He will never lose a coin. What we need to ask ourselves is "Am I a son?" He will never lose us then. Shame on us if we go astray.

"And because ye are sons, God hath sent forth the Spirit of His Son into your hearts, crying, Abba, Father" (Galatians 4:6).

BEAM 68

PAID IN FULL

ROMANS 4:5

Many people are aware of the use of pottery among the ancients. It was not just a baked clay of beauty, with painted images or flowers upon it, but it served useful purposes in the home. It was easily broken but the pottery itself could last for centuries, as they have. Now and again a pot was broken. It was not thrown out. If it could no longer hold wine, or oil, or some other liquid, it could still be used for lentils, or beans, or some dry victual.

Every now and then it would be smashed into what we call shards. But were they thrown out? No, no.

They still had a use. The Greeks could use these for writing letters. These little pieces of broken clay pots were used to vote with. The pieces are called "ostraca" and it gives us our English word "ostracize," because these votes could remove an undesirable person from their city. He was ostracized by being voted out.

They also used them for paying their taxes. The interesting thing about this is that they got a receipt on these little pieces of clay that stated "Paid in Full." These were kept in case Uncle Sam, or perhaps Uncle Alexander, wanted to collect the tax again. This was the proof. The taxes were paid, here was the receipt, and they could not be asked to pay the taxes twice.

Which brings us to a beautiful story. We have, or had, a great debt which we owed God. "For all have sinned and come short of the glory of God" (Romans 3:23). And like the king in the parable Jesus told in Matthew 18:25, whose servant owed him a tremendous debt, we have no way of paying our debt. What can we do? The man in the parable fell down and worshiped and prayed. But that still does not pay anything on the debt. In the parable the lord, to whom the debt was owed, forgave the man.

Romans 4:5 tells us that we may work for the Lord, not to be saved, for we cannot work until we are alive. Dead men can do little work. But if we have been made alive, then when we work we may be given a reward. But how can a dead man be made alive so he can work? Romans 4:5 tells us that it is by faith.

He that believeth on Him, that is Jesus, his faith is counted for righteousness. That word "counted" means it is put down to his account, or imputed to him, that he is righteous. It is the "Paid in Full" receipt that our sins have been paid for by another. Someone else, the Lord Jesus, paid the debt and we now have it down in the books that we are righteous; we owe nothing. This may sound like bragging for us to say we owe God nothing, because the debt was paid, but we have nothing to boast of. The glory belongs to Him, Who paid the debt.

And, like the income tax receipt, we cannot be asked to pay the bill twice. It was paid in full. What is the penalty for sin? Death. How many times can the penalty be paid? One time, that is it. If Adolph Eichmann killed 6 million Jews during Hitler's reign, he still only paid the penalty of one death. That may not sound reasonable but that is the way it is. He cannot be executed 6 million times. Our penalty has been paid by another, Who took our place and died in our stead. His death has paid the penalty for sin. He did no sin. He took ours, and paid the price for ours, and His righteousness becomes ours. It is "Paid in Full" by Him. What a beautiful story.

"For what saith the Scripture? Abraham believed God, and it was counted unto him for righteousness" (Romans 4:3). It was put down on his account that he, Abraham, was righteous. Open up an account!

It doesn't cost anything but faith!

BEAM 69

SLAVERY HAS ITS ADVANTAGES

PHILIPPIANS 1:1

This can be a touchy subject. Advantages of being a slave? Wow! Let's look at it. Paul says in a number of places, like here in Philippians 1:1, that he is a slave. He uses the word *doulos* which is the word for a slave. He is a slave of Christ. What are some of the advantages?

If you are a slave you do not have to worry. The worries are left up to the slave owner. If he wants the slave to work for him then he must take care of the slave. That means he must provide the food, the clothing, the shelter, the health insurance. Everything the slave needs must be provided for him if he is to do a good job for the master. If he is sick he can be of little service. He needs the food to have the energy to do the work. He needs rest, also. He also needs guidance. Someone must tell him what to do.

The slave of Christ only needs to know the will of the Master, that's it. The Master makes the decisions. So our prayers should be for guidance through every day. The slave really has no worries at all. It is up to his Master to care for him, protect him, guide him. It really makes the life of slavery simple. Let the Master make all the decisions. The slave has one important work to do: obey the Master. And our Master is a loving, kind, gracious Master, whom we should love, and love to serve.

In the Old Testament under the Law of Moses, which is really the Law of God given to Moses, a man might have to serve as a bond slave to pay his debts. He could work for his master for six years. "In the seventh he shall go out free for nothing" (Exodus 21:2). So if someone paid his debts for him that one had to calculate how much he would be repaid in six years of service. The servant served six years and that was it. Then he was free to go back to his own family and farm. But sometimes the master was such a good master that the slave did not want to go free. He liked working for his master. In fact, he could love his master and want to stay a slave to him for ever.

Then the ritual was that if he desired to serve his master, he told his master, who then called for the judges to witness this. The master brought the would-be slave to the door of his house or yard. "Then his master shall bore his ear through with an aul; and he shall serve him for ever" (Exodus 21:6). If you really, really, loved your master, then you became his for life, and you had the marks to prove it.

Our Master is better than any other master could possibly be. But, unlike other masters of this world, He will not force anyone to be His servant. But for those who do become His slaves, they find Him gracious and loving and good, as well as powerful and almighty. They love their Master and like Paul they are His servants (doulos). We may not have our ears pierced but we may bear other marks upon our body, for in His service we may suffer persecution. Paul was well aware of the sufferings for Christ, and he rejoiced in those sufferings.

However we may suffer, we have so many other advantages. Some bus company says to "Leave the Driving to Us." Well how about "Leave the Worry to Me?" It is His responsibility to care for the slave. The slave only has one thing to do. Serve Him! We should be willing to be slaves for this Master. Are we? And like the Old Testament slave that stayed with his master forever, and lived at his master's house forever, we have a glorious home that we will spend with our Master–for ever and ever. Wow! There is an advantage in being a slave. This is only true if our slave master is a good slave owner. Who would want any other kind? But is there a slave master that is better than Jesus? No way.

"O taste and see that the Lord is good; blessed is the man that trusteth in Him" (Psalm 34:8).

BEAM 70

THE SEPARATION OF ABRAHAM

God wanted Abraham all to Himself. So He had to separate Abraham from everything else. He did this a little at a time. It might have been because Abraham would not have been able to stand it otherwise.

First, God calls on Abraham, who was called Abram at that time, to leave his country, his kindred, his father's house, his home land, and go to a new land that God had prepared for him (Genesis 12:1). All of his blessings were tied up to this land of Canaan. So Abraham goes about half way to Haran. He goes with his father Terah, and his nephew Lot, along with his wife Sarai (Genesis 12:5). He did not leave all, as God said. But God is not through with Abram. Now Abraham's father, Terah, dies in Haran. Then Abraham goes on to this new land of Canaan.

Next, there is a famine in the land of Canaan, a test from God. So Abraham goes down to Egypt. It is never good for God's people to go into Egypt. The blessings of God were connected to the land of Canaan. So Abraham gets backed into a corner in Egypt and lies about his wife, Sarai. He feared that the Egyptians would kill him for her. God preserves him and he is sent away with his wife, and much wealth he got as gifts from Pharaoh (Genesis 12:16). He also got a maid for Sarai, Hagar, who caused Abraham many headaches.

Now he is back in the land. But he has not been separated yet from his nephew Lot. They both have so many cattle now that the land is getting crowded and they need to separate. So Abraham does a kind thing. He allows Lot to choose first. "You take the right side," he says "and I'll take the left, or if you like the left side, I'll take the right." So Lot chooses and now Abraham is separated from Lot.

That promised child has not yet arrived so Sarai tells him to take Hagar and have that child by her. Abraham does so and later on he regrets it. Ishmael is born of Hagar. This means trouble. Now the maid, Hagar, is acting like she is the boss for she has born Abraham a male child. Then God tells Abraham that the promised child is one who is to be born of Sarai. Sarai, who is now almost ninety years old, laughs at the thought. She changes her mind though when she becomes pregnant and when her son is born she names him "Laughter," or Isaac. Now Ishmael is mocking Isaac. Sarai says Hagar must go, and take Ishmael with her. So Abraham is separated from his son Ishmael.

God still does not have ALL of Abraham. Now Abraham has this one son who, God promised, would bring forth a nation of children and heirs of Abraham like the sands of the seashore and the stars of the heavens. Then God asks Abraham to take his son, and He calls Isaac Abraham's "only son" (Genesis 22:2), and offer him up on Mt. Moriah. So Abraham was separated from his homeland, friends, relatives, his father, his nephew, his other son Ishmael, and gets down to his one and only last possession, his son Isaac. But Abraham gives up his long awaited and beloved son Isaac. He believed that God, Who promised him a great nation through Isaac, would somehow raise Isaac up from the dead, if need be, and God would keep His promise.

Now God had Abraham all to Himself. Abraham passed the test. Now God provides an animal for a sacrifice and spares Isaac. As they went up to the mount to make this sacrifice, Isaac asked where was the lamb for an offering? Abraham said "My son, God will provide Himself a lamb for a burnt-offering" (Genesis 22:8). This is a picture of the cross in the Old Testament. God spared Abraham's son. God did not spare His only begotten Son at Calvary, but offered Him up for us all. What a beautiful story! What a gracious God! What a wonderful Savior to go to the cross willingly for sinners! What love! But Abraham is an example. God wants all of me. God wants all of you. He wants us for our own good.

He deserves all of us. He gave His all for us.

BEAM 71

THE KINDNESS OF GOD

2 SAMUEL 9:1–7

Mephibosheth, try saying that one, had everything against him. He was in the wrong place, he was in the wrong family, and he was crippled for life. His name means "utterance of Baal." He was of the house of Saul, born of Jonathan, Saul's son. Now Saul is dead and David is king. This made him a contender for the throne, so David could put him to death. That was the custom. When one of Gideon's sons wanted to be king, he killed 69 of his half brothers upon one stone (Judges 9:5). And he did this at his father's house at Ophrah. Jerubbaal is Gideon's other name and it happens to mean "contender with Baal."

Mephibosheth was at the wrong place. He lived in Lodebar which means "no pasture." If this were not enough, he was a cripple. When he was five years old, the news of Saul's death and Jonathan's death came to his nurse who picked him up to flee. She stumbled and fell on Mephibosheth and crippled his legs for life. He is in the wrong family, wrong city, and had the wrong nurse, as a child anyway.

David had a few years of civil war with the house of Saul but now he is established on the throne as king over all of Israel. One of the first things he does is to send for Mephibosheth. It does not look good. Mephibosheth can expect to be put to death so there will be no more rivalry, no more civil war between David's house and Saul's.

When David's servant, Ziba, brings Mephibosheth to David, Mephibosheth falls on his face and does reverence (2 Samuel 9:6). It looked like the end for him. Then David did a marvelous and merciful thing. He says he

(1) Will show kindness to him for his father, Jonathan's, sake.

(2) He will spare his life.

(3) He will give him all the land that was his grandfather Saul's.

(4) He will have his servant Ziba and Ziba's children work the land that he has given to Mephibosheth.

(5) He will have Mephibosheth eat at his (David's) table continually.

You can see why Mephibosheth is overwhelmed and wonders why King David would even look "upon such a dead dog as I am?" (2 Samuel 9:8).

Why is this story told? Because it is another Old Testament picture of the cross in the New Testament.

David did not just say I will show mercy to him. No! He asked "Is there not yet any of the house of Saul, that I may shew the kindness of God unto him?" (2 Samuel 9:3). That is the difference. Look at the difference.

Like God's kindness toward us, David showed kindness to one who was his enemy. "When we were enemies, we were reconciled to God by the death of His Son" (Romans 5:10). "That in time past ye (Gentiles) were without Christ . . . having no hope, and without God in the world . . . but now in Christ Jesus . . . are made nigh by the blood of Christ" (Ephesians 2:11'-13).

Like God's kindness toward us, David did it for the sake of another. He made a covenant with Jonathan, and it was because of Jonathan he did this to an enemy. There is nothing in Mephibosheth that was so loving and good that David should do this, just like there is nothing good or loving in me, or you, that God should do this for us. "By grace are ye saved through faith, and that not of yourselves, it is the gift of God" (Ephesians 2:8–9).

Like God's kindness toward us, David invited Mephibosheth to eat at the king's table, like we will some day eat at God's table. There is a beautiful story here. He was lame in both feet but David said "He shall eat at my table, as one of the king's sons" (v. 11). So where were his crippled feet? Out of sight. We are invited also to sit at the King's table and rejoice with Him, and eat as one of God's sons. All our sinfulness, all our failures, all our ugliness, all our shortcomings, are hidden from God's eyes and we are seen without a flaw. We are to be treated as one of His sons, like His only begotten Son. What a love story of grace!

Because of God's loving kindness we can come to His table as one of His sons, and be part of the family of God. Our sins are gone because of the crucifixion of His Son. He died to make all of this possible.

"For we ourselves also were sometimes foolish, disobedient, deceived, serving divers lusts and pleasures, living in malice and envy, hateful, and hating one another. But after that the kindness and love of God our Saviour toward man appeared" (Titus 3:3–4).

BEAM 72

WHO IS THE LORD THAT I SHOULD OBEY HIM?

EXODUS 5:2

This is the question that Pharaoh asked Moses. It is a good question for all of us. Who is God? What can we say? He is God of all creation. I know there are some, who call themselves "scientists," who believe all of this around us just sprang into existence of its own accord. You wonder about these people. Where was the brain, or brain cells, before there was a brain, that thought of doing all of this? And millions, or billions of brains all agreed on which way to go? No back-seat drivers at all? They all agreed? Amazing!

Talk about putting the cart before the horse, how about putting the brain before the cells. If alligators were going to evolve into humans why didn't they just become humans right from the start? Why spend those billions of years as apes? They should have skipped that part. And why do we still have apes? Paul says that the things we see give positive proof of God's existence and power so that they are without excuse (Romans 1:20).

He is also a God who knows everything, and knows it from the beginning before it happens, and knows how it will all turn out. Isaiah puts it this way: "I am God, and there is none else; I am God, and there is none like Me, declaring the end from the beginning, and from ancient times the things that are not yet done, saying My counsel shall stand, and I will do all my pleasure" (Isaiah 46:9–10). It is hard for us humans to think of a God who never had to learn anything, a God Who knows the end of everything before it even happens. He never had to say, "Oh, I see," or "Oops." He did not have to wait to find out.

He is also a God who is present everywhere. That is not to say that He is a part of everything as pantheists teach. You are not sitting on God when you are in your chair, nor walking on God when you take a stroll. He is present no matter who you are or where you are. You can fool mother nature, I guess, but you can't fool God. He is a God who never had a beginning and will never have an ending. He is the maker of time, as we know it, but He is not captive to it. He is God

Who is holy, absolutely holy. He is righteous. He is God Who is long-suffering and patient. He is God who is gracious and forgiving, He is God Who is absolutely greater than we can imagine. He must be. If my little brain can understand all about Him then He is too small to help me. I must have a greater God than my little brain can fathom.

But there are some things that even this God cannot do. He cannot lie. Some men can lie as easily as they can breathe. They look at you and smile while knifing you in the back, or telling you about that lifetime warranty. Not God. "God is not a man, that He should lie, neither the son of man that He should repent; hath He said, and shall He not do it? Or hath He spoken, and shall He not make it good?" (Numbers 23:19). We may not like what He says, but He will do what He says. Then again we may love what He says, because He loves sinners and is gracious toward them.

He cannot sin. When Isaiah saw the Lord sitting upon a throne, the angels cried "Holy, holy, holy is the Lord of hosts, the whole earth is full of His glory" (Isaiah 6:3). "The Lord is righteous in all His ways, and holy in all His works" (Psalm 145:17). The list goes on and on. He is just and merciful and longsuffering and kind.

There is another thing He cannot do. He cannot save a sinner apart from Christ. "Neither is there salvation in any other for there is none other name under heaven given among men whereby we must be saved" (Acts 4:12). Are we under heaven? Are we among men? Then there is one way of salvation. Jesus is the way. Who is the Lord? He is. Worship Him. He invites you to come and have eternal life.

BEAM 73

THE MISS UNIVERSE CONTEST (OF 519 BC)

You never heard of it? Well they had one and it was a big one. There was a party given at the White House, I mean at Shushan the palace. This was a blast. It lasted six months (Esther 1:4), and while the king was drunk with wine he decided to call in his wife, Vashti, to show her off to the guests. He may have had more in mind than simply showing how beautiful she was. He may have wanted her to do a dance such as Herod had Herodias' daughter dance before Herodias asked for the head of John the Baptist (Matthew 14:8). It may have been indecent, or worse. This was a drunken audience and a drunken king.

Vashti refused to come to the party. This was a dangerous thing to do. You could not approach the king without endangering your life, unless he bade you to come closer. And, before NOW, it would be a terrible thing to refuse your husband's request, even if he were not king. She refused, endangering her life. The king's advisors said this act would be heard of throughout the kingdom and women everywhere would start refusing their husband's requests. "We can't let that happen," was the verdict of the wise men. "Put her away" (Esther 1:17–19). So the king spared her life, but she was removed as queen. Then what about the king? He would not have a wife anymore. What about him?

A Miss Universe Contest–that was the answer. Young maidens, virgins, from all over the empire, from every province of the kingdom would be gathered at Shushan. They would be given everything needed for purification. They would have cleansing, cosmetics, adornments, raiment, everything for a fashion show that would put to shame what we do today. Everything and anything that a maid needed to make her look outstandingly beautiful would be provided. Then she would be brought before the king. The winner got a crown that she kept. She would be the queen of Persia.

There was one Esther, who was a Jewess. She was a cousin of a Jew, Mordecai, who was carried away from his home in Jerusalem. Both of her parents were dead, so Mordecai reared Esther like his own daughter. He worked in the palace at Shushan and without divulging his race he brought his cousin, Esther, to the palace to have her entered in this beauty contest. Guess who was the winner? Esther was the beautiful and lovely Number One, the Winner! Still no one knew about her nationality. Then comes the evil one. A certain enemy of all Jews, Haman, who because Mordecai would not bow down to him, wanted to kill all Jews throughout the empire. The king listened to Haman and sent out the decree, not knowing that he, the king, had married one of those people he had just given over for destruction.

Where is the love story? Mordecai hears of the king's commandment and informs Esther that she will not escape if she keeps her race a secret. This really puts Esther in a bind. Shall she tell the king? Even the queen could not approach the king without endangering her life. She could be put to death, unless the king put out his golden sceptre (Esther 5:2). Esther asked for prayer and fasting for three days. Mordecai said to her "Who knows, perhaps this is why you have come into the kingdom for just this very thing (Esther 4:14 free translation). God hears their prayers and answers their prayers.

The king hears Esther's plea and allows the Jews to defend themselves. He learns of Haman's hatred. He hangs Haman on the gallows that Haman had built for Mordecai. He elevates Mordecai over the other cabinet members in the place of Haman. What a beauty she must have been. And what a trust she had in God to risk her life. A nation is saved by prayers and fasting and also by a Jewish Beauty Queen being in the right place at the right time. She was willing to be used by God. Who knows what God will do through us if we trust Him? "How unsearchable are His judgments, and His ways past finding out" (Romans 11:33). He only uses volunteers. Are we ready to be used?

BEAM 74

IF A MAN DIE SHALL HE LIVE?

JOB 14:14

Sometimes what Job actually said is misread. The King James translation says it like this, "If a man die shall he live again?" To be fair we should write like the King James does. "If a man die shall he live *again?*" The italics are sometimes missed and it is read incorrectly. The King James is a beautiful translation. It does sometimes put in a word or two to help the meaning. When it does, it puts those words in italics so we will know that they are not in the original. This is done to help with the meaning. Most of the times it does help. We find that other translations may add words that were not in the original and the translators do not tell us. Some do not even give a good translation but rather give us a paraphrase. That is OK if they tell us it is a paraphrase and not a translation.

Matthew 2:18 speaks about the weeping over the slaughter of innocent children in Bethlehem by Herod. We read of Rachel weeping *for* her children. Here it makes it clear that she is weeping FOR her children, which sounds better in English than to say "Rachel weeping her children." So "for" is in italics.

Again in Zechariah 14:4, speaking about the return of the Messiah, the King James reads "the mount of Olives shall cleave in the midst thereof toward the east and toward the west, *and there shall be* a very great valley" sounds better than to say "and a very great valley." It helps the meaning.

In Job 14:14 however, it may confuse some who may not be aware of the reason for italics in the King James. Here, and in a few other cases, it may not help with the meaning. But the translators did tell us about the italics and we should be aware of their meaning. What Job said was "If a man die, shall he live?" To say "If a man die shall he live again?" sounds like Job is asking if there is a resurrection. What Job is saying is, if man dies, is there life after death? Shall he live after he dies? Not again, at some future resurrection, but does he somehow go on living after death?

Job had a number of questions. We have the answers. He may

not have been sure, but we can be positive. Yes, a man goes on living somewhere after death. And yes, after some time, there will be a resurrection also of both the saved and the lost. The Lord told His disciples about the rich man and Lazarus in Luke 16:19 ff. This is not a parable. He never says it is a parable. And, unlike parables, this man is mentioned by name.

He says in verse 22 that the beggar, Lazarus, died and was carried by angels to Abraham's bosom. He says the rich man died and was buried. Nothing about any angels. And he says that in hell, which is really the word "Hades," the place where the dead went, he lifted up his voice in torment. We are sometimes told incorrectly that "we cannot take it with us." That is true of most things. There is at least one thing that we do take with us; our memory. In Hades the rich man lifts up his voice and cries to father Abraham for a little bit of water to cool his tongue. Father Abraham says "Son, remember" (Luke 16:25). We take our memories with us. We will have them for all eternity. Shall we regret what we have to remember? The missed opportunities? The many chances we had?

But Job had a great confidence in having life sometime after death. He made that remarkable statement "I know that my redeemer liveth, and that he shall stand at the latter *day* upon the earth and though after my skin worms destroy this body, yet in my flesh shall I see God, Whom I shall see for myself and mine eyes shall behold and not another" (Job 19:25–27). And this was before the cross and before a resurrection of the Messiah. I do not believe Job had any trouble believing that if a man died he would still live. The question for us is where? If Jesus is my Savior, then I will live with Him. If not, I will be in that awful place where that rich man was, who cried out in his suffering. Let's not go there.

BEAM 75

PENIEL, THE FACE OF GOD

GENESIS 32:22–32

Peniel means "Face of God." This is a beautiful story here about Jacob meeting God face to face.

Look at the MAN.

He was a rascal. You had to look carefully at the fine print when you signed a contract with him. You even had to count your fingers after you signed it. He was a rascal. His name means "Supplanter" and that is what he did from the beginning. He came into the world grasping at his twin brother's heel and kept on grasping. He got his brother's birthright. Yes, Esau sold it to him, but Jacob took advantage of his brother's hunger. He could have given him food. This was his brother. Later he tricked his own father into giving him Esau's blessing. His father, Isaac, had poor eyesight. This did not go over well with Esau and Jacob had to leave town before Esau killed him. Jacob only had one good work about him, if you could call it that. He loved Rachel. He really loved her and served her father seven years to get her for a bride.

Then Jacob gets a dose of his own medicine. Laban, his father-in-law, switches women on him on that beautiful wedding night and Jacob wakes up with Leah, Rachel's sister. What you sow, that is what you reap. Now, after working for his father-in-law, and stealing as much as he could from him, he decides it is getting too hot at Laban's place. Laban has sons who do not like the way Jacob has been stealing their inheritance. What is he to do now? About the only thing he can do is head back home where Esau is and beg for mercy. Maybe Esau has softened somewhat and will spare him. What a man. Crooked, conniving, cheating Jacob. So he heads back home.

Look at the MEETING:

Along the way Jacob still tries one of his old tricks. He sends the women and children across the river in separate groups hoping that Esau would see the little ones and have mercy on their father, Jacob. He is alone now, still protecting himself. If Esau is going to kill him, he will be the last one Esau will find along the way. Then God appears to Jacob. We read that Jacob "was left alone; and there wrestled a man with him until the breaking of the day" (Genesis 32:24). Now this was not some stranger that appeared out of nowhere. It was God appearing in a pre-incarnate form. That is before Jesus took on human flesh and became the God-man. God appeared in the Old Testament in various forms, but temporarily. This was one way of appearing before men without the glory of God blinding them and even killing them. It permitted God to be near and to get their attention and to speak to them. We are told by Jacob that it was God. He wrestled with Jacob all night. Of course God could never lose a wrestling match or any other fight. It was done so that Jacob might get a good look at himself. He must have also wrestled with his past sins and wished he had not done the things that he did. Don't we all?

Look at the MERCY:

We read that the "man" could not prevail against Jacob, so he touched Jacob's thigh and crippled Jacob. This was all a part of God's mercy. If God could cripple Jacob He could have won any wrestling match. He could have killed Jacob on the spot. But God is in the saving business. He wanted to save Jacob. God asks Jacob to let Him go. Can you imagine God asking any man to let Him loose from a wrestling hold? Impossible! But look at what happened. The "man" (God) asks Jacob to let Him go. Jacob is crippled so he is hanging on to the "man." This is beautiful! When a sinner, even one who is not crippled, is hanging on to God and asking for His blessing, God cannot take away those arms that are around His neck to cast off the sinner. God is merciful and full of grace. He cannot turn away from a sinner who is clinging to Him for mercy. It was called "Peniel," the Face of God. God's face today is seen in Jesus. "He that hath seen Me hath seen the Father" (John 14:9). Have you seen Him? He cannot tear away arms that are clinging to Him for mercy. What a gracious God we have! He loves to save sinners.

BEAM 76

THE HIGH PRIESTLY ROBES REMOVED

LEVITICUS 16:4

The High Priest had special and beautiful garments made for his ministry. Exodus 28:4, ff tells us about some of these garments that were really glorious attire. These were holy and beautiful and glorious garments that spoke of the glory of the High Priest. They were symbolic of the glory that Christ had before He entered into the world through a virgin birth, before He took on the nature of man. These were made of the very best materials.

There was a breastplate. On this there were 12 stones for the 12 tribes of Israel. This could mean that the High Priest carried the names of the children of Israel on his heart, as Jesus, the One True High Priest, carries the names of His brothers on His heart.

There was an ephod. This was made of gold, purple, scarlet, and fine twined linen. It was made to hang by two chains of gold from the shoulders, where two other stones, one on each shoulder, had the names of the tribes of Israel.

There was a robe. This was all of blue.

There was a coat. This was embroidered of fine linen.

There was a mitre. This was a plate of pure gold with "Holiness To The Lord" engraved upon it.

There was a girdle. This was of fine needlework.

We are told that these were made "for glory and for beauty" (Exodus 28:40).

These were so beautiful and glorious that God made special arrangements to have them made. We sometimes are told that God never filled anyone in the Old Testament with His Spirit. We are told this filling is strictly a New Testament revelation. But we read in Exodus 31:2–3 that God "filled him (Bezaleel) with the Spirit of God" to do the work of the Tabernacle and the garments of Aaron and his sons (v.10).

Yet, all of this was removed on the Day of Atonement. Leviticus 16:4 tells us Aaron was to remove all of these glorious garments and put on plain, simple, but clean linen garments when he entered into the Holiest of Holies. What is the beauty of this?

Revelation 19:8 tells us that "fine linen is the righteousness of saints." The beauty is that Jesus "Who being in the form of God, thought deity not something to be grasped" (Philippians 2:6, Scofield margin) but emptied Himself of the manifestation of glory. He can never be separated from His glory because He is God, but the manifestation of it He set aside. He "took upon Him the form of a servant, and was made in the likeness of men" (Philippians 2:7). He entered into the Holiest of Holies, on the cross, manifesting only His humanity which was sinless. Isaiah 53:2 tells us that there was no comeliness in Him, no beauty that we should desire Him. He looked like an ordinary Joe. It was not physical beauty in Him that made Him different. It was that He was without sin. He laid aside the manifestation of His glory to die as the sinless man who could save sinful men.

He enters the Holiest Place as a simple, but sinless, man, clad only in the white linen garments of His righteousness to save those whose righteousnesses are as filthy rags (Isaiah 64:6), and repugnant to God. "For there is not a just man upon earth, that doeth good, and sinneth not" (Ecclesiastes 7:20). "And this is the name whereby He shall be called, THE LORD OUR RIGHTEOUSNESS" (Jeremiah 23:6).

But His glorious righteousness was given to us in exchange for our sins (2Cor. 5:21). He died a sinless One without all the heavenly glory being seen on the cross. He still had it, but did not show it. What a love this is!

BEAM 77

LITTLE DOGGIES AND THE CRUMBS

MATTHEW 15:26

At first this sounds rather crude and harsh when we read it. A poor woman who had a sick daughter comes to Jesus to get help. And He refuses to help her. And, does He call her a dog? She was a Gentile and Gentiles were called many names by the people of Israel, including dogs. They were called the "Goyim" or Gentiles, and are stilled called that today. This doesn't sound like Jesus. But why? Was He really rude to this woman? The woman cries out so much the disciples want Him to send her away, she is bothering them. We can understand that. The disciples are not as patient as the Lord. But He still does not seem to heed her cry. Why? What has she done? Why doesn't He do what she asks, like He has done so many times in the past?

She called Him "Son of David" (Matthew 15:22). She had no right to come to Him as an Israelite unless she had been a proselyte. If she had become an Israelite, He would not have spoken to her this way. In verse 24 He says "I am not sent but to the lost sheep of the house of Israel." That sounds like a negative, like "go away, you're bothering Me."

Now she changes her approach and says "Lord, help me," no longer coming to Him as an Israelite but just someone in need. He tells her "it is not meet (proper, good) to take the children's bread, and cast it to the dogs." That does sound harsh but there are two words used in the New Testament translated "dog." One is "kuon," the hound dog, the common scavenger of the street. The other is "kunarion," which is the doggie, or puppy, a house dog. That is the word Jesus used, "doggie" or "puppy." This, I believe, is a test for this poor woman. She answers Him "Truth, Lord: yet the dogs eat of the crumbs which fall from their masters' table." She passes the test. She is saying what Israel does not want, she is glad to accept. The Lord came to Israel first. If Israel does not want Him as their Messiah, she will be glad to receive Him as Lord and Savior. She will take whatever falls from Israel's table.

Then the Lord says "O woman, great is thy faith, be it unto

thee as thou wilt" (15:28). There were few times that the Lord Jesus marveled at the faith of some sinner. This is one example. Another is when the centurion, another Gentile, came to ask Jesus to heal his servant in Matthew 8:5–13. The centurion said the Lord Jesus did not have to come to his house to heal, He could just speak the words. Jesus marveled at his faith.

What a love story! We do not have to be of any particular race, or country, or religion. We do not come on nationality, or through some priesthood. We take our place as sinners, with the rest of the world of sinners. Yes, "For all have sinned, and come short of the glory of God" (Romans 3:23). When we come that way His ears are open to our cry and His heart is opened to help. Yes, even the doggies are grateful for whatever the children did not want. The doggies are glad they can have what falls from their table.

She is saying she will take Him any way at all. She was in need.

When he went back to His hometown, Nazareth, He marveled because of their unbelief. He could do no mighty work there, "save that He laid His hands upon a few sick folk, and healed them" (Mark 6:5–6). So unbelief does have a way of stopping what the Lord would like to do. Even though He healed some, the unbelief was so great He could do no "mighty work" there. Far better to have Him marvel at our faith, than our unbelief. Which is it with you? Are you willing to receive Him as crumbs from the table, when the master of the table does not want Him? Are we ready to receive Him any possible way we can? That way, of course, is by faith. Receive Him. He is ready to do us good.

BEAM 78

DR. JEKYLL AND MR. PAUL

(MR. HYDE HIDING INSIDE)

There are some good Bible teachers who want to protect the Apostle Paul's reputation. The Apostle Peter made many blunders before the filling of the Spirit on the day of Pentecost. I am glad the Bible shows us how Peter was like many of us. He put his foot in his mouth many times. That gives me hope. The Apostle Paul likewise, was made out of the same stuff as we all are. He tells us so. In Romans 7, he tells us about the tug of war that went on inside this apostle. It is between the new nature that he received when he was saved, and the old nature that he was born with, which he still had within him. The new man might be called Paul, while the old man may be called Saul.

Paul writes in Romans 7 "For we know that the law is spiritual, but I am carnal, sold under sin" (verse 14). He tells us about the battle that he must fight. The battle over who is in charge. He says "For that which I do, I allow not, for what I would, that do I not, but what I hate, that do I" (verse 15). He is saying there are times when he should do something that is right, but he doesn't do it because he still has a sin nature that still loves to have its own way. And, he says there are some things he should not do, but he does them anyhow, for the same reason. That old sin nature. This is not the norm for Paul's life. He certainly is not living in sin, but he is telling us that he also must struggle with this two nature thing, just like the rest of us. The old nature wants to run our lives and we know that the new nature should be in charge.

Some would have us believe that Paul never sinned after he trusted the Lord Jesus. However, any sixth grade schoolboy could understand Acts 21:4. It states plainly enough that there were some disciples "who said to Paul **through the Spirit**, that he should not go up to Jerusalem." That sounds clear enough. It was not their words, but they spoke by the power of the Holy Spirit. It does not matter that Paul was ready to offer up his life for the Lord Jesus. He was told not to go to Jerusalem. If God tells me not to go to Chicago, and I go anyhow, even if I am willing to be tortured in Chicago, isn't it wrong for me to go?

Paul had taken up a collection before at various churches, to send to the poor saints at Jerusalem. In 1 Corinthians 16:3 he tells the saints at Corinth that "whomsoever ye shall approve . . . them will I send to bring your liberality (their offerings) unto Jerusalem." But in Acts 21 Paul disobeys the Lord's command to not go to Jerusalem. He desires to go there himself and suffer for the Lord. Long before this, Samuel said "to obey is better than sacrifice" (1 Samuel 15:22). But some defenders make Paul an exception. Why?

What happens when Paul disobeys the Lord's command? He takes a Jewish vow, and shaves his head. Then he is about to have a priest offer up **an animal sacrifice**. This is the apostle who said "Christ is the end of the Law for righteousness to every one that believeth" (Romans 10:4). In Galatians 3:10 He writes "For as many as are or the works of the law are under the curse, for it is written Cursed is everyone that continueth not in all things which are written in the book of the law to do them."

So God has Paul arrested before he does more things to be ashamed of. Yes, Paul was willing to suffer for the Lord Jesus. But who knows what more he might have done if he had obeyed? We do not have to defend Paul's reputation. He, like Peter, gives us hope. We also have a Mr. Hyde inside of us that wants to run our lives. But he does not have to. We can let the new man have charge of our lives. But even if we fail, God shows us that He is still gracious, as He was with Paul. He can still work things together for good to them that love God (Romans 8:28). What a loving God He is! Let's try harder. Let the Holy Spirit be in charge. We will have less to regret later.

BEAM 79

LEAVEN–WHAT IS THIS STUFF?

1 CORINTHIANS 5:6

What is this leaven and what does it have to do with us? It was a sour dough that was fermented and when put into any other dough it fermented that dough. This may have made the dough more palatable to the taste. It stood for pollution in the Old Testament sacrifices. The Feast of the Passover was followed by the week of unleavened bread. Honey was another additive that was forbidden. It was prone to ferment also. But honey made things sweet. It was therefore out of place in any sacrifice that portrayed the death of the Savior on the cross. Nothing could be symbolically used that would seem to make the picture of the cross sweet. The cross was a bitter ordeal, a bitter sacrifice.

Leaven stood for a type of corruption. It permeated any kind of dough it entered. The Lord said "Take heed and beware of the leaven of the Pharisees and of the Sadducees" (Matthew 16:6). The apostles were confused about this product. They thought the Lord was speaking about literal dough for bread. He said "How is it that ye do not understand . . . it is not . . . concerning bread, . . . then they understood." It was the "doctrine of the Pharisees and the Sadducees" (Matthew 16:11–12).

Because it represented corruption it was forbidden in most of the Old Testament sacrifices. The Passover Sacrifice represented Jesus' sacrifice on the cross. There could be no leaven in this sacrifice for He was without sin, a perfect sinless sacrifice for sinners. Leaven would have spoiled the picture. Some years ago I read a lesson from a good and conservative Bible teacher. He said that the Lord Jesus declared that "the Kingdom of heaven is like unto leaven which a woman took, and hid in three measures of meal, till the whole was leavened" (Matthews 13:33). From that one verse he took it to mean that the kingdom of heaven is like leaven. Many others do the same thing. They say leaven stands for evil everywhere else in the Bible, except in this passage. So they teach that the Gospel is like leaven, and all the world will get the message some day and be converted. That is a strange way of interpreting Scripture. In all other places it means evil but here it means good, the Gospel. Huh!

But the Lord Jesus did not say the kingdom of heaven is like leaven. No, He did not. Once in a Sunday School Class I said "I never had parents help me with my homework." (They could not read, nor write.) Now did I say I never had parents? Sure I did. Did I say I never had any parents? Surely not. That would be an impossibility. What I said was I never had parents help with my homework. That's another story. Jesus did not say the kingdom of heaven is like leaven. He said the kingdom of heaven is like leaven which a woman took and hid in the meal. That's a different story. Leaven still stands for evil, corruption. And that corruption is in the church and will get worse. "Now the Spirit speaketh expressly, that in the latter times some shall depart from the faith, giving heed to seducing spirits, and doctrines of devils" (1 Timothy 4:1). And that is what this is all this about, doctrinal corruption in the church in the last days.

The world is not going to get permeated with the "leaven" of the Gospel until the world is converted to Christianity. It would be wonderful if it would. Do you believe things are getting better? Read the newspaper! What does the Bible say about it? "But evil men and seducers shall wax worse and worse, deceiving, and being deceived" (2 Timothy 3:13). Good ole Peter also agrees with Paul. "Knowing this first, that there shall come in the last days scoffers, walking after their own lusts, and saying, Where is the promise of His coming?" (2 Peter 3:3–4).

I know one may be on shaky ground to use a parable to teach doctrinal truth, but I feel I am on solid ground right now, I think. In Matthew 13 we have the parables about the kingdom of heaven. There is the one about wheat and tares growing together until the harvest. Then the Lord Jesus said "I will say to the reapers, Gather ye together first the tares and bind them in bundles to burn them; but gather the wheat into my barn" (Matthew 13:30). If leaven is the Gospel, you would think that there would be no more tares, they would all turn into wheat. But there I go again, getting theological. Sorry about that.

Nevertheless, there were some sacrifices that depict the sinner in fellowship with God. In these, leaven was to be used. It all fits together perfectly, because we still have that old sin nature, even after we are saved. An example of this would be the peace offering. In this offering the sacrificer partakes of the sacrifice, just as a believer shares the peace of God with God. In this sacrifice he offered "Besides the cakes, he shall offer for his offering leavened bread with the sacrifice of thanksgiving of his peace-offerings" (Leviticus 7:13). Yes, we can never get rid of that old sinful nature, even after we are saved, until we get those new bodies that know no sin. We still have leaven in us.

Honey cannot be used to sweeten the cross, leaven cannot be used because His death on the cross is a sinless sacrifice. But leaven, that picture of sin and corruption, can be used when it is the man who is pictured and not the Savior. One day, my leaven will be entirely removed once and forever. Hallelujah!

BEAM 80

TEMPTATION

We pray "lead us not into temptation." But we also know that there will be temptations because the enemy, Satan, still wars against God our Savior. We also know that "there hath no temptation taken you but such as is common to man" (1 Corinthians 10:13). And we have a promise from God that He "will with the temptation also make a way to escape, that ye may be able to bear it" (10:13). Yet we fail and fall in temptation. Let's look at the avenues of temptation to see how we are attacked. And how to escape.

John tells us there are three avenues of temptation. He writes "For all that is in the world, the lust of the flesh, and the lust of the eyes, and the pride of life is not of the Father but is of the world" (1 John 2:16). Three things mentioned here are ways in which we are tempted.

THE LUST OF THE FLESH. That would include too many things to list here. The flesh cries out for satisfaction. It is the thing that most of us feel must be satisfied. Here is a partial list of the desires of the flesh. "Now the works of the flesh are manifest, which are these; adultery, fornication, uncleanness, lasciviousness, idolatry, witchcraft, hatred, variance, emulations, wrath, strife, seditions, heresies, envyings, murders, drunkenness, revellings, and such like" (Galatians 5:19–21). Even Paul did not finish the list. The flesh is never satisfied. It cries out for satisfaction, but when it gets one thing it lusts after, it then lusts after another. There is no satisfying the flesh. We think it is, but it is only temporary.

THE LUST OF THE EYES. Here is another avenue where Satan gains entrance. What the eyes see, the eyes want. We hear the phrase "shop till you drop," and that is just what some people do. What the eyes want, they crave for, and that is what we give them. It was David's eyes that led to his sin of adultery and murder. He should have been with his men fighting the Lord's battles. "But David tarried still at Jerusalem" (2 Samuel 11:1). Then we read in the next verse David saw a woman washing herself. After his eyes saw, then the flesh lusted. It started with his eyes.

A third avenue is THE PRIDE OF LIFE. My how that gets so

many people. They want you to know that they are "somebody." Of course they are. They are sinners like the rest of us. But no, they have a college education, or they have a mansion to live in, or they have an excellent job as a CEO of something. Sometimes it is just in their name. They are not John Brown, no siree. They might be, but the name is changed to Johannes Spinklenburg Brownley III.

All three of these avenues were used against Eve in the Garden. She saw the fruit and it "was good for food (the lust of the flesh), and that it was pleasant to the eyes (lust of the eyes), and a tree to be desired to make one wise (pride of life)" (Genesis 3:6). She failed the test.

The same three were used against Jesus when Satan tempted Him. After Jesus fasted forty days and nights, Satan says to Him, "If thou be the Son of God command this stone that it be made bread" (Luke 4:3). The lust of the flesh. Then he shows Him all the kingdoms of the world (lust of the eyes) and says he will give them to Jesus if Jesus will worship him. (They were not his to give.) Then he brings Him to a high pinnacle of the temple and says cast yourself down. God has given His angels charge over you so you will not get hurt. Yes, and all the people down below will marvel. You won't need to go to the cross. Anything to keep Jesus from the cross, for that is the only way we could be saved. Without the shedding of blood there is no forgiveness of sin. Yes, the pride of life. But where is the cross? And without the cross there could be no salvation for sinners. That was Satan's plan. Jesus did not fail. Jesus answered him just like we can, by using the Word of God. "It is written," He says. He did not use His divine power. He did what any of us can do. He used the Word of God. Have we? How are we doing with the three avenues? Our defense is in the Word of God. "It is written," He said. That's what we need to say.

BEAM 81

STONING STEPHEN AND WHAT GOOD DID IT DO?

ACTS 7: 54–60

There was a controversy in the early church. Greeks versus Hebrews, over the way the Greek widows were neglected in the daily services. What a way to end controversies in the church. Those Hebrews said to the Greeks pick out some of your good Greek servants to watch over these widows. That is the way. You want more done. We won't stand in the way or give you any reason to feel that we are biased. Pick out some Greeks. This pleased the whole multitude, so they picked out seven Greeks to serve, while the Hebrews (the Apostles) gave themselves to the Word of God (Acts 6:1–5). These seven were "workers" and we call them "deacons," for that is what the word means.

One of these workers was Stephen, which means "crown." He was such a witness for the saving power of the Lord Jesus that he was stoned to death when he said that he "saw the glory of God and Jesus standing on the right hand of God" (Acts 7:56). It looked like Jesus was standing to receive Stephen, for we read elsewhere that after He made "one sacrifice for sins for ever, sat down on the right hand of God" (Hebrews 10:12). This also says something about His perfect sacrifice for sin. The tabernacle and the temple never had any chairs in them. This signified that the work of redemption from sins was never done, until Jesus came. Then He could sit down. He said "it is finished" (John 19:30). Now He is seen standing to receive Stephen. And this "Stephen" receives his "crown" as the crowd stones him to death.

But there was another young man there named Saul, of Tarsus, who held the clothes of those who threw the stones (Acts 7:58). I believe Saul was sorry he got stuck with that job. From what we read elsewhere I believe Saul wanted to throw stones, not hold robes. But this was God's way of overruling. Saul heard Stephen forgive the people who were stoning him, just like the Lord Jesus did when He was crucified. Saul, I believe, remembered this act of grace. It may have been a thorn in His side for some time.

This same Saul did his best to obliterate this "new worship" of this group of Jews, who worship a Jesus, as the Messiah. He did all he could to wipe them out. Then the Lord Jesus meets Saul and wants to know why Saul is persecuting Him, the Messiah. This says something. When you hurt the church, you hurt Jesus. After Saul becomes Paul the Apostle he goes into all the world preaching that same message he once tried to destroy. Paul is then hated, like Stephen was, and is stoned like Stephen at Lystra. I believe that Paul was stoned to death at Lystra (Acts 14:19). They were good stoners in those days. Later, Paul tells us how he was caught up into the third heaven and whether he was alive or dead he did not know (2 Corinthians 12:2). I believe he was dead at Lystra. Unlike Stephen, Paul was raised up again.

So what! Well after some time Paul comes back on another missionary journey and comes through Lystra again. Did they stone him? No! However, a young man named Timothy joins Paul's group and becomes one of his closest helpers. Could it have been from watching this Paul getting stoned, just like Saul was watching Stephen getting stoned? I do not know, but it could be, and I believe it happened that way. Stephen is stoned and forgives his stoners. Paul is stoned and comes back to Lystra, so he must have somehow forgiven his stoners. And there is Timothy seeing the whole thing, I believe. Is it a coincidence? I think not. The suffering of the saints brought glory to the Lord and a crown to the saints. What a beautiful story. God brought good out of suffering.

"And we know that all things work together for good to them that love God, to them who are the called according to His purpose" (Romans 8:28).

BEAM 82

THE GLORY OF GOD'S GARBAGE

EXODUS 25:4–5

Can you imagine a world without color? There is no theological must that says the earth must be more colorful than, say, the moon. Suppose everything was gray. We could still appreciate the wonder of God's universe. Its immensity and power would still awe us into a bewilderment of God's wisdom and creative power. That which is clearly seen would still testify to that Creator, which is not seen.

If we had never seen color, we would not know we were living in a drab world. Our children would still be precious to us, even though they would all be shades of gray. We can imagine hugging our little ones, wiping gray tears from gray cheeks, running gray hands through gray locks. We can even imagine cleaning "dirty gray" spots from gray clothes to make them "sparkling gray" clean.

Look-alike houses in look-alike neighborhoods would be look-alike shades of gray. Only their shapes could be used to distinguish them. Mountains would still be there to be conquered. "Sunny" clouds and storm clouds would all be dark clouds hovering about the peaks.

God could have created the world in this manner, or made mankind's eyesight to be color blind, and not compromised His attributes and character one iota. He would still be holy, righteous, omnipotent, omniscient, and unchanging in justice, mercy, love, et. al. Aren't you glad He didn't? The God of glory, Who is incomprehensible in wisdom and unsearchable in His loving purpose, has ordained a glorious world of splendor that surpasses the capacity of the eyes of the most critical artist.

Take the tree for example. How many trees are there in the world? Billions? Quadrillions? How many leaves do you suppose are on those billions of trees? Those leaves serve their purpose in feeding the trees all summer. After their purpose is fulfilled, they are discarded to become a mulch to fertilize those same trees, and any other plant that may be in need of mulch. They are really garbage that God is about to scrap in His providential way.

People travel hundreds of miles to visit some states that are noted for the color of their trees. The next time you are driving along that country road in October, and marvel at the splendor of the world around you, remember God is merely painting His garbage before He tosses it away. Behold, what manner of God this is! How can words describe the beauty of color that is displayed before our eyes each Autumn? All for a few weeks before He tosses out His glorious garbage.

And what about sunsets, or sunrises? How about the clouds and how they dress up that beautiful blue sky? And flowers? Are they not more beautiful that the entire splendor that Solomon had in his palace?

The Lord said so. "Consider the lilies how they grow . . . I say unto you, that Solomon in all his glory was not arrayed like one of these" (Matthew 6:28–29). Yet they are here for a few weeks and then gone, like the tree leaves. And the birds. Some of them may be more beautiful than the flowers. And how long are they with us? No long. But oh, the beauty they carry with them in their little coats of feathers. What a drab world it would be without color. And yet, this is just the dressing stage for what is coming.

If God so clothes the earth with such magnificent splendor for a few weeks, what must He have in store for those who are redeemed and are to share His glory for eternity? If He glorifies His garbage for a few weeks before He tosses it, what must He have for His eternal residents? We should thank Him for all of this "extra" that He has allowed us to see with these eyes. Greater things are coming. Will you be there with the saints to enjoy the new creation? You can. Jesus is the Door. Come on in!

BEAM 83

WHOM CAN YOU TRUST?
OLD PROPHETS? NO WAY!

1 KINGS 13:11

Trust only in the Lord. "Trust in the Lord with all thine heart, and lean not unto thine own understanding. In all thy ways acknowledge Him, and He shall direct thy paths" (Proverbs 3:5–6). The Lord is the One whom we can trust, always and ever, under any circumstance. Sometimes you can trust man, sometimes. But you can trust the Lord always and forever.

In 1 Kings 13 we read that God sent a prophet to Jeroboam, a wicked King of Israel. He was to cry out against the false altar that Jeroboam set up and to tell him of the future destruction of this false altar of worship. Jeroboam did not like what this prophet uttered and stretched forth his hand to order his men to grab this prophet. His hand withered completely, in a moment, so that he could not pull it back. Then Jeroboam asks the prophet to pray to the Lord for him to restore his arm again. And this prophet does so (1 Kings 13:4–6). Even a wicked king can be thankful at times, so Jeroboam asks the prophet to come home with him and he would give him a reward.

Now we come to the heart of this story. The prophet refused and tells why. God told the prophet not to eat food, nor drink water, nor return the same way he entered into the city of Bethel. God told him. So the prophet refuses the offer of a good dinner and other rewards and returns home another way (13:9).

But there was an old prophet in Bethel. His sons tell him about this new young prophet and what he did to Jeroboam. By the way, the new young prophet is called "the man of God" (1 Kings 13:12). He is unnamed but called a "man of God." The old prophet, by riding on his donkey, heads him off at the pass. He says to the "Man of God" prophet, "Come home with me and eat bread." The young prophet refuses because the Lord had told him not to. Then the old prophet says he is a prophet also, and an angel of the Lord told him to bring the young prophet home to eat with him. But he lied! (Verse 18). So the young prophet goes home and eats with Old Liar. Then the Lord speaks through Old Liar, against his will no doubt, and says the young prophet shall be slain because of his disobedience. And he is. When he leaves Old Liar he is killed by a lion.

So what's the point? You cannot believe everybody, even when they say they are a prophet of the Lord.

You cannot believe someone because he is an old man either. You can believe the Lord, because He never lies, He cannot deceive, He cannot do wrong.

There are many false prophets stating things in the name of the Lord, and there will be many more in the Last Days. "Beware of false prophets which come to you in sheep's clothing" (Matthew 7:15). Satan loves to be in the pulpit on Sundays preaching "You can be good. You don't need a cross."

Jesus said "I am the way the truth and the life: no man cometh unto the Father, but by Me" (John 14:6). We cannot trust anyone who tells us differently. He is not One of many ways. He is not one of the Doors. He is the only Door. He is the only way to God. He is the only way of salvation.

Is this narrow mindedness and bigotry? Yes, it is. Jesus is very narrow minded, because He is the only Way. He does not want us deceived because someone says an angel told him something. There is one we can trust. "God is not a man, that He should lie, neither the son of man the He should repent" (Numbers 23:19). You can trust Him completely for anything that He says. Are you? Why not?

BEAM 84

GOD CHOOSES A MAN

NEHEMIAH

There was a time when Israel was no longer in their land of Judea, which was Canaan land, not Palestine.

It was because of their sins, their idolatry, their many gods and idols that they worshiped instead of the one true God of Abraham, Isaac, and Jacob; the one God who sent Moses into Egypt to bring His people out. God let Nebuchadnezzar carry them away captive into the land of Babylon. There in Babylon they were to remain for 70 years. This number was given in 2 Chronicles 36:21 to fulfill the word of the Lord by Jeremiah the prophet that it would be seventy years so that the land might enjoy its Sabbaths. The nation did not believe God, or at least they did not obey God, when He said every seventh year the land should rest. They should not sow nor reap. But He would provide them enough in the sixth year so that they would have an abundance to last for two years.

There is some confusion about these seventy years though. Some Bible scholars take it that the land had not had any rest for 490 years. That makes a nice number of 70 years. However, I do not mean to be a spoil sport, but simply take the Scriptures at their face value. After all what is the purpose of Bible study, if it is not to learn? Every fifty years there was a year of jubilee in which every man who had sold himself because of poverty, or any other reason, would be returned to his liberty. The land that was in hock would be returned to the owners. That meant if someone held a mortgage on your land, they had to calculate how many years till Jubilee, when they had to return it to you.

The year of Jubilee was also a Sabbath year of rest for the nation. This is overlooked by those who calculate 70 Sabbath years come out of 490 years. In Leviticus 25:11 we read "a jubilee shall that fiftieth year be unto you; ye shall not sow, neither reap that which groweth of itself in it, nor gather the grapes in it of thy vine undressed." God said He would provide them with enough to last for two years and then till the harvest of the third year. They did not believe Him. So counting one jubilee for every 50 years it would only take about nine years less than 490 years to make 70 Sabbaths of non-rest. It could be 10 years depending on when these years started.

But back to Nehemiah. We see a man that was CONCERNED. After those 70 years were about up, Nehemiah became burdened for his city, Jerusalem. In Nehemiah 1:2, he asks them about the Jews that had escaped the captivity and about Jerusalem. In 1:4 we read that he sat down and wept and mourned and fasted and prayed. Do we ever get so burdened that we weep over the lost, or fast for them?

Then we see a man that was CONVINCED. In 2:5 he asks the king if he might be the one sent to Jerusalem to build it. He was so burdened that the king wonders if he is sick (2:2). It was not nice to be sad in the presence of the king. But Nehemiah could not refrain. He was convinced that he should be the one to build it again.

We see also a man CONSECRATED. In 1:6 he confesses his sins and the sins of the children of Israel. He prayed day and night for them. I wonder if we ever get that burdened and convinced that we consecrate ourselves for the sake of the lost. This is the kind of man that God chooses. The king consents and he is sent back to build the walls of the city and fight off enemies that wanted to hinder that work. Do we ever get that consecrated that we lose our appetite and pray continually for the lost? That is the kind of man that is after God's own heart. In Romans 1:15, Paul states "I am ready to preach the gospel to you, that are at Rome also." Are we ready? We should be. God needs feet, and hands, and tongues to take His message to a lost world. Will you be that man that God chooses? You can be. Try it.

BEAM 85

WIMPS AND NERDS

2 CORINTHIANS 11:23–29

Not so long ago a politician made some remarks about church goers and religious people that were not complimentary at all. He felt that those who go to church and study the Bible are a bunch of wimps. Some may be. This may be the way many non-church-going people think of Christians. They have the idea that church members just go to church and pray and don't have any fun. Ah hah! Yeah, they just bury their heads in some old book and read and that's about all the fun they get out of life. Ah hah! Well let's see how Wimpy these Christians can be.

I wonder if this politician ever heard of the Apostle Paul? I wonder if he ever read anything about Paul's wimpiness? Here are a few of the things that Paul went through for his Savior. He says five times he received 39 lashes. This was not simply a whip of leather. It was a three prong instrument with lumps of lead or stones embedded in the leather. Plain old leather was not punishment enough. And the number was just short of the maximum of forty. Forty was the most that could be given as punishment by a judge under the Law (Deuteronomy 25:3). One more could make the brother "seem vile." Just in case the lasher did not count correctly, they stopped short by just one. You did not want to overdo it.

Let's see what else Paul, the Wimp, went through. Three times he was beaten with rods. The word rod is used in many different ways in the Scriptures, but it was a stick or piece of wood or a thin club when used for punishment. Paul says he was stoned once. This would have been at Lystra. There is some argument as to whether Paul was stoned to death or not. I believe they were good stoners. He tells us in chapter 12 how he was caught up into the third heaven and saw revelations that were unspeakable. He even says he did not know if he were alive or dead when he saw these visions (2 Corinthians 12:3, 7). Sounds to me like he was dead.

Paul was in a shipwreck three times, and spent a night and a day in the deep. Sounds like Paul was a sissy doesn't it? And they had no busses for Paul to go from one country to another. They walked those many, many, miles. Look at all the perils this Nerd was in. "In perils of waters, in perils of robbers." Yes, they had them in his day too. In perils of his own countrymen, in perils by the heathen, in perils in the city. Sounds like New York or Chicago. In perils in the wilderness, in the sea, in perils of false brethren. And the list goes on. He also suffered from weariness and pains and hunger. He was human you know. Sometimes he suffered fastings and other times he just did not have anything to eat. He says he was in the cold and in nakedness. What a wimp!

And these are just some of the physical things that he went through. There was the burden of the many churches, the constant prayers for the saints. You should read his prayer list and see how many saints he prayed for. Yet he did not boast of his sufferings. He carried in his heart the burdens of all the saints. What a wimp? Yes, he just went to church and read some old book about religion. I wonder if this politician ever suffered just one flogging, or shipwreck? I doubt it. Those wimpy Christians can be thankful if they have not gone through all the sufferings that Paul went through, yet there have been many saints that likewise have suffered for the Lord Jesus. Fanny Crosby suffered from an incompetent medical treatment that left her blind for life, yet she wrote over 2000 beloved hymns that we sing today. Yes, I guess she was just another wimp. It is too bad that so many untaught people think that Christians are just wimps that can't make it in the world. Just look at Paul. Doesn't he look wimpy? Just one of those religious nerds. Yes, the world says, "Come on and get a life." Paul had one. And we can have an eternal life because of the sufferings of another. Come join the Wimps and see what a little suffering can do for you. Come see what a real life is all about. Come on! Get a life! Get eternal life! Oh! How? Jesus will give you life, if you come to Him.

BEAM 86

JOB IN SATAN'S SIEVE

JOB 23:10

It is easy for us to look back on what happened to Job and see how it all worked together for good. Satan had implied that God must bless someone abundantly to get that one to love and serve Him. Every time Satan speaks in the Scriptures it is a lie. There is no exception here. But without knowing there was a contest between God and Satan over Job's loyalty, it is another story. Job did not understand why all of these troubles were happening to him. He tried to be faithful and serve God. No, not perfect, as none are, but he was far above most of us. A true worshiper and a rich man who confessed his sins and prayed continually for himself and his children.

Then everything was suddenly gone. No herds, which meant wealth, no houses, and worse than all of that, no children. Ten children all gone in one swift calamity. How does anyone take that? And then his own wife comes to him, as his last temptation, and tells him to curse God and die. Many a soul today would feel the same way. What kind of a God could do that, or allow that to happen? If He is a God of love how can He let such awful judgments fall upon one of His own? Many would feel that it cannot be true that God is love and at the same time God is almighty. If He has all power, then why doesn't He stop all of this tragedy? After all, didn't God know that Job loved Him?

Job was not like most men. He is in a class by himself. This is certainly true because at the beginning of the book it was God who pointed Job out to Satan. "And the Lord said unto Satan, hast thou considered my servant Job, that there is none like him in the earth" (Job 1:8). Satan could see someone that showed all of the character that should be manifested in a true worshiper of God. This is what angered Satan. He made the challenge. Take away your abundant blessings, God, and Job will no longer love You, nor serve You. That was how it happened.

We know the behind the scenes story, but Job did not. Look at how the man received what looked like a terrible judgment from God. He says that God "KNOWS THE WAY I TAKE" (Job 23:10).

Nothing surprises God. He knows all about me. He knows just how I am behaving and He knew it ahead of time. He knows that I humbly bow before Him and confess my own unworthiness. He knows that I am a sinner and I have confessed that I am a sinner. He knows that I depend on His grace and goodness to forgive me. He knows all of this. God's knowledge sustains Job. We see Job's patience.

Secondly, Job says "WHEN HE HATH TRIED ME." Job knew there was a purpose behind his suffering. There is always a purpose in what God allows to come into our lives. "That the trial of your faith, being much more precious than of gold . . . might be found unto praise and honour and glory at the appearing of Jesus Christ"(1 Peter 1:7). "They were stoned, they were sawn asunder, were tempted, were slain with the sword . . . being destitute, afflicted, tormented; (Of whom the world was not worthy) And these all, having obtained a good report through faith" (Hebrews 11:37–39). Sufferings had a purpose.

Third, we have Job's prospect. Job says that his sufferings are like the melting pot. When it is over he says "I SHALL COME FORTH AS GOLD." We must all go through some smelting to get rid of the dross of this dirty world. But the day is coming when we, like Job, will come forth as gold. God's testings are not because He loves us less, but rather loves us more. He is refining us to be better witnesses here and blessings to others while we are here. Later, there will be no need for more fire to purge us from our dross. It will all be gone and we shall shine like the stars for ever. "They that be wise shall shine as the brightness of the firmament, and they that turn many to righteousness as the stars for ever and ever" (Daniel 12:3). Satan loses again. Job wins. I do not know why this is happening to me? I know that God knows, and I can trust Him that it is for a good purpose.

BEAM 87

SILENT SAINTS

NOT TO BE LIKE THEM

2 KINGS 7:9

Here are four lepers outside the city of Samaria. This was in the time of Elisha the prophet. Benhadad king of Syria had laid siege to Samaria. It got so bad that women were joining together to eat their own children. We read how horrible it was. Two women come to the king and one complains that she and her neighbor agreed that they would kill and eat her son one day and eat the other woman's son the next day.

Then after they boiled and ate her son, the other woman hid her son (2 Kings 6:29).

These four lepers were outcasts from society, so they were not in the city but at the gate. They said to themselves that if they went into the city they would starve to death. If they stayed where they were they would die. So why not go to the camp of the enemy. If they were killed, what would be the difference?

They said, very logically, we will die one way or another, so what? And, they thought, the enemy might have pity on us. If not, so what. We will just die.

But the Lord performed a miracle to fulfill the prophecy of Elisha. He prophesied there would be plenty of food in a day. He was doubted, no doubt. One of the king's lords said "If the Lord were to make windows in heaven" this thing might happen (2 Kings 7:2). God made windows in heaven. He provided an abundance of food, but the king's lord did not taste of it. He was killed in the stampede by the people to get to the food (2 Kings 7:17). So much for unbelief in God's word.

The Lord caused the armies of Behadad to hear a great noise of chariots and horses and a great army. The armies of Benhadad fled. They were in such fear because they thought the Samaritans had hired the Hittites against them. They fled so fast in such terror they did not take down their tents, nor take their animals, their horses and donkeys, nor did they take their food. They just tore out of that place in a fearful rage and headed home.

This happened at night, so the starving people of Samaria did not know it. Neither did these four lepers. So the lepers chose to go to the enemy and seek mercy, and perhaps some food. Imagine their surprise when they find a banquet of food waiting for them, and no troops? They ate and drank. I imagine that was the first thing they did. Then they carried out silver and gold and clothes and hid their treasures. Then it dawns on them. There are people in the city starving to death. If anything happened to the lepers those people would keep on starving, while there were acres of food waiting just outside the city. They say what they are doing is not good. "This is a day of good tidings and we hold our peace" (2 Kings 7:9). They may have been persecuted or abused by some of the city dwellers but still, it was not right for them to keep this good news to themselves. They must tell the good news. They could not be silent. And that is the point.

They said "This is a day of good tidings." They had food for the hungry. But food only keeps us alive for a short time. We have what the angel said to the shepherds. "I bring you good tidings of great joy, which shall be to all people" (Luke 2:10). We have the good tidings that are for all. We have good tidings of the true bread of life, that if a person eats of that bread "he shall live forever" (John 6:58). It is not good to be silent when we have such tidings of great joy to all people. Silent saints! Why keep it to ourselves? We are to go into all the world and tell the glad tidings (Mark 16:15). For the Lord Jesus came into the world "to seek and to save that which was lost"(Luke 19:10). Why keep it to ourselves? Silent saints? No way! It is too good to keep to ourselves. Let's broadcast it. Let's shout it out. Well, at least tell others about it. OK?

BEAM 88

THE "IF" GOD

IF I HAD DONE IT THAT WAY

MATTHEW 11:23

I wonder if you have ever thought about how different things might have turned out "if" you had made a different choice back there? Suppose you had taken that job in Cleveland, or the one that was offered in Westminster? You might even think of that house, and wondered what would have happened if you had bought that one instead of one you did buy? And the schools? You could have changed schools, but you didn't. There was that Sunday School Class you could have taught. Wonder what happened to it?

We can only guess at what might have happened. We have a God who knows the outcome even of those things that did not happen. He is the God Who knows what would have happened if I had taken that job in Cleveland, or bought that house in Dallas. He knows the results of everything that happened, or will happen, or if it had happened. Jesus says here "If the mighty works which have been done in thee (Capernaum), had been done in Sodom, it would have remained until this day." He knows what would have happened even though it did not happen. We should know something about what happened to Sodom. He says it will be worse for Capernaum in the judgment.

So what does this have to do with me? Was I wrong in not going to Detroit? Did I not buy that house because of my selfishness? Sometimes we wonder if the Lord is leading us, or we are doing what WE WANT to do. Sometimes there are obstacles in the way. They could be tests to see if we are willing to trust the Lord to bring us out. I have heard many years ago about a woman who said "If the Lord told me to jump through that wall it would be my job to jump. It would be His job to make a hole for me." Oh! If it were that easy. To know for a certainty that it is the Lord telling us to do something, and not we ourselves doing it because that is what we want to do. He knows what would happen "if." So how do we handle this? What can we do?

FIRST of all, if we are told to do something that is contrary to

His word, we know that He is not the one talking to us. He will never have us go contrary to His revealed will in the Word.

SECONDLY, we must be willing to do His will. If we are not ready to do what He asks, or go where He sends, or say what He tells us, we might as well forget all the talk of wanting to do what is right, or what He leads us to do. We must have a willing heart.

THIRDLY, we are to commit our way unto the Lord. "Trust in the Lord with all thine heart: and lean not unto thine own understanding. In all thy ways acknowledge Him, and He shall direct thy paths" (Proverbs 3:5–6). "The steps of a good man are ordered by the Lord: And He delighteth in his way" (Psalm 37:23). Sure, sometimes we make mistakes. But it should be failing to recognize the Lord's guidance. It should never be one of refusing to do the Lord's will.

FOURTHLY, it should be a matter of prayer for light. We want to do His will. What we need is knowledge of what that will is. If it were as simple as some make it, we would not be walking by faith, but by sight. Walking by faith is not knowing for sure, but we are trusting that this is what the Lord wants us to do. No problem doing it, once we know that this is what He wants.

He knows what would have happened and how differently things would have turned out if I had taken that job in Cleveland. But, there is nothing wrong with Cleveland. I just was not supposed to take that job there, that's all. But that house? I'm still not sure. We did pray about it. I believe this is what he wanted.

"Teach me to do Thy will; for Thou art my God" (Psalm 143:10).

"I delight to do Thy will, O my God; yea Thy law is within my heart" (Psalm 40:8).

BEAM 89

PRIDE AND PREJUDICE

NAAMAN THE LEPER

2 KINGS 5

What have we to be proud of? Well, some have a great deal of this earth's treasures so that they think it proves how "great" they are. Someone has said that "all men are created equal, but some are created more equal than others." I suppose if you have the right name, and the right fortune that goes with it, you are more equal than others.

Naaman was a man that had much to be proud of. He was not just a general of the Syrian army but he was the five star general in charge of the whole army of Syria. He was a great man with his master, the King of Syria, because he had won great battles for the king. He was not just an armchair general either. He was a mighty man of valor. He was a wealthy man. He was a politically powerful man. He was what many a man would like to be. But his poorest slave girl would not trade places with him, because he was a leper. That deadly disease had latched on to him and was slowly bringing him to his grave.

This dreaded disease is an outward appearance of the deadly inward disease called sin. Like sin, it gets on to a person and slowly and surely brings him to his death. Like sin, leprosy keeps corrupting the body until the whole is corrupted. Like sin, leprosy is incurable and brings one to a certain horrible death. It is never said that someone is "healed" of their leprosy in the Old Testament. They are "cleansed." That may not seem to be much of a difference, but it shows that this disease is different. Unless God intervenes, the leper perishes, just like we would perish in our sins if God did not intervene.

God did intervene in Naaman's case. Naaman was told to go to the prophet Elisha. In fact, it was a little slave girl that Naaman had captured who told him of the prophet who could cleanse him of his leprosy. Naaman comes loaded with gifts to reward the "healer." Elisha tells his servant, Gehazi, to tell Naaman to go down to the Jordan River and wash in it seven times. Here is where it becomes crazy.

Naaman gets angry and storms away in a rage. Is this crazy or not? The very thing that he came for, he did not have. The one thing that he so desired, the cleansing from leprosy, was forfeited. He did not just walk away. He raged in anger. And he started back to Syria. But he was going back the same way he came. He came as a leper and he was going back home again as a leper. There is a lesson here. If we hear the Word preached and do nothing about it, we go home the same way we came. If we came to church lost, we go home lost.

Some of his unnamed servants saw how crazy this was and came to him, I can imagine somewhat timidly, and said to him this very thing. "Master," they say, "if the prophet had asked you to do some great thing you would have done it, right? Why not do a simple thing like this?" This was an Old Testament picture of a New Testament truth. It was not the Jordan that had any cleansing power. It was a picture of the Cross, and belief in what the Old Testament prophets say about the Cross. It was a simple matter of faith. So the General was persuaded to turn around and do what Elisha told him to do.

What was it that made him so angry? One of the things was HIS PRIDE. He did not like it when a servant came out to tell him what the prophet said. He was a big man in Syria. He did not take too kindly to having some unseen prophet send a servant to speak to him, not to this five star general. He could come down with his armies and wipe out this place. And he may have thought he would do that, if this prophet keeps messing with him

We do not want to come to Christ as other sinners do. "After all, I am not so bad. I go to church. I am certainly not as bad as that drunken bum in the gutter over there." We want to come to Christ as doctors, or teachers, or wealthy people. We're not just plain sinners, like other sinners. But the ground is level at the cross. We all must come as sinners needing God's mercy.

Another thing that may have made him angry was HIS PREJUDICE. That Jordan was not a clean river. He had cleaner rivers back home. Why couldn't he wash in them? He says Abana and Pharpar were clean enough to drink from. Why this dirty, muddy Jordan? But the prophet said Jordan. The New Testament prophet says Jesus and Jesus it must be. It was a matter of obedience, that's all. Well, after thinking it over Naaman does change his mind and goes into the Jordan. He dips himself seven times. He does not get one seventh clean after the first dip, etc. He is still a leper until he does what the prophet told him. Seven times, and his flesh is as the flesh of a young child and he was clean. He did not come up with a new outlook on life, or an effort to do better, or somewhat cleansed. He came up completely cleansed all over, wholly clean. That is the way it is when sinners come to the Cross. They do not just get a desire to try harder, to make an effort to do "good," or be more sincere. They come up new creations in Christ, with a new birth, and the Holy Spirit dwelling within them to guide them through this new life. They, who were dead before, are now made alive in Christ.

What a beautiful story. It was done freely by God's grace. Naaman comes back to Elisha's house to reward him abundantly, and he could afford it. Elisha turns him down. The picture God was painting would be spoiled if Elisha took reward. It would have looked like we have a part in our own salvation, if Naaman paid anything to Elisha. It was turned down because "For by grace are ye saved, through faith, and that not of yourselves it is the gift of God: not of works lest any man should boast" (Ephesians 2:8–9).

Pride, yes, and prejudice, almost kept Naaman from the most precious thing that he could desire. Let it not happen to us. Don't let anything stand in our way. The Old Testament prophet said Jordan. The New Testament apostles say Jesus, and Jesus it must be.

BEAM 90

THE THREE ENTRANCES INTO JERUSALEM

MARK 11

There were three offices that God kept separate. You could not be king and priest. You could not be a prophet and a king. Yes, David and Solomon could prophesy, but they did not hold the office of a prophet.

Samuel was a priest who also prophesied (1 Samuel 3). Later there developed an office of prophet. We read of the sons of the prophets in 1 Kings 20:35. Nathan was a prophet who was sent to David after David committed his awful sin.

The priest was appointed to approach God on behalf of man. The prophet did the opposite. He came from God to man with God's message. The king could not be prophet or a priest, but he was to rule in God's stead. However, as is it is in other cases, Jesus was the exception. He alone could be all three, Prophet, Priest, and King.

During His last week, before His crucifixion, He stayed outside the city of Jerusalem at night in Bethany, which was about two miles from Jerusalem. Each day He then came into the city of Jerusalem.

THE KING COMETH (Mark 11:8–11). I choose Mark to show that His triumphal entry was not on Palm Sunday but rather on Palm Saturday. But who is going to change tradition? The crowds cast palm branches before the King and shouted Hosannas to Him and said "Blessed is He that cometh in the name of the Lord" (Mark 11:9). Then He entered the temple. He enters the temple, as Mark says in verse 11, looks about, does nothing and leaves. He did nothing because it was a Sabbath day and those Pharisees and Scribes, who condemned Him for healing on the Sabbath, would not do any money exchanging on the Sabbath day. Then He left to go out to Bethany.

THE PRIEST COMETH (Mark 11:15–16). Now on the first day of the week He comes into the city again, as Priest. He enters the temple again and this time He drove out the money changers and turned over their tables and would not let them carry any vessel through the temple. He said they had made God's house a den of thieves (11:17). This still goes on today in some in circles.

THE PROPHET COMETH (Mark 11:19–20:27–28). The next day He again comes from Bethany and enters the city. This time He is Prophet. He enters the temple again and they, the chief priests, scribes, and elders, ask Him how He had the authority to do what He did. That would be the cleansing of the temple the previous day. He tells them. Rather, He asks them. If they answer His question correctly, they will know how He had the authority. He was ordained by a priest, John the Baptist, the son of a priest. So He, Jesus, as a priest, had every right to cleanse the temple. The question was about John the Baptist. Was he a man sent from God or not? John was the one who pointed out Jesus and declared "Behold the Lamb of God, which taketh away the sin of the world" (John 1:29). They saw where Jesus was going, so they refused to answer the question.

THE SAVIOR COMETH (Luke 1:47). "My spirit hath rejoiced in God my saviour." Some day we must give an account of what we have done with this same Jesus. Because He also came to save sinners. "For the Son of man is not come to destroy men's lives but to save them" (Luke 9:56). They mocked Him and said "He saved others; himself He cannot save. If He be the king of Israel, let Him now come down from the cross, and we will believe Him" (Matthew 27:42). The first part of that statement is true. He did SAVE OTHERS. He COULD NOT SAVE HIMSELF and ALSO save others. He had to die for others for them to be saved and have eternal life. It cost Him a horrible death on a cross. If He saved himself, others could not be saved. How much did He love the world of sinners? He willingly laid down His own life so they could be forgiven of ALL of their sins, and live with Him for ever and ever. What a loving and kind savior. How can anyone not love Him?

BEAM 91

I SHOT AN ARROW INTO THE AIR AND IT HIT AHAB

1 KINGS 22:34

With God there is no accident. We sometimes speak of "accidents," but these never happen with God. In the Mosaic Law we read about God delivering one into the hands of a neighbor. Exodus 21:12 states "he that smiteth a man, so that he die, shall be surely put to death." This is spoken of a murderer. That death penalty has never been repealed. Verse 13, however, says that "if a man lie not in wait, BUT GOD DELIVERS HIM INTO HIS HAND," then God will appoint a place for him, for refuge. In Numbers 35:11 we read about these cities of refuge where the slayer may flee "which killeth any person at UNAWARES." Today we would call that manslaughter. That is when someone did not plan, or premeditate, or plot to kill someone. Manslaughter is said to be when God delivers him into his neighbor's hand. We would call it an accident, when the axe head comes off and kills a bystander, just as today we say someone was killed in an automobile "accident." Not so with the Lord. He brings to pass what He will. "For I am God, and there is none else; I am God, and there is none like Me, declaring the end from the beginning and from ancient times the things that are not yet done, saying, My counsel shall stand, and I will do all my pleasure" (Isaiah 46:9–10).

Here was a wicked king, Ahab. He had brought much idolatry and wickedness upon the people of Israel. He married Jezebel, who was more wicked than he was. God warned Ahab, but Ahab would not turn from his wicked ways. The prophet Micaiah warned Ahab, but Ahab says "I hate him, for he doth not prophesy good concerning me, but evil" (1 Kings 22:8). How about that for a reputation? How can he say good things when Ahab was only evil?

Finally God told Ahab his number was up. Micaiah, the prophet, said that IF Ahab went to battle at Ramoth-gilead he would die. Ahab's answer was to put Micaiah in jail until he returned from battle. Micaiah's answer was if Ahab came back alive then God had not spoken by Micaiah. This is the way to tell a true prophet from a false one, even today. If a prophet prophesies something, anything, and it does not come to pass, that prophet is a false prophet. Beware of those who predict the Lord's return. One wrong prediction and that predictor is a liar and a false prophet.

So Micaiah is put in jail. Just to be sure though, Ahab disguises himself (1 Kings 22:30). It looked like things were going to turn out OK. His partner in the battle, the king of Judah, was dressed as a king and they almost killed him thinking he was Ahab, king of Israel. Things looked pretty good for Ahab.

Then we read that a certain man "drew a bow at a venture" (1 King 22:34) and shot an arrow into the air. Perhaps he had run out of arrows and had just one more left, so why take one arrow home. So without taking any particular aim he just shoots the arrow into the air. It fell to earth and hit the king of Israel, Ahab. This was not an injury. It killed Ahab. Just like that. God said it would happen to Ahab IF, and WHEN, he went up to battle at Ramoth-gilead. And it did. Ahab would not listen to God, ever.

Whatever God says will come to pass. Whatever God purposes to do He will do. He declares the end from the beginning. He will do all His good pleasure. And it is good pleasure. He says that whosoever comes to the Lord Jesus will never be cast out. "This is the Father's will which hath sent Me, that of all which He hath given me I should lose nothing, but raise it up again at the last day" (John 6:39). Nothing can prevent God from fulfilling His will. Are you in His will? It's gracious that the God of all creation would even count us to be a part of His will. You can be an heir. Believe and receive!

BEAM 92

UNDERWEIGHT

DANIEL 5:27

It was some party. Belshazzar knew how to throw a bash. The name means "The Lord's Leader," but he did not lead his people toward the Lord or anything that was good. But he knew how to throw parties.

He made a feast for a thousand of his lords and wine was running like water. Some of these bashes could last for six months. In the book of Esther we read where Ahasuerus had a party for 180 days. Beshazzar's may not have lasted quite that long. That may have been because his number was up.

Belshazzar drank wine with his lords and was having a ball. He thought they should bring in the gold and silver vessels his ancestor, Nebuchadnezzar, had taken out of the temple that was in Jerusalem. He is called "father," but only in the Bible sense of being an ancestor, like David was a son of Abraham. These were holy vessels and Belshazzar was showing his contempt for the God of the Hebrews by drinking from these holy vessels. Then they praised the gods of gold and silver and brass and iron and wood and stone. They really had a hatred for this God of the Hebrews, Who, the Hebrews said, was the only true God, the only one God of the universe.

Then the party was over, at least for Belshazzar. A hand appeared out of nowhere and the fingers began to write on the wall of the king's palace. What was written no one understood, but it was enough to make the hair on Belshazzar stand on end and his knees began to knock against one another (5:6). What did this mean? He could not read it, maybe it looked like Greek to him, but he knew enough to be terrified so that the joints of his loins were loosed, whatever that means. He was falling apart?

Send for the magicians, the astrologers, the psychics, the con artists. Whoever can interpret this shall be clothed royally and be the third ruler in the kingdom. He said third, because the number one was out of the kingdom fighting, and Belshazzar was number two ruling in the absence of number one. Not one clairvoyant could read the writing. Not one astrologer could, not one psychic. Then someone remembered Daniel. They remembered that he was an interpreter of dreams in the past. Get Daniel, was the cry of the queen. He had wisdom from the gods, she said. Daniel is brought in and has no trouble deciphering this mysterious writing. Belshazzar feared greatly and must have had that feeling that the message bode no good for him. And he was right.

The message was that God had numbered Belshazzar's kingdom, his number was up. And it went on, "You have been weighed in the balances and are lacking. Your kingdom has been given to the Persians."

Weighted and wanting, that is lacking. That is the Old Testament message for the New Testament people. We must all be weighed. And every one of us is lacking. God's righteousness demands that anyone coming into His heaven to live with Him must be absolutely perfect. Not one of us is. "For all have sinned and come short of the glory of God" (Romans 3:23). "There is none righteous, no not one" (Romans 3:10).

What can we do? We must all step into the scales and be weighed. We must step in alone. My mother cannot go with me. My wife cannot step in with me. My pastor cannot step in with me. And I cannot make up for God's righteous demands, not by my life. I am lost and undone. How can I step in and be weighed when I have no righteousness? There is only one way to solve this sin problem. There is One, Who has promised to never leave me if I come to Him. He, Who cannot lie, has promised that He will never cast away that one who comes to Him (John 6:37). He has promised "I will never leave thee nor forsake thee" (Hebrew 13:5). If I have to step into God's scales, then He will step in with me. He makes up for all of the righteousness that God demands of me. He alone has all the righteousness that God's holiness demands. He is perfect. He is without sin. He alone could meet God the Father's demands. With Him stepping in with me I need not fear. What a beautiful story.

By the way, that great city of Babylon was impregnable. No one, no army, could possibly take that city in any kind of a war or siege. According to Herodotus, the city of Babylon was 14 miles long on each side making it nearly 196 square miles in area. It enclosed water and pastures and everything needed to sustain a siege. But what a wall!

You have heard of the seven wonders of the ancient world. One of them was the hanging gardens of Babylon. It seems Nebuchadnezzar's wife liked the hills back home and missed them. (I believe she was from West Virginia?) So Nebuchadnezzar built those gardens for her. Poor homesick Momma! The outer walls, those around the city to protect it, were an amazing feat for those people. They were 311 feet high and 87 feet thick at the bottom. They were wide enough for chariots to pass one another at the top. And there was a canal from the river Euphrates flowing through the city so they could not be starved by an enemy army. Who could break through those walls and take that city? So why should Belshazzar worry? Because God said it would be taken.

While Belshazzar and the Babylonians were having their ball, the Medes were marching under the wall of the city. They had diverted the water from the canal and nobody in the city noticed it. The water went down and the soldiers came in. They marched under that tremendous wall and they took the city. Belshazzar was slain that very night. He was warned and he did fear. Perhaps it was not too late for him to see the light. Have we? Ready to be weighed? Not me, not alone that is. But, I don't have to go it alone. Neither do you. If we come to Him, He will step in the scales with us. He meets all of God's demands. With Him, I lack nothing. I am not underweight, not in God's sight anyway.

BEAM 93

BARABBAS KNOWS SUBSTITUTIONARY ATONEMENT

HE SHOULD KNOW

MARK 15:7

Here is a man who has a terrible criminal record. Matthew says in 27:16 "They had a notable prisoner, called Barabbas." That is not the kind of notoriety we would want. Not only is he a robber and a criminal but he also is a murderer. Mark says that he had "made insurrection" and "had committed murder in the insurrection" (Mark 15:7). Here is one who would be on the most wanted list. A rebel and robber, and a murderer. He is in jail awaiting the sentence to be carried out. In that day the sentence would have been crucifixion. Crucifixion was not for every criminal, but was for the very worst, and also for slaves that rebelled against their masters.

Crucifixion was a slow and agonizing death. Sometimes the person crucified would suffer for a day, and longer. It was a horrible way to die. When Jesus was crucified the hour of the Passover approached. In order to not have anyone hanging on the cross they would break the victim's legs. This made his rib cage collapse and his breathing was stopped, so he died shortly afterward. This is what His enemies sought of Pilate so that the three on the crosses might die quickly before the Passover (John 19:31). But Jesus was dead already when the soldiers came.

This was the kind of death Barabbas was looking forward to. He is jail. There is a big commotion going on outside. He may not have known what that was all about. He was preparing to pass out of this world in a most horrible way. The hours slowly pass by. The time of execution approaches. Whatever prayers Barabbas might have been saying, if he prayed at all, he would be uttering them now. "Well," he thinks, "when are they going to come and get me? What is going on anyhow? Why don't they come? This waiting is almost as bad as the execution itself. How long? When will they get on with it?"

Ah! Now he sees someone coming. "Here come the jailers. Now we can get this thing over with." I do not know if he was given any last requests, like a last meal, etc., but I doubt very much if they were that merciful to these outrageous criminals. "Well finally, let's get this over with," Barabbas thinks to himself, or maybe says it out loud. So they open the jail and come in. He expects them to say follow us. They say to Barabbas, "You can go now." "Huh?" "I said you can go now. We have no reason to hold you any longer." Barabbas says, "What are you talking about? I was sentenced to be crucified. What do you mean I can go? Go where? You mean to the cross?"

"No," the jailer says, "You are free to go home. We are through with you. Someone else is taking your place." "What do you mean someone else is taking my place? Who would want to take my place and die on a cross?" Then he is told. "The people were given a choice of you or Jesus and they chose Jesus." "You mean that One who has been going around healing people and saying He is Messiah. You mean they want to let me go and crucify Him?" "Yes," the jailer says. Barabbas cannot understand it. Why would anyone do a thing like that? He has had someone else take his place on the cross so he could go home free. How can this be? But it is true. Someone else took Barabbas' place and died in his place, so Barabbas could go free! This is substitutionary atonement. This is what theologians talk about. This is what saints rejoice in. Someone else took the place of the sinner, so the sinner can go free.

"For He hath made Him to be sin for us, Who knew no sin, that we might be made the righteousness of God in Him" (2 Corinthians 5:21). Barabbas may be the first to understand what it means to have another take your place and die in your place, so that you might have His righteousness, which you do not deserve.

Do we understand it? Barabbas could explain it to us. It is simple. "Jesus died in my place" he says.

Jesus died in my place, and your place, for every sinner. He was our substitute. We get His sinlessness while He got our sins. But it only matters if we believe in Him. If we do not believe, then we do not receive.

BEAM 94

DEAD AND BLIND
BUT HOW CAN YOU TELL

JOHN 1:7

How bad off was man when the Light of the world came into this world? John 1:7 reads that John "came for a witness, to bear witness of the Light, that all men through him might believe." How bad? I once was teaching a Sunday School Class and turned off the lights. I then asked the class if the lights were on or off? Then I turned the lights back on again, and again I asked the class if the lights were on or off? Guess what? They got it right both times. That may sound somewhat stupid but it had a purpose.

When I turned the lights back on I asked the class if they were sure they were on. "Suppose someone says 'I don't know' what would that say," I asked. They were right again. They said that person must be blind. That's the thing about light. You do not need to have someone tell you it is on. You just have to look at it, that's all. Unless you are blind. If you are blind, lights on are the same as lights off. You see neither one and it makes no difference. You are still blind. I have a stove that tells me that I just turned the stove light out. I think "What for?" If I can't see that light is now off, I must be blind. If I am blind, it would not make any difference to tell me the light is out. I could not read what it is saying anyhow.

In Isaiah 9:2 we read "The people that walked in darkness have seen a great light, they that dwell in the land of the shadow of death, upon them hath the light shined." Matthew 4:16 tells us that this was fulfilled when Jesus came to Capernaum. You can walk when you are blind, as everyone knows. You can sit down in the darkness, also, when you are blind. Mankind was so bad off that mankind sat down in the darkness and was blind also. If they could see, no one would have to tell them that the Light had come. But they were blind. So they needed someone to tell them.

John the Baptist was a bell ringer, an announcer, a herald, proclaiming to those who sat in darkness and were blind that the Light had come. What a pitiful condition for man to be blind and sitting in the dark. And there is no need to be blind nor in the dark. The Light has come. Believing on Him who is the Light gets one's eyes open. His blindness is removed and he can then see the Light. He is on his way out of the tunnel of darkness with this Savior, Who has come to bring men out of the darkness of sin into His glorious Light.

I am a poor example of John the Baptist, but I want to tell everyone that the Light has come. If you believe, you can open your eyes and see the light. Who would want to sit in the dark for the rest of his life? And there is a worst future for those who keep sitting in the dark. This Light of the World, Who came to bring men out of sin and darkness into His glorious life–He is what life is all about. We are here for a little while. James says our lives, even if lived to what is called a "ripe old age," whatever that means, is like "a vapour that appeareth for a little time, and then vanisheth away" (James 4:14). You see that vapor coming out of your warm mouth on a cold winter day. How long does that last? A few seconds and then it is gone. Even a ripe old age means little when we think of eternity. The Light has come. You can see Him, if you believe. He will take away the blindness. Is there light at the end of your tunnel? How can you see it if you are blind? Believe and you will see. That is the order. Not seeing is believing but believing is seeing. See and live. You can have it all; light, life, love, forgiveness, living with God in a glorious heaven forever. Believing is seeing and seeing is receiving.

"The Lord is my light and my salvation; whom shall I fear? The Lord is the strength of my life; of whom shall I be afraid?" (Psalm 27:1). "While ye have light, believe in the light, that ye may be the children of light" (John 12:36).

BEAM 95

IS JESUS GOD?

ROMANS 9:5

I once heard a minister say from the pulpit that he did not know any Scripture that actually said Jesus is God. I almost fell out of my pew. I was too young and unlearned in how to deal with a minister who is pastor of a church and preaching something that I knew was wrong. What does a young man say to a more experienced and older minister of the Gospel? Since that time I have heard many more ministers say even worse things from the pulpit. Some even lie. They say the Greek word doesn't mean this, or it does mean that, thinking no one in their audience would know anything about the Greek, or Hebrew. This man was a pastor of a church that had been built up by a faithful pastor who preached the Word and had sent many missionaries into the world, as well as students to seminary. That man retired after a long and blessed ministry in that church.

Without bothering to go into the Scriptures where Jesus makes the claim Himself, saying that He is the "I Am" of Israel, which his enemies understood, there are some other verses that clearly state the fact. The Scriptures certainly do state that Jesus is God. Here are just a few.

In Romans 9:4–5 Paul lists some of the advantages of being a Jew. He says they had the adoption, a nation that was claimed by God to be His people. They had the glory. This was the Shekinah glory, the visible manifestation of God's presence. No other nation had such. He goes on to state that they had the covenants. This would be the Law of Moses and also the covenant God made with Abraham. He goes on to say that out of those fathers, concerning the flesh, Jesus came, "Who is over all, God blessed for ever, Amen." This is not a benediction. A benediction is the other way around. We say blessed be God, not God blessed. Paul is stating here very simply and clearly, if we would hear, that Jesus is over all, God, blessed for ever.

In 1 John 5:20 the apostle John states that "the Son of God is come, and hath given us understanding, that we may know Him that is true, and we are in Him that is true, even in His Son Jesus Christ."

Then he states "This is the true God, and eternal life." Any English teacher would tell you that the demonstrative noun refers back to its nearest antecedent. That would be Jesus Christ. He is the one spoken of and John says "This is the true God." If we want to hear it.

One of the strongest passages I know of is one that many memorize, and it is a good one to remember. It is Titus 2:13 where Paul states that we should live a godly life in this world "Looking for that blessed hope, and the glorious appearing of the great God and our Saviour Jesus Christ." Isn't that one clear enough? He is not only declared to be God, but He is called THE GREAT GOD. I wonder if that minister took this verse to mean that the church was looking for two people to make their appearances? Or did he suppose that Paul was talking about the appearance of God the Father and God the Son? It should not give anybody a problem, unless you are a theologian. As sure as two and two are five they will stumble over such a clear and simple verse of Scripture.

Yes, Jesus is God and the Bible clearly states that He is God. So we should humbly bow down and accept His death on the cross. God, the righteous God and Savior, took the sinner's place and died in our stead. We should be thankful. No man was good enough, and perfect, to meet God's righteous demands. Only the God-man could do it. That was why God had to take on human flesh so He could die in man's place. God cannot die but the God-man could.

Another point, if you don't mind. If, if, there were a perfect man who would die for sinners, he could only save ONE sinner. One life for one life. He could not save even two sinners with one death. But God is infinite. His death can save any finite number of sinners. So the God-man does both. He can die, while God cannot. He can die for any finite number of sinners because He is infinite. And He did. What a loving God we have. Is He yours?

BEAM 96

INVITATIONS

ISAIAH 1:18

R.S.V.P.

The invitations are too numerous to count. In this verse God invites sinners to come and reason together with Him. Think of that. The God Who created the universe, the Holy God of righteousness, the gracious, longsuffering, loving God Who is from Eternity, invites poor, ignorant, sinful, fragile, and weak, frail man to a powwow.

But the Scriptures, from one end to the other contain this same manner of communication. Man is invited to come together with the Almighty, omniscient, omnipotent, omnipresent God to talk things over.

In the beginning it was God Who came looking for Adam, after Adam sinned. In Genesis 3:9, we read "God called unto Adam, and said unto him, Where art thou?" You would think it would be Adam who would smite his breast and call out for God to help him. Adam would be the one to cry "My God, my God, where art thou?" But no, it is God, who seeks Adam.

In Genesis 7:1 we hear the Lord saying unto Noah, "Come thou and all thy house into the ark." He did not say "Go into the ark." God is inviting man to come. He is in the ark.

In Isaiah 1:18 He again invites sinners to come, and He says He will cleanse them from their sins. They shall be as white as snow. I might say in passing that sins are not black according to God's reckoning but red, or scarlet.

In the New Testament we read again the invitation of God. "Come unto Me, all ye that labour and are heavy laden, and I will give you rest" (Matthew 11:28). You cannot get those sins clean, you cannot get rid of the stains, you labor in vain, you cannot do it. Come to Me. I can wash away those stains and make you as white as snow. And so the invitation goes on and on through the Scriptures.

And at the end of the Book we read the invitation stills stands. It is almost the last word in the Bible.

"And the Spirit and the bride say, Come. And let him that

heareth say, Come. And let him that is athirst come. And whosoever will, let him take of the water of life freely" (Revelation 22:17). God still invites sinners to "Come, let us reason together."

In most cultures there is a certain formality when inviting guests to come to a party, or a banquet, or some special occasion. This is proper so the Host can make proper preparation for the number of guests who will show up. They send out the invitation with a RSVP at the bottom. This stands for the French words "repondez s'il vous plait" which means "please reply." Have we replied? We have been invited to a great marriage feast with God. Not only are we invited to come to this banquet, but we are invited to come as the Bride of the Only Begotten Son. The church is called His bride (Matthew 22:2; 2 Corinthians 11:2).

What a beautiful story! What a beautiful invitation! Have we answered yet? Have we given our RSVP, we will be there. I cannot RSVP for you and you cannot RSVP for me. But you can for you, just as I can, and do, for me. What love! Please RSVP now. Why keep God waiting? It is not polite and it is not wise.

He is preparing a place for those who come. He needs to know if you will be there.

"I will bless the Lord at all times: His praise shall continually be in my mouth. My soul shall make her boast in the Lord: the humble shall hear thereof and be glad. O magnify the Lord with me, and let us exalt His name together" (Psalm 34:1–3).

BEAM 97

WHAT ME WORRY? CHIPMUNKS DON'T

MATTHEW 6:25–34

Did you ever see a heron pray? How about a chipmunk? Can you imagine a robin, before it settles down in its nest, praying that God will supply it with some food the next day, and also thanking Him for the food that it had this day? Maybe birds are more thankful than man, but from what the Lord said they certainly do not worry about their next snack, or dinner. But man–well that's a different story. The Lord tells us that man worries about what he will eat, what he will drink, what he will wear.

If man has trusted the Lord Jesus, he is now in God's family. Can we trust that God will take care of His own? The Lord points out here in Matthew 6:25–34 that man worries over whether he will have food and clothing and a place to sleep. He worries about the less important things of life rather than the important things. Jesus said the fowls of the air don't worry about food and they do not sow any grains, nor reap any. God takes care of them. As for clothes, some people are so fashion conscious that to them life means the proper style of clothes. But Jesus points out that even Solomon, with all the wealth he had, could not clothe himself as beautifully as the lilies of the field, which are here today and gone tomorrow.

And what can we do about it? He asks if worry will help us to live a day longer? In verse 27 it is translated "add one cubit unto his stature." If He were talking about height, adding 18 inches would be no little thing. However, He is talking about length of days. The word "stature" here does not mean how tall one is but how long one lives. Luke 12:26 refers to length of time, not how tall. "If ye then be not able to do that thing which is least, why take ye thought for the rest?" You cannot gain a day by worrying. So why worry? Birds don't, lilies don't, chipmunks don't. But the rest of the story says that your Heavenly Father feedeth them. "Are ye not much better than they?" (Matthew 6:26). So it all boils down to whether God is our Heavenly Father. If He is, we have nothing to worry about. That is life's question. And if we are not sure yet, then we should make it sure. Here is what Jesus says for us to do to have this life without worry.

"Seek ye first the kingdom of God and His righteousness; and all these things shall be added unto you. Take therefore no thought for the morrow, for the morrow shall take thought for the things itself" (6:33–34). Sure, we should have plans. We should have insurance for those who will be left behind. Perhaps a trust, or at least a will. But we should remember our Heavenly Father is rich and delights to give His children good things. "For the Lord God is a sun and shield; the Lord will give grace and glory; no good thing will He withhold from them that walk uprightly" (Psalm 84:11). Again we read in Psalm 37:4, "Delight thyself also in the Lord; and He shall give thee the desires of thine heart." That is even more than the necessities of life, like food and raiment.

Matthew 6:32 states that "Your heavenly Father knoweth that ye have need of all these things." We should seek first the kingdom of God before all of these things. God did not make sparrows in His image, nor lilies, but man. We are more precious in His sight, and for man's sake He sent His Son to die so that man might enjoy living with his heavenly Father forever. So if He is our heavenly Father, we do not have to worry. So we come back to the BIG QUESTION. Is He our Father? If Jesus is our Savior, then He is our brother and we are in God's family. Why worry when we can pray. "He that believeth on the Son hath everlasting life" (John 3:36). Why worry? Spend your time in telling others the good news. Jesus came into the world "to seek and to save that which was lost" (Luke 19:10). That means us. No need to worry. Chipmunks don't.

"Trust in the Lord, and do good; so shalt thou dwell in the land, and verily thou shalt be fed. Delight thyself also in the Lord; and He shall give thee the desires of thine heart" (Psalm 37:3–4).

BEAM 98

THE TORN VEIL

MATTHEW 27:51

Before this time God had appointed one method of approach. A sinner could come to a Holy God by following the Law of Moses. One would need to bring an offering to a priest and have the innocent animal slaughtered for the sins of the one who brought the animal. One would have to come by faith, "for he that cometh to God must believe that He is, and that He is a rewarder of them that diligently seek Him" (Hebrew 11:6). And one would have to come through the nation Israel, through the Mosaic sacrificial system. In the Book of Ruth we hear Ruth say "Thy people shall be my people, and thy God my God" (Ruth 1:16). She did not say it in reverse, "Thy God, my God, and thy people, my people." You needed to be Jewish or a proselyte in order to approach the God of Israel.

In Exodus 26:31 we read "And thou shalt make a vail of blue, and purple, and scarlet, and fine twined linen of cunning work." To make this simple it should be noted that this was a beautiful curtain that was made to separate the Holy Place from the Holy of Holies. The Holy Place was a part of the Tabernacle where the priests ministered daily. And they could enter it daily. There was an incense altar, a table for bread, and a lamp stand. All of these pointed to the coming Messiah. He is the Bread of Life, represented by the shewbread. He is the Light of the world, represented by the candlesticks, or lamps. He is the One Intermediary of Prayer (we pray in His Name), represented by the altar of incense. OK?

But the Holiest of Holies was on the other side of the veil. It contained one thing: the Ark of the Covenant, the box that contained the tablets of the broken Law, some manna, and Aaron's rod that budded. This room was so sacred that only the High Priest could enter it, and only on one day of the year, the Day of Atonement. He could only enter it then if he had the blood, which he was to sprinkle on the lid of this ark, called the Mercy Seat. That was for the sins of the nation of Israel and himself. If he did not follow the rules, he was a dead man.

So, the veil was a separator that kept any sinner from approaching a Holy God, on penalty of death. It was God's "Keep Out" sign. All of this was to show that sinful man had no way of approaching a Holy God, except through the blood sacrifice of an innocent one, whose blood was shed for the guilty one.

Hebrews 10:3 states that the blood of animals could not take away sins. The sins were covered. That is what "atonement" means, a covering. They were forgiven, but only on an IOU basis, until the Lamb of God would die, and then sins would not only be forgiven, but also taken away.

So what is this all about? When Jesus died on the cross, that veil was torn from top to bottom. This showed that man did not accidentally tear the veil, from bottom to top. It also showed that there was no longer any restriction keeping sinners from approaching a Holy God, if they came by the blood of Jesus. It said there is no longer any particular race, or nation, or religious belief that has a monopoly of God. All are invited to come into His presence, if, if, we come through the Lord Jesus by faith. We no longer need to bring a lamb, or a goat, or a bullock. That is done away with now. It is all by grace. We are no longer under the Law of Moses. John the Baptist said "Behold the Lamb of God, which taketh away the sin of the world" (John 1:29). He has opened the door to God. The "Keep Out" sign is gone. God tore it down.

God's presence is open to all who come by faith trusting the shed blood of Jesus the Lamb of God. We can come to God, freely, on our own, by faith. No special helpers needed. What a love story. The Holy God of the universe allows sinners to come into His presence on the basis of the shed blood of Jesus on the cross. The Door is now open. Jesus is the Door. Have you come in? There is a welcome to all who come!

BEAM 99

THE GREEKS HAVE A WORD FOR IT AND PLENTY OF VARIATIONS

I suppose everyone has heard the old saying "The Greeks have a word for it." They sure do. And it was not an accident that the New Testament was written in Greek. In Galatians 4:4 we read "But when the fulness of the time was come, God sent forth His Son." What all this means may take too much time at this point. Here are a couple of things that might be said about it.

First, there was the Greek empire. Alexander the Great conquered the known civilized world and made an empire that spread from the Middle East all the way to India. There his homesick men rebelled and wanted to go home to see their families again. But wherever Alexander conquered he gave the cities and countries much liberty in the realm of religion and law. But, there was a big but. They had to learn the Greek language. They spoke a common language called the "koine" that is used to give us the New Testament.

There are many hues and variations of meaning in the Greek. One does not need to know Greek to understand the Bible. There is not a doctrine that is missed by not understanding Greek. But there are some **shades** of meaning that really brighten up some of the doctrines that we know from the King James English.

One of them comes to mind. The double negative. In the Greek it is "ou me," both of which are negatives. It is saying "no' and then another "no." In English we are told not to use a double negative. This is because of grammarians thinking like mathematicians. Sure, two negatives make a positive? So when junior says, "I don't want no spinach," he means he wants some. Pile it on his plate. Not so in Greek and some other languages. In the Greek, a double negative means a greater emphasis. This is what is beautiful about it.

In John 6:37 the Lord Jesus says, "Him that cometh to me I will (and here it is) in no wise, under no circumstances, never, ever, ever, cast out." That is comforting. He not only says He will never, but He says never, ever, in no way, under no conditions.

There are many more like this. One more that is comforting is in John 10:28. "I give unto them eternal life and they shall (here it is) never, under no circumstances, never, ever perish." What a comfort. Another one of these "ou me's" is in Hebrews 13:5 where the writer says "For He (Jesus) hath said I will never (ou me) never, ever leave thee, nor forsake thee." I like those double negatives that tell us how He has promised to keep His promises even when we fail. He will never fail.

Another little tidbit from the Greek that might be helpful is the way the Greek puts some words out of order, or at least what we Englishmen would say is out of order. This is done to emphasize what they are saying. A good example of this is in John 1:1. It states "In the beginning was the Word, and the Word was with God and the Word was God." It actually says "And GOD was the Word." It emphasizes the fact that Jesus was and is God. GOD was the Word. Someone may come to your door and point out John 1:1 and say that the original says that Jesus was "a god." That is not true. John emphatically states that GOD was the WORD and the WORD became flesh and dwelt among us.

There is another Greek shade of meaning that is beautiful. It is called the perfect tense. This means that there has been a completed action, called an aorist, and the results continue to be in that completed state. We read in Ephesians 2:8–9 that "by grace are ye saved through faith." This, with the perfect tense, would mean "by grace you ***have been and continue to be saved,*** by faith, and that not of yourselves, it is the gift of God."

Here it is again. "Who hath **saved us and continues to save us,** and called us with an holy calling, not according to our works, but according to His own purpose and grace, which was given us in Christ Jesus before the world began" (2 Timothy 1:9).

Still, you don't need to know Greek to get this from the King James Version of the Bible. It's there in English.

What a beautiful salvation we have! All by God's grace. The price has been paid by another. And it lasts for ever!

BEAM 100

HYSSOP

HEBREWS 9:19

If you ever see pictures of the walls of Jerusalem you will notice the little green patches that come out of the wall. Some are growing quite high up on the wall. The whole area looks so dry you may wonder how anything could grow, even in the ground. You see the rocks and the sand and wonder how so much fighting can take place over such a place that looks so desert and barren. It was not always like this. It was a place so beautiful and fruitful it was called a land flowing with milk and honey. God came to Moses and told him to go back into Egypt and tell the people of Israel that He had come down to deliver them and "to bring them out of that land unto a land flowing with milk and honey" (Exodus 3:8). That means a rich and fertile land.

But because of their sins and idolatry God withdrew the rainfall and His blessings on the land. Amos 4:6–9 tells how God withheld His blessings in order to turn Israel around from its sinful ways. It then became such a barren piece of rock and sand that one would wonder why all the fighting over it?

Still, these little green things grow out of the wall. You might think of them as one thinks of dandelions, which are not so dandy to people who want a nice green lawn. But dandelions are vigorous as lions and put up a ferocious battle of survival. These little green things growing out of the walls are like that. They are hyssop, a persistent and vigorous green bush. We read about this hyssop in 1 Kings 4:32–33. Solomon spoke of the trees of Lebanon and "the hyssop that springeth out of the wall." It seems that the vigorous plant can be found just about anywhere. So what does this have to do with the price of butter? Hyssop is a biblical lesson. After David's great sin David cried out "Purge me with hyssop and I shall be clean" (Psalm 51:7).

The blood of the Passover was to be taken "with a bunch of hyssop, and dip it in the blood" and then it was to be put upon the sides and the top panel of the door (Exodus 12:22). You did not put it on the threshold. You were not to walk upon that blood. The Day of Atonement sacrifices were sprinkled by taking hyssop and dipping it in the blood and then sprinkling it upon the Mercy Seat. So what does all of this mean? The blood was applied with hyssop. How is the blood applied today? By faith. Hyssop is an Old Testament picture of a New Testament teaching. Faith is the way the blood of Jesus is applied. We are not saved by the handle. Faith is the handle, but we are saved "by grace through faith" (Ephesians 2:8).

So what does this teach? Faith is bountiful and easily grasped. It is available everywhere, wherever and whenever we need it. We exercise faith when we use an elevator, or cross a river by driving over the bridge. Oh it looks strong enough. However, when some of those monstrous trucks loaded with enormous weights go over the bridge and the bridge vibrates, you may wonder. We know nothing about who built the bridge or installed that elevator. But we trust them, total strangers. We fly in planes and do not know who did the maintenance, if he did it. But we trust him. Faith is all around us and we use it every day. The most important use of all is to apply the blood of Jesus, spiritually of course, to our sinful lives so that we can have forgiveness, like David wanted. "Purge me with hyssop and I shall be clean, wash me and I shall be whiter than snow." You can't get whiter than that. Snow! All sins put away. All sins forgiven!

It just takes a little hyssop, a little handle, to accept what God offers. Take it. It's free. It only takes a little hyssop, a little faith, that's all. Nothing enormous, just faith. "Daughter, thy faith hath made thee whole, go in peace, and be whole of thy plague" (Mark 5:34). "Thy faith hath saved thee, go in peace" (Luke 7:50).

BEAM 101

BEAUTIFUL, ISN'T IT?

REVELATION 21:1

My isn't it beautiful out? We have had a long and cold winter but now it is Spring. Isn't the sky beautiful, so blue with those puffy white clouds slowly drifting along. And the trees are putting out their leaves. My it looks so good, like the world is coming alive again. And there are the birds. What would Spring be without the birds? There are the robins and some finches. They gather round the feeder and have a great time. We do too, just watching the little critters.

Sometimes there is another critter who is getting the feed that the birds knock down to the ground. Perhaps a chipmunk is a pest to some people, but he has to live too. He will take what the birds drop. And then there are the flowers. Jesus said that "Solomon in all his glory was not arrayed like one of these" lilies of the field (Matthew 6:29). Even the wild flowers are more beautiful than all that Solomon could put together for his apparel, and he had a lot of wealth that could buy just about anything. He had so much gold it was like dirt in the city of Jerusalem. But he could not capture the beauty of the simple little flower. What a glorious array of colors God has given to the flowers. Man cannot replicate them.

What a beautiful world! The blue sky overhead, the white clouds, the birds, the flowers. And oh yes, the oceans. Those wonderful waves that come rolling in. So many love to ride those waves. And others just walk on the sandy beaches and get tanned. It is beautiful! And then at night, to look up and see the thousands of stars shining so brilliantly in the heavens. Even without a moon there is a majestic beauty about the heavens. What a beautiful world we live in! But this is a temp.

You think this is beautiful? It is all to be destroyed, finished, done away with, kaput! Once before God destroyed the earth by water. He then gave a promise that He would not destroy the earth again by water.

He gave a token of this covenant with mankind, a rainbow in the sky (Genesis 9:12–13). He never would again destroy mankind with waters. But, when mankind continues to disobey God's word and becomes more wicked, God has another way of destroying this world. He says it will be by fire.

Peter says "The Day of the Lord will come as a thief in the night: in the which the heavens shall pass away with a great noise and the elements shall melt with fervent heat, the earth also and the works that are therein shall be burned up" (2 Peter 3:10). All of this beauty gone? Ah, but what is going to replace it? You think this is beautiful? You should see the replacements. There is to be a new heaven and a new earth.

John writes about this new earth in Revelation 21:1. "And I saw a new heaven and a new earth for the first heaven and the first earth were passed away; and there was no more sea." How beautiful must this replacement be if what we see now is "beautiful"? It must be beyond our imagination. We cannot comprehend what God has in store for those that love Him. This beautiful earth, and the beautiful heavens also, done away with! What must heaven be like if the new earth is beyond our imagination?

Paul tells us in 1 Corinthians 2:9 "But as it is written, eye hath not seen, nor ear heard, neither have entered into the heart of man, the things which God hath prepared for them that love Him." What a beautiful thought! It is so magnificent and so beautiful that it is more than our minds can imagine in this present life. But the time is coming. The Day of the Lord is coming. The new heavens and the new earth are coming. And this new earth, which is beautiful beyond description, is to be enjoyed for ever and ever. No more floods. No more fire. No more destruction. Enjoy for ever and ever. If you have Him as Savior, this is what God promises you. A new world that will make this one look like a pig sty.

Beautiful, you say? You ain't seen nothing yet! You will see something that is really beautiful. We can have this, if we have Him. Have we? It's up to us. He did it for us on the cross. Have we thanked Him?

BEAM 102

LOCK-JAWED LIONS

DANIEL 6:22

This man Daniel is a remarkable person who teaches us lessons in godly behavior, trust, testimony, and many of the trials of life. We can learn a lot from Daniel. Look at his behavior. He made enemies of course. The members of the king's cabinet were jealous because Daniel was preferred over them (Daniel 6:3). Paul reminds us, if we needed to be reminded, "all that will live godly in Christ Jesus shall suffer persecution" (2 Timothy 3:12). Daniel was such a devoted servant of God that his enemies could find no fault with him except in his devotion to God (Daniel 6:5). What a testimony! I wonder if anyone ever says that about me? The only fault in him is his devotion and worship of Jesus Christ. I wonder.

So what did his enemies do to get revenge on Daniel? They knew Daniel prayed toward his city of Jerusalem three times a day. He did this in private, in his house, but with the windows open. That was his habit. So these members of the king's cabinet thought of a way to trap Daniel. They got the king to pass a law that no one could pray to any god, only to the king, for 30 days. If anyone broke this law he would be fed to the lions (Daniel 6:7). They kept the lions hungry so they would be glad to eat anyone, or anything, thrown to them. Now, they think, let's see if Daniel is still devoted to his god. Daniel went right on doing what he had been doing. When a law forbids us to worship God, or pray to God, we must disobey that law. In the last days it may come to that. I wonder how many of us will continue to pray to God if we know we will go to jail, or worse?

The king liked Daniel. This is something different. He did not want him to become a Danielburger for the lions. But the law was the law. Even the king could not change that law. So Daniel is thrown into the lions' den while the heathen king says "Thy God whom thou servest continually, He will deliver thee" (6:16). This is astounding. A heathen king has been so impressed by Daniel's life of worship and devotion to the God of Israel, even this heathen king believes Daniel's God is able to deliver. Whether He wills to do so is another question.

This same king cannot sleep that night. He is worried about Daniel. Will he be alive in the morning?

The king's band plays music to soothe the king's nerves, but he still can't sleep. Early in the morning the king goes to the lions' den, which had a stone over its mouth. The king then cries out "O Daniel . . . is thy God able to deliver thee?" (6:20). The answer comes back from the lions' den. "Yes, O king, my God has sent His angel and has given these lions lock-jaw. I had lions' manes for my pillow last night. It actually wasn't so bad. I am OK, O king" (free translation 6:22).

What can we learn from this? God's will must come FIRST. No matter what government passes laws against worshiping and praying to Him, we still worship and pray to Him. SECONDLY, lives should be consistent. We should live on Monday and Thursday as Christian as we do on Sunday. We are not to be Sunday believers and something else on Monday. THIRDLY, God may not deliver us, but we still will obey Him and suffer the persecution for Him, if that be the case. We know God is able. We do not know if this be God's will at this time. FOURTHLY, we should be known by everyone, friend and foe alike, that we are servants of the Lord Jesus Christ.

We can be like Daniel. We may not have a heathen king watching how we live, but we do have neighbors who watch. Let them see the Daniel in us, or rather, the Lord Jesus living through us. He who gave the lions lock-jaw can do greater things with us, if we let Him. How about it? Will we let Him?

"I sought the Lord, and He heard me, and delivered me from all my fears" (Psalm 34:4).

"And call upon me in the day of trouble: I will deliver thee, and thou shalt glorify Me" (Psalm 50:15).

BEAM 103

A BOY'S LUNCH

MARK 6:37

That's all it was. When we read about loaves and fishes it was not the family loaf that we buy for the week. It was not even a long submarine bun, or a hoagie. This was what a young boy had for his lunch.

They had crossed over the Sea of Galilee to get some rest. They went near to a place called Bethsaida in a desert area. The Sea of Galilee is 13 miles long and 7 miles wide at some points, and 695 feet below sea level. Their quest for rest was hindered because the crowd followed them. In fact, they outran them. They wanted to hear more from this Savior and to receive healing for those who needed it (Luke 9:11). It was not long before the day was drawing to an end. There were no McDonalds along the way. The crowd needed to start homeward. It was desert area so some might faint along the way if they did not get started soon.

The disciples said "This is a desert place, and the time is now past; send the multitude away" (Matthew 14:15). This miracle, by the way, is recorded by all four Gospel writers. But the Lord Jesus said "Give ye them to eat" (Mark 6:37). They thought "Buy food for this multitude? It would take a fortune. Two hundred pennyworth (that is 200 days wages) would not be enough for every one of them to have a little (John 6:7). What are we to do?" Then that introducer, Andrew, Peter's brother, says "There is a lad here with five barley loaves, and two small fishes: but what are they among so many" (John 6:9)? He may have wondered what could they do with such a little bit, but he must have had some idea that the Lord Jesus could do something with them. Else, why bring it up?

The Lord tells them to have the crowd sit down on the grass in ranks by hundreds, and by fifties (Mark 6:39–40). That tells us how they could be so sure of the number, "about five thousand men, beside women and children" (Matthew 14:21). He took the bread and looked up to heaven. He blessed that boy's lunch, then He broke up the lunch, then gave the broken pieces to His disciples to give to the crowd. I can see Peter now. He has a little bite of fish and a small piece of bread. He wonders what can he do with something that is less than a boy would eat for lunch? But the Master told him to give it out to the multitude, so that is what he is going to do, even if he cannot understand what good it would do, these little scraps.

Peter goes over to his group of a hundred. Of all the luck. The first person on the end of the row is a Sumo Wrestler, 517 lbs., a Sabbath day's journey around. Peter wonders "How can I get this past him so his wife can have a little bite. Well, the Lord said pass it out so that is what I am going to do." So Peter says, "Take a little, and pass the rest." Peter watches as this 517 pound giant takes a little piece and passes the rest. Then Peter sees his wife take a little and pass the rest. Peter looks and it seems like they have more in their laps than Peter had to start with. Then he looks down the row. There are fifteen or twenty people all eating and their laps have more in them now then what he started with.

Then it dawns on Peter. He is seeing creation before his very eyes. There is more bread and fish coming back in the next row than when he started. And the people have more in their laps also. When the disciples are through there are twelve baskets still left over that were not distributed. This is not garbage that the multitude left. This is what was not taken by them. It is for the apostles. And do not forget that little lad who must have had his eyes bulge out of his head. "Wow! Look at that! Look at my lunch!" I believe he ate his lunch with Andrew, the introducer. Just another miracle that no one could disprove. Even His enemies could not deny that the Lord Jesus did miracles. No hocus pokus. He stilled the raging sea. He created bread and fish. He raised a dead body from the grave, after Lazarus was dead four days. He could do these things because He was God in the flesh. "In the beginning was the Word, and the Word was with God, and the Word was God" (John 1:1). Is He our God? Is He our Savior? He should be.

"For by Him were all things created, that are in heaven, and that are in earth, visible and invisible, whether they be thrones, or dominions, or principalities, or powers: all things were created by Him and for Him" (Colossians 1:16).

BEAM 104

WEDNESDAY CRUCIFIXION

MARK 11:11

There is much confusion about the last week of our Savior's earthly ministry. Much of it, most of it, comes from tradition. We have little chance of changing tradition. It is like the leaven which a woman took and hid in three measures of meal, till the whole was leavened (Luke 13:21). You try to get yeast out of some dough after it has permeated the dough. Good luck!

Mark tells us that the Lord Jesus came into the city of Jerusalem on a Sabbath Day, a Saturday. Mark says He looked about on all things and left and went out to Bethany with the twelve. He did nothing because nothing was going on. It was a Sabbath Day. The strict Pharisees would not be buying and selling in the temple on a Sabbath. But as sure as two and two are five theologians will not see it, or will not believe it if they do. This would be His entrance as KING. He never stayed in Jerusalem during that last week. He went to Bethany, a city on the other side of the Mt. of Olives, a Sabbath Day's journey away.

Some might feel that the four writers do not always keep the chronological order in their writings, and they are right. However, this same writer, Mark, then goes on to tell us about the next day, Sunday. He says Jesus came into the city and began to cast out them that sold and bought in the temple (Mark 11:12, 15). This would be His entrance as PRIEST.

Monday He comes back into the city and they argue with Him in the temple (Mark 11:19, 20,27–28). They wanted to know by what authority He did these things, casting out the money changers, etc. Here we see Him as PROPHET in the temple. Again He leaves the city. On Tuesday He institutes the Lord's Supper with His own (Mark 14:22). He tells them one would betray Him and Judas leaves to do that very thing.

He goes into the garden named Gethsemane (Mark 14:32). There He prays. Then He is arrested. All of this is from the same writer so we should not be confused about the order. He is sent to Annas, the father-in-law of Caiaphas the High Priest (John 18:13). After that, He is sent to Caiaphas the High Priest (John 18:24). He is then sent to Pilate (John 18:28). When Pilate heard Jesus was from Galilee he sends Him to Herod, who happened to be in Jerusalem at that time (Luke 23:6–8). Like a politician, Pilate wanted to have no part in this matter. Herod cannot get a word out of Jesus. Jesus "answered him nothing" (Luke 23:9). Woe to that man who cannot get Jesus to say anything. He cannot learn about his need if Jesus says nothing. Then Herod sends Him back to Pilate (Luke 23:11). That day, Wednesday, Jesus is crucified around 9 AM. He is on the cross until about 3 PM. Then He is taken down.

There is no such thing as "two silent days" theologians talk about. There were none. Can anyone imagine that in that last riotous and rebellious week there were two "silent days" when nothing happened? But that is not all. Someone will say that under Jewish reckoning a part of a day is taken as a whole day, sometimes. But we are told, quite emphatically, that as Jonah was "three days and three nights" in the whale's belly so "shall the Son of man be three days and three nights in the heart of the earth" (Mathew12:40). There is no way you can get three days and three nights from Friday evening to Sunday morning.

That still is not all. Jesus came from Jericho six days before the Passover (Matthew 20:29; Mark 10:46, 11:1; Luke 19:1; John 12:1). If that Passover was on a Friday, that makes six days before a Sabbath Day. Jesus would be breaking the Sabbath by journeying from Jericho to Jerusalem on a Sabbath Day. That is why the writer makes it clear that Bethany was a Sabbath Day's journey away (Acts 1:12).

Still that is not all. The Passover lamb was to be taken on tenth day of the month and penned up for four days (Exodus 12:3, 6) to show that the lamb was perfect, without blemish. Then it was to be slain on the fourteenth day between the evening of the 14th and the 15th. This certainly comes out to a Wednesday, four days from Saturday to Wednesday, if we believe what Mark says about His triumphal entry on a Saturday.

The trouble with the theologians, or should I say one of the troubles with the theologians, is that they still believe that the Passover was on Friday when it really fell on a Full Moon Day, since the Jewish month was based on the lunar calendar. That means the Passover could be on a Thursday, Sunday, Tuesday, etc. The month began with the New Moon and 14 days later would be a full moon, no matter what day of the week it fell on. That means that when the Holy Days were celebrated they were Sabbaths, and then the regular weekly Sabbath made TWO Sabbaths in one week. Amazing, isn't it! Two Sabbaths in one week! We have a Sunday and then in the same week we have Labor Day, a holiday. Two "laborless" days in the same week. How about that! Why is it so hard to see that Israel had two in one week?

Now after the crucifixion Jesus' body was removed and put on a shelf in a cave. That's what it was. No dirt was ever shoveled on His body. Then the Passover began, on Wednesday night. The stores would be closed. On Thursday the stores would be open and the women would be able to buy the spices they wanted for His body. Then the regular weekly Sabbath began that Friday night. After that, on the first day of the week, Sunday, they went very early to the tomb.

From Wednesday night to Saturday is three days and nights. Early Sunday, the first day of the week, He is risen. Another point, if I may, is that the Jewish day starts with the evening first, then the daylight follows. God said in the beginning, "the evening and the morning were the" first day, or the second day, etc. I do not believe the Lord Jesus stayed in the tomb longer than He had to. We read that Mary Magdalene came to the grave "when it was yet dark" (John 20:1). That is, it was Sunday but not yet light. He was already risen from the dead. It is only my interpretation, but I believe when Saturday ended in the evening, and the new day, Sunday, started at sundown, the Savior rose from the dead. That would be three days and three nights. Why would He stay in the grave from Saturday night till Sunday morning (our time) when He had already paid the price for sins? It was finished. Wednesday to Saturday, then He rose on the first day of the week, Sunday, which in Jewish reckoning is our Saturday at sundown.

Well, the leaven is still there and it will never be taken out of the bread. But there will be some who will appreciate the teaching. Yes, it was Palm Saturday. Four days later is a Wednesday crucifixion, according to Mark. Start there and you end up with three days and three nights and a first day of the week resurrection.

BEAM 105

A MYSTERY

EPHESIANS 3:5–6

This is not a whodunnit. The word "mystery" in Scripture simply means something that was a secret before but is now revealed, something that is known to the initiated. Paul tells us what that mystery was. In Ephesians 3 he says that it was not known in past ages that Gentiles should be fellow heirs and of the same body and partakers of God's promises in Christ by the gospel. In the past Gentiles were without Christ, aliens from Israel and the covenants (promises to Israel). They had no HOPE, and were WITHOUT GOD (Ephesians 2:11–12). Can words describe a worse condition than that? No Christ, so no hope, and no God. Does that say there is only One Door? It certainly does.

When Ruth came to the land of Israel (Bethlehem) from Moab, she said to Naomi her mother-in-law, "thy people shall be my people" then she said "thy God my God" (Ruth 1:16). Not the other way around. When the Passover sacrifice was given to Israel, God said no foreigner or servant should partake unless he was circumcised first (Exodus 12:42–43). He became a proselyte or an Israelite first, then he could partake of the Passover.

The promises were to Israel, and the adoption, and the glorious presence of God's visible glory in the tabernacle (Romans 9:4–5). Now all of this is changed. We now have those who were without hope and without God joined with Jews; Gentiles and Jews in one body, His church. Something unheard of in the Old Testament. Now they are one in Christ.

Before the cross there were two groups of people in the world, Jew and Gentile. Now there are three. We are told in 1 Corinthians 10:32 "Give none offence, neither to the Jews, nor to the Gentiles, nor to the church of God." That makes three groups now. Only a theologian could mistake that verse to mean two groups. But as sure as two and two are five they will miscount or misunderstand the verse. Don't do that. It sure looks clear enough to me. There are three groups; Jews, Gentiles, and the Church.

The mystery was not revealed before! A church would be formed out of both Israel and Gentiles to become the Bride of Christ. What a beautiful story! And you are the bride, if He is your Savior. Mystery-lovers help yourself. Do not just read about the mystery but become part of the mystery. We poor lost sinners, who were without any hope and without God in this world, and you cannot have it any worse than that, are now joined to the one and only Savior, to be His bride and share in His glory forever. You cannot have it any better than that!

What a mystery! What glory! But now the secret is out. There is no more separation between one race and another. We all come to Him in the same way. We are all sinners. We all need His grace. And He will receive any one who comes to Him.

Yes, the church is in the Old Testament in types. Anyone reading about Joseph should see that he is a perfect type of Christ in the Old Testament. Then his Gentile bride would be a type of the church. Genesis chapter 24 tells about getting a bride for Isaac. Rebekah then, is another type of the church. And there are more. The book of Ruth tells about the Gentile girl, who is redeemed by the rich and powerful Boaz, who is a "Goel," or kinsman-redeemer, who buys her back with her land and then marries her. He is a clear picture of Christ in the Old Testament. Ruth is a picture of the church. She becomes the great grandmother of David.

But the actual church was not spelled out. It is now. Do you belong to it? Not the first so and so church, but the universal church. This church is not a building. It is "people" who have trusted the Lord Jesus. Whenever believers gather together to worship Jesus, they are the church.

Paul speaks about the church which met in homes. In Colossians 4:15–16, he says "Luke, the beloved physician, and Demas, greet you. Salute the brethren which are in Laodicea, and Nymphas, and the church which is IN HIS HOUSE." And again in Philemon 2 he says, "And to our beloved Apphia, and Archippus our fellowsoldier, and to the church IN THY HOUSE." The "church," made up of Christians, was outlawed until the fourth century, when Constantine made it a lawful form of worship in AD 313. The "church" of believers met in a building, someone's home, but the building was not the church. It was simply a place where the "church" met. When the church, the believers who worship the Lord, leave that building they meet in, it is just a building. That is all it is, just a building.

That group of worshipers is the "church" we must be a part of. Are you? You should be and you can be! You become a "member" when you believe on the Lord Jesus.

BEAM 106

LORD OR LUNATIC? WHICH IS HE?

C .S. Lewis pointed out how ridiculous it would be if a person went around saying that he was a poached egg. We would naturally think that he is nuts.

"Therefore the Jews sought the more to kill Him, because He not only had broken the Sabbath, but said also that God was His Father, making Himself equal with God" (John 5:18). Jesus Christ went around saying, He is the Son of God, the Only Door of salvation, the only Redeemer, the Lord of All. Is this bigotry? It sure is, unless it is true. If it is not true, then Jesus Christ is mentally insane and should be treated like someone who says he is a poached egg.

But, but, but. Does a lunatic do the things that He did? Does a lunatic heal all manner of illnesses and diseases? Does a lunatic walk upon the water? Does a lunatic raise dead bodies? Does a lunatic come back from the dead after he is killed and has been dead three days? And the things He said? Do His sermons sound like the ravings of a lunatic? If He is a lunatic, then history should forget such a person.

If He is not a lunatic, then what He said must be true. Then He must be Lord, the only Savior, the Son of God. Then we can no longer ignore Him. We can no longer neglect so great a salvation that He has offered us. "How shall we escape, if we neglect so great salvation" (Hebrews 2:3).

There is another possibility. He may be a deceiver trying to fool people into believing something that is not true. But what did He get out of it? He said He did not have a place to lay His head. He had no home, even though the birds of the air have nests and foxes have holes, He had none. Why do people hoodwink other people? Usually to get the money. That's what counts in this world. Get it and get as much as you can. What did He get? A cross! Do deceivers plot so they can be put to death by a mob? And look at all the miracles He did. Miracles that even His enemies could not deny. Why would a deceiver do that? He certainly did not gain anything by being a deceiver.

Is He just man? I once heard a group of ministers at one of their gatherings sing a song from one of the Broadway shows, "He's Just a Man." If Jesus is "Just a Man" then he is unlike any other man that ever lived. Does "Just a Man" walk on water, or raise the dead, or feed thousands with a boy's lunch? Why are they worshiping a man? Or are they? If He is "Just a Man" then it would be blasphemy to worship him. Just like it would be blasphemy to worship a lunatic.

Lord or lunatic or a deceiver? Which is He? He must be one of these. He changed the world. Has any lunatic done that? He still divides the world this very day. Is he deceiving anyone? He did tell us about persecution we may suffer if we follow Him. And the countless millions of lives that have been changed. How does one account for that? Does any deceiver do that? Then He must be Who He said He is, God in the flesh. He is Lord.

If He is Lord, then we must worship Him. If He is Lord of all, then we must bow to Him and confess our need of Him. If He is Lord, then He alone deserves our devotion, He alone deserves our service, He alone deserves our sacrifice. One day every knee shall bow and every tongue confess that He is Lord (Philippians 2:10–11). How is it with you? Is He your Lord or a lunatic? "Believe on the Lord Jesus and thou shalt be saved." We can bow now or we will bow later. Now is much better!

BEAM 107

DON'T CALL ME SHADRACH

DANIEL 1:7

Years ago I listened to a baritone with a beautiful voice singing a song about these three Hebrew children. It was a hit for a while. Their names made a good group for a songwriter. It was "Shadrach, Meshach, and Abed-nego." Few people would know what those names mean, but they sounded good in a crazy sort of way in the song. Even the furnace got into the song. It was heated seven times hotter than it ought to be.

There is a lesson in the meaning of Biblical names. One did not just call him "Junior" to keep his father's name alive. The names had a Godly meaning and a Godly lesson. Some children may not have been named until some time after their birth, until their behavior came out, or they may have been renamed. No trouble with Jacob. He was a supplanter from the beginning, coming into this world grabbing the heel of his twin brother. Later he is renamed Israel "Ruling with God." Abram meant "High Father" even though he had no children. Later he was renamed Abraham which meant "Father of a Multitude" even though he had only one child, and that not by his wife Sarah.

When Abraham was told he would have a son by Sarah, who was now about ninety years old, and Abraham was about 100 years old, she laughed, in unbelief. Later, when the Lord fulfilled what He promised and a son was born to her, she named her son "Isaac" which means "Laughter." This time she laughed in thanksgiving for what God had done.

The three Hebrew children were taken captive to Babylon. They had God-given names. Daniel means "God is my judge." Hananiah means "Jehovah is Gracious." Mishael means Who is Like God is?" Azariah means "The Lord is my Help." The Prince of the Eunuchs was given charge over these prisoners. He knew he could not have someone named "Jehovah is Gracious" running around in Nebuchadnezzar's palace. Nor could he have a "Who is like God (the God of Israel) Is?" So he changes their names to suit the heathen environment they are now in.

Hananiah says, "Guess what I am being called now? Shadrach, "Illumined by the sun-god" What do you think of that?" Mishael says "How about me. Now I am called Meshach, 'Who is like Venus.'" Then Azariah speaks up. "You aint heard nothing yet. Now I am known as Abed-nego, 'The servant of Nego.' I wouldn't serve Nego if my life depended on it." Daniel says "You are not alone. He changed my name from 'God is my Judge' to Belteshazzar, a heathen name that means 'Whom Bel Favors.'"

These four had the name of God in their names, the God of Israel or Jehovah. That was a testimony to all that they were believers in the God of Israel. They were identified by those godly names. Why should I bother to remember those heathen names? The children of the Lord should remember their saintly names.

The New Testament saints also got new names. No, they did not change Philip "Lover of Horses" to Philatheos, "Lover of God." But they were first called "Christians" at Antioch (Acts 11:26). This most likely was in the form of derision, but they were told that they would suffer persecution for His sake. We are still called by His name today. If it means persecution for us, so be it. That is little to suffer for Him Who gave His all for us. Many people call themselves "Christian" because they joined a church or give money to a church or sing in the choir. These early "Christians" were those who followed Him. They were called disciples of the Lord. Do people know us by our new name, "Christian?"

What are you known as? What is your name? No, I mean your new name? Is it Christian? Do your friends know that you are one of those "Christians?" If not, why not?

BEAM 108

A GOOD WOMAN IS HARD TO FIND

PROVERBS 31:10

Years ago there was a song that said "A Good Man Nowadays is Hard to Find." That is still true today. Maybe even harder to find. But let's look at the woman. Women, some women anyway, feel that the Scriptures make them second class citizens, or Christians. It is true that in some things only one can be first. At creation, God chose man. He made Adam first. Then from Adam's innermost being he made a woman. Perhaps that is saying something about how the woman, his other half, is his better half.

It is also true that there can only be one head to a body, unless we are talking about some horrible monster that Hollywood would put in a horror film. Here again God chose to make man the head of the body in the home. He chose twelve apostles, all men, to spread the Word of the Gospel.

But the curse that came upon mankind from the Fall was not because of the woman. She was deceived by Satan. The man, Adam, was not deceived. He willfully sinned, knowingly, against God's command.

1 Timothy 2:14 "And Adam was not deceived, but the woman being deceived was in the transgression."

It is to be noted that she took of the fruit first, then Adam. (And it was not an apple.) If she had taken it after Adam she could have said to God that she was only obeying her husband.

But God has given many passages for the woman to rejoice over. She is to be loved, protected, sheltered, and honored. The most beloved passage would be that in Ephesians 5:25 where we read "Husbands, love your wives, even as Christ also loved the church, and gave Himself for it." It would have been a loving passage if it just said "Love your wives as Christ also loved the church." But Paul wants us to understand it. It is sometimes said that "only a theologian could misunderstand that." Paul wants theologians to understand what he just said, so he makes it clear, "And gave Himself for it."

That is tremendous love. A woman who is loved like that will have no trouble submitting to her husband as Paul states in Ephesians 5:22. Does he really mean the husband is to give himself for his wife? I always think of the great ship that "even God could not sink," the Titanic. There you are, or I am, with my wife. But we are both in the freezing water. Here comes a lifeboat. Ah! But there is only room for one more passenger in it. Now comes the test. Do you help your wife to get up on the boat, or do you push her down so you can climb over her to get in the boat? This is the test. Love puts her in the boat.

Proverbs 31:10–12: "Who can find a virtuous woman? For her price is far above rubies. The heart of her husband doth safely trust in her . . . she will do him good and not evil all the days of her life."

What good are rubies? They would look best ON her. You can't eat them and they do not cook or clean house. Rubies do not take care of the children, or the dishes, or the clothes. And this was spoken by Solomon who lived in a palace. He probably had many babysitters and cooks and dishwashers.

These days "A good woman IS harder to find." But they are there. And they do all of these things without a salary. Man's work is from sun to sun, but a woman's work is, well you know how it goes. And they fulfill what Solomon wrote about. They do their husbands good. They are to be sheltered, and protected. For in the marriage the two became one. So, Paul says "So ought men to love their wives as their own bodies. He that loveth his wife loveth himself" (Ephesians 5:28). So she may well be my better half. At the least she is half of me, since we two became one. Without her I am not a complete person.

Perhaps you have not found that woman who is above the price of rubies. Keep trying. Look in the Sunday School Class. You may find her there.

BEAM 109

POOR MARTHA

LUKE 10:40

There are some seven women named Mary in the Scriptures, so it might be necessary to name which Mary one is talking about. This Mary was the sister of Lazarus and Martha. She might need some defense too.

In Luke 10:40 we read "But Martha was cumbered about much serving, and came to Him, and said, Lord, dost Thou not care that my sister hath left me to serve alone? Bid her therefore that she help me." Of course He cared. He cares about everyone and everything.

But read verse 39. There we are told that Mary "also sat at His feet, and heard His word." It might look like Mary did not help Martha at all, but let her do all the housework, serving tables, cooking, etc. But notice that little word "also." It is missed by so many. It can mean one of two things. It could mean that Martha sat at His feet, and Mary ALSO sat at His feet. Or, it can mean that Mary served, and ALSO sat at His feet. The first meaning is obviously incorrect from the statement that Martha makes.

So we have here two women who loved the Lord Jesus. They have opened their hearts and their home to Jesus. He is invited in to a meal, something that they had done on other occasions no doubt. After doing some of the housework, Mary sits at His feet and listens to Him give out the Word. Martha is too busy doing the cooking and cleaning and dishes and whatever else needed to be done. She is just too busy for her own good. She is missing something that is more important and is so necessary.

Jesus says to her "Martha, Martha; thou art careful and troubled about many things: But one thing is needful: and Mary hath chosen that good part, which shall not be taken away from her" (Luke 10:41–42). What is He saying to us? Sure there are some necessary things that must be done. Who wants to live in a dirty house? And cooking? Somebody has to do it. And the washing and sewing and the grocery shopping? Sure, these must be done. But some time needs to be spent listening to Him. This is "that good part." In other words, spending time with the Lord.

Today we are not able to sit at His feet, like Mary did, but we listen to His word and we can talk to Him in prayer. That means we must take some time AWAY from the little things of life. Yes, they are little. He is the important thing in life. Martha was a good person and one who loved the Lord. I am sure she was always glad to welcome Him into her home. But, she was too busy with the dishes. His word was more important. Sure, she had to cook, but she could also take a little time to hear what the Master was saying.

Turn that oven down to low and take a break.

This may explain how it was that Mary understood what Jesus was saying about going to the cross, and dying on the cross, and then rising again from the grave. No one else seemed to understand that. This Mary was the one who came to the house of Simon the leper and anointed the Lord Jesus for His burial. She was the Mary who poured out her "pound of spikenard, very costly, and anointed the feet of Jesus, and wiped His feet with her hair" (John 12:3). Martha did not choose "that good part" then but I am sure she learned a lesson. Put first things first. He is first. Sit at His feet now and later we will sit with Him in His kingdom. First things first.

"Worship the Lord in the beauty of holiness" (Psalm 29:2).

"Exalt ye the Lord our God, and worship at His footstool; for He is holy" (Psalm 99:5).

"The Lord said unto my Lord, sit Thou at my right hand, until I make thine enemies Thy footstool" (Psalm 110:1).

BEAM 110

NOT UNDER THE LAW

GALATIANS 3:10–13

I was in a Sunday School class once when a young lady said she did not have to learn the Bible. She was born with a Bible knowledge. I thought wow! That's more than the Apostle Paul could say. He had to go away into the desert of Arabia for some years and learn the Scriptures over again. And he already knew the Old Testament (Galatians 1:17–18). He now had to learn how Jesus was that Messiah the Old Testament foretold. How one can be lost and have an understanding of the Bible before they are saved beats me. She was born with it. Aah hah! Well, Paul says "The natural man (that is the unsaved man) receiveth not the things of the Spirit of God; for they are foolishness to him; neither can he know them, because they are spiritually discerned" (1 Corinthians 2:14).

Then she went on to tell the class that we must keep the Law of Moses. Aah hah! Well, I thought, she already broke that Law if she turned on the lights in her home or cooked a meal the day before, Saturday, the Sabbath. By the way, who gave man the right to call Sunday the Christian Sabbath? God said it was on Saturday. No man can change what God has said. If Sunday WERE a "Christian Sabbath," we would be breaking it by traveling to church on Sunday

Hear what Paul says about the Law of Moses. "Cursed is every one that continueth not in all things which are written in the book of the Law to do them. But that no man is justified by the Law in the sight of God, it is evident for, The Just shall live by faith. And the Law is not of faith . . . Christ hath redeemed us from the curse of the Law, being made a curse for us: for it is written, Cursed is every one that hangeth on a tree" (Galatians 3:10–13). That sounds plain enough to me. If you are under the Law, you are under a curse. If you are under the Law, you must do every iota of the Law to keep the Law and no one ever has except the Lord Jesus. And it also says that "if righteousness come by the Law, then Christ is dead in vain" (Galatians 2:21). That sounds clear to me. If we are under the Law of Moses, then Jesus died in vain, that is for nothing. I guess I can be glad I was not born with the knowledge of the Bible. I have to learn the hard way, by working at it.

So the Christian is not under the Law. No, but he is under a higher law. We may miss this when we think about the Law of Moses and the 10 commandments. It must be understood that the 10 commandments are NOT ALL OF THE LAW of Moses. They are only a BEGINNING of the Law. Chapter after chapter we read "And the Lord also said unto Moses, or the Lord spake unto Moses," etc. Exodus 20 is only a beginning.

But what about the higher law that the Christian is under? He has a higher standard to live up to. He also has the Holy Spirit living within him so he can live on a higher plane. Look at the comparison. We will use Exodus 20 for the 10 commandments and compare.

EXODUS 20	NEW TESTAMENT
1. Thou shalt have no other gods before Me.	Phil. 2:10 "That at the name of Jesus every knee should bow, of things in heaven, and things in earth, and things under the earth: and every tongue should confess that Jesus Christ is Lord to the glory of God the Father." Not only do we have no other gods but we have One whose name is above every name.
2. Thou shalt make no graven image.	Hebrews 1:3 "Who being the brightness of His glory, and the express image of His person." That word "express image" is the word "charactar" which gives us our word "character." Jesus is the very "Character" of God. God incarnate.
3. Thou shalt not take the name of the Lord Thy God in vain.	2 Thess. 1:12 "That the name of our Lord Jesus may be glorified in you."
4. Remember the Sabbath day to keep it holy.	Eph. 5:16 "Redeeming the time because the days are evil." COL2) Luke 9:23 "let him deny himself, and take up his cross daily, and follow Me." All of our time is His.
5. Honor thy father and mother.	Eph 6:1 "Children, obey your parents in the Lord, for this is right." This is more than honor them.
6. Thou shalt not kill.	Matt. 5:44 "Love your enemies, bless them that curse you."

7. Thou shalt not commit adultery.	Matt. 5:28 "Whoso looketh upon a woman to lust after her hath committed adultery with her already in his heart."
8. Thou shalt not steal.	Eph 4:28 "Let him that stole, steal no more but let him labor . . . that he may have to give to him that needeth."
9. Thou shalt not bear false witness against thy Neighbor.	Colossians 3:8–13 "But now ye also put off all these; anger, wrath, malice, blasphemy, filthy communication out of your mouth. Lie not one to another," etc.
10. Thou shalt not covet thy neighbor's wife.	1 Cor 12:31 "But covet earnestly the best gifts."

We have a higher standard to live up to. We are not saved by living up to it. We have to be alive to be able to live up to anything. But we have a higher standard to live for Him Who died for us. And some day we may hear Him say "Well done, thou good and faithful servant. Enter into the joy of thy Lord." His well done is worth it all. But we cannot live for Him until we are alive in Him. That is by grace through faith without works so there can be no boasting in His presence. We are sinners. We need a Savior. We have one, if we have believed.

BEAM 111

THE HUMBLE KING

MATTHEW 21:4–5

He did not show His humility by riding on a colt, the foal of an ass. That is a misunderstanding. He was not showing His humility by riding on the animal which today we call a donkey. This was a royal animal. Way back in the 17th century BC it was thought inappropriate for a king to ride a horse. There were thousands of tablets found in a place called Mari, in Syria. These told the story. The donkey was a royal animal, not the horse. We today think the horse is proper, but we are out of step with the ancient world.

You do not need to go outside of the Bible to find this out. We see the attempt to become kings in the Book of Judges. In that book we read that one of the Judges, Jair, the eighth judge, had thirty sons "that rode on thirty ass colts" (Judges 10:4). They were already pushing to be made royalty. A twelfth judge, Abdon, had forty sons and thirty nephews "that rode on threescore and ten ass colts" (Judges 12:14). He likewise was seeking to be known as royalty. His sons wanted this honor.

Later on when there is a king, David, we read this. David was driven out of town by his son Absalom. A servant, Ziba, met him with a "couple of asses saddled, and upon them two hundred loaves of bread" and raisins and summer fruits (1 Samuel 16:1). In verse 2, Ziba says "the asses be for the king's household to ride on." These were royal animals. Horses, no! Donkeys, yes!

What Zechariah 9:9 tells us is that this Messiah, this coming One, is meek and lowly and riding on a royal animal. He is not showing His humbleness by riding on the donkey. He is royalty, but unlike other royalty, this King is humble and lowly. You might think of the royal carriage of Great Britain when the king or queen is crowned or making a trip during some ceremony. There we see a royal coach. It is glorious with all of its gold and fine craftsmanship. It speaks of royalty. We recognize it by sight.

This King was riding on a royal steed. But unlike other members of a royal family, He was meek and lowly in heart. If ever One had the right to be proud, He certainly did. We sing of Him in the Hallelujah Chorus that He is King of Kings and Lord of Lords. And He is. One day this world will see Him in His glory. Every knee shall bow and every tongue shall confess that He is Lord.

Philippians 2:10–11, "That at the name of Jesus every knee should bow of things in heaven, and things in earth, and things under earth, and every tongue should confess that Jesus Christ is Lord, to the glory of God the Father." We all are going to bow and confess this. The question for us today is when? Do we do it now, or later? One way or another we all are going to bow and confess. He is Lord, He is King of Kings. But when He came the first time He was lowly and humble and meek. The next time He comes He will rule and reign over all of the earth. Now is better than later. What a King! What a Savior! A humble One!

"The Lord lifteth up the meek; He casteth the wicked down to the ground" (Psalm 147:6).

"Better it is to be of an humble spirit with the lowly, than to divide the spoil with the proud" (Proverbs 16:19).

"Humble yourselves in the sight of the Lord, and He shall lift you up" (James 4:10).

"My soul shall make her boast in the Lord; the humble shall hear thereof, and be glad" (Psalm 34:2).

BEAM 112

PO FOLKS

YET RICH INDEED

LUKE 2:24

In Leviticus chapter 12 we read about the sacrifice that a woman offered up when she bore a child. After eight days the male child is circumcised. Then after 32 more days the woman offers up her sacrifice for her uncleanness. During those forty days she is not to touch any hallowed thing nor come into the sanctuary (verse 4). After this time she then brings her offering. We read in Leviticus 12:6 that she is to bring a lamb of the first year for a burnt-offering and a young pigeon, or a turtledove, for a sin-offering.

Leviticus 12:8 tells us that if she "be not able to bring a lamb" that is, if she is too poor and cannot afford to bring a lamb, then she "shall bring two turtles (doves), or two young pigeons, the one for the burnt-offering, and the other for a sin-offering." This is the poor man's offering, or the poor family's offering. A couple of birds is what the poor could bring, if they could not afford a lamb, which was not very expensive. The lamb was not as rich an offering as a bullock or a sheep or goat. So the Lord provided for the poor. They could bring a couple of birds for the cleansing.

In Luke 2:24 we are told that Joseph and Mary brought a couple of birds to the priest in the temple to be offered up. This shows how poor they were, unless of course you believe they were a couple of hypocrites and were hoarding their money. Hardly! Mary had found favor with the Lord and was chosen to bring the Messiah into the world. But what has this to do with the price of butter? The problem is that shortly after this period, nearly two years later, the wise men came from the East seeking this new king of Israel, this Messiah. He is not the baby any more. When they arrive, and finally find where this young child-king is staying, He is a young child in a house in Bethlehem. He is not in any stable. He is not a babe. And when Herod finds he has been mocked, he sends his soldiers to kill all the children in Bethlehem who are "two years old and under, ACCORDING

TO THE TIME WHICH HE HAD DILIGENTLY ENQUIRED of the wise men" (Matthew 2:16).

But before this slaughter of the innocents of Bethlehem could happen, an angel of the Lord warned Joseph in a dream and told him to take the "young child" (Matthew 2:12–13) and flee into Egypt. There they stayed until they heard of Herod's death. That might have been a year later, more or less. The question is how did they live in Egypt? Since it is evident that they were poor, how could they travel to Egypt and live there for some length of time? They had no monthly check coming in.

Back to the wise men again. When these people came from the East, and the Scripture never says there were three wise men, they presented gifts to this Messiah-king. I am sure there was a caravan of people from the East, but however many there were, they presented gifts to the Savior. And I am sure more gifts were given than those mentioned. But there are three mentioned. Matthew 2:11, they "fell down, and worshipped Him: and when they had opened their treasures, they presented unto Him gifts; gold, and frankincense, and myrrh." It seems reasonable to believe that these gifts, and others that are not mentioned, would be used to pay the expenses of this poor family that could not afford to offer up a lamb.

He came into a world that He created, and the world knew Him not. He was born in a stable. He was born into a poor home that could not offer up a lamb. Yet He did it to make us rich. "Though He was rich, yet for your sakes He became poor, that ye through His poverty might be rich" (2 Corinthians 8:9).

What a beautiful story. What a wonderful Savior! They were not so poor after all. They had Him for a son.

BEAM 113

GOD RULES THE EMPIRES TOO

DANIEL 4:25

Far too many times I have heard preachers and teachers teaching about the temptation of Jesus where they seem to say that God rules in heaven above and Satan rules on the earth below. Not so! In Matthew 4 we read that the devil took Jesus up into a high mountain and showed Him all the kingdoms of the world and the glory (such as it is) of them. And then he said to Jesus "All these things will I give thee if thou wilt fall down and worship me" (Matthew 4:8–9). And then they say "since Jesus did not deny what the devil said, it must be true. The devil gives the kingdoms of this world to whomever he pleases." Not so. This is an argument from silence which is never a good argument. Just because I say nothing when you say you are the president of the United States, does not make you the president of the United States.

Daniel had another dream to interpret. It seems Nebuchadnezzar was getting quite a number of dreams, but these were not from eating pizza before he went to bed. These were revelations from God. And, none of the fortune tellers could help. No, not one astrologer, or tarot reader, or palm reader. No magician, no horoscope, could help poor Nebuchadnezzar. It was God's purpose to reveal His will to this king and it was through Daniel again, who interpreted a dream for Nebuchadnezzar before. You would think that he would have learned his lesson the first time and called for Daniel at the beginning. You might think that Daniel would be the head of his Security Council. But sometimes we just don't learn. After all his magicians and fortune tellers fail, then he sends for Daniel.

Daniel gives him the interpretation. It isn't good news for Nebuchadnezzar, but that is the way things go. Daniel says Nebuchadnezzar has gotten too big for his britches, too proud. He says that he has done a great job in building Babylon. After all, everyone has heard about the hanging gardens of Babylon. It is one of the seven wonders of the ancient world. (What about the bricklayers? Do they get any credit?)

Daniel says that Nebuchadnezzar is going to go crazy for a while. He is going to live like an animal, sleep like an animal with the animals, and eat grass like an animal. He is going to do this for seven years and then God, in His wonderful grace, will restore him to his kingdom. That is amazing. It is amazing that someone else did not take over his kingdom and even kill him like an animal, since he is acting like one. But God rules in the earthly affairs of men.

This is what Daniel says to him. "Till thou know that the most High ruleth in the kingdom of men, and giveth it to whomsoever He will" (Daniel 4:25). There he says it. God above rules in the kingdoms of this earth. It is not Satan's to give. God gives kingdoms to whom He pleases. Yes, even a Nebuchadnezzar, or a Hitler, or a Hirohito. God is in charge. So he lives like an animal for 7 years as Daniel said. Then he is restored to his throne. The change did him good. Now Nebuchadnezzar believes in the Jehovah God of Daniel. He blesses the Most High, and praises and honors Him (Daniel 4:34).

Satan is mentioned many places in the Scripture, but there are only three conversations where we read what he says. He lies each time. In Genesis 3:4 he lies about God. He says to Eve "Ye shall not surely die." That was a lie. They ate and they died.

In Job 2 and 3 he lies about man. He says to God "Oh sure, Job loves you and serves you, because you pay him so much with so many blessings. But take them away and he will curse You to Your face" (Job 2:5). That also was a lie. Job took suffering and still loved God.

In Matthew 4:9 he lies about himself. He says he will give all these kingdoms. They are not his to give. God rules on earth in the kingdoms of men and He gives them to whom He will. In John 8:44 Jesus said of Satan "He was a murderer from the beginning, and abode not in the truth, because there is no truth in him . . . he is a liar and the father of it." He is not to be listened to.

Be careful what you hear and more careful of what you believe. You can believe Jesus. He not only tells us the truth but He is the truth. And He did not say that He was A way. He said He is THE way, THE truth, THE life, THE only way to God. You can believe what He says. He cannot lie. And it is still God's world. He rules over it. Amen!

BEAM 114

COME ON, IT'S FREE

ISAIAH 55:1–3

There are some people who cannot resist something if it is free. We have heard that there is no such thing as a free lunch, you really pay for it somehow, but many a person still likes to hear "It's free, it won't cost you anything." Sometimes it is a gimmick, or a scam. Beware! You don't get something for nothing. Somebody has to pay for it. Do you think they could stay in business if they gave things away for free?

However, here is an invitation that is different. We are told to eat and drink without money and at no cost. Is this another of those "free is phony" things? In one sense it may not be entirely free, but in another it is absolutely free. God says if you thirst "come ye to the waters, and he that hath no money, come ye, buy and eat, buy wine and milk without money and without price"(Isaiah 53:1). He says why do ye spend money for that which is not bread (food) and labor for what will not satisfy? Not only are we invited to the banquet table, but we are also invited to come, if we believe, and our soul shall live. He says He will make an everlasting covenant with us and we shall live forever. Is this for real? Is this all free?

In one sense it is. We do not have to pay anything. In the first place, we have nothing to pay with. We have no righteousness to bring before God. In the second place, we are dead to God and all He stands for and all He wants from us. What can a dead man do to please even a merciful God? Yet the invitation is there. Come, it is free. Accept the invitation and you will not only feast but you will have God's everlasting promise for good. You will have eternal life.

Yet in another sense it is not free. It cost everything, only it was not OUR everything. It was the Lord Jesus' everything. He paid it all, and since He paid it all, there is nothing left to pay. We only need to come to Him. He gave everything He had to pay the price, but He did this willingly. "The Son of man came not to be ministered unto, but to minister, and to give His life a ransom for many" (Matthew 29:28). He wanted to pay it all for us because we had nothing to pay. "And you hath He quickened (made alive) who were dead in trespasses and sins" (Ephesians 2:1).

He did this willingly, at no cost to us, but it cost everything to Him. "For the Son of man is come to seek and to save that which was lost" (Luke 19:10). The only requirement for us to have is to be lost. That should not take a lot of effort on our part. We are sinners. We just have to ADMIT TO GOD that we are sinners. We only need to come and take of the free offer of His grace. Then we have everything we need for now and eternity because He paid for it. What a beautiful story. What wonderful grace that He should even invite us. It is free! Let's take it.

Some people are always looking for bargains. If it is on sale, even if they don't need it, they buy it. Here is a real bargain. Are you hungry? Are you thirsty? Are you inquisitive about the Scriptures and what they teach? Come! It's free, truly free. No gimmicks. Take, eat, drink, and be filled with God's goodness.

"Come unto Me, all ye that labour and are heaven laden, and I will give you rest" (Matthew 11:28).

"A certain man made a great supper, and bade many, and sent his servant at supper time to say to them that were bidden, Come, for all things are ready" (Luke 14:16–17).

"Being justified freely by His grace through the redemption that is in Christ Jesus" (Romans 3:24).

BEAM 115

JAIRUS' DAUGHTER

MARK 5:21–42

I can see the anxiety on the face of Jairus. His daughter is at the point of death and he asks Jesus to come down to his house and lay His hands on her that she may be healed and live. He did not have the faith of the centurion in Luke 7:1–10. He said Jesus did not have to come down to his house. He could just speak the word and his servant would be healed. Jesus marveled at him and said He had not found so great a faith in Israel (7:9). This was a Gentile who had heard about Jesus. Jairus did believe that Jesus could heal his daughter. He just did not have faith to believe that Jesus could heal from a distance.

Jesus starts on His way with Jairus. Then everything stops. Jesus said someone had touched His clothes. He was aware of a poor sick woman in the crowd, who believed if she could but touch His clothes she would be healed. She had an issue of blood for 12 years and wanted healing. She believed Jesus could do it, and He did do it. He knew someone touched Him by faith. But He wanted her to have more than healing. He wanted her to know that His clothes were not magical. And by faith in Him her sins were taken away also. So He stops, and wants this woman to come forward. You can see the look on Jairus' face now. "Why are we standing around talking when my daughter is dying? We're wasting time. Let's go!"

But Jesus stood around and waited for this woman to come forth. Then He says to her, "Daughter, thy faith hath made thee whole; go in peace, and be whole of thy plague" (5:34). Now comes the bad news. "Your daughter is dead. Why bother the Master. It's too late." But it is not too late, not when Jesus starts out to do something. He had time for the woman and He had time for Jairus. What he starts out to do He will finish. Paul says he is "confident of this very thing, that He which hath begun a good work in you will perform it until the day of Jesus Christ" (Philippians 1:6). He has started out to do a work in us, also. We are to be "conformed to the image of His (God's) Son, that He (Jesus) might be the firstborn among many brethren" (Romans 8:29). God wants more than one son in heaven.

But what about Jairus? Did he believe it was too late? She was dead now. Could Jesus do anything after a sick child dies? Yes! He has the power to do what He starts out to do. He started out to heal Jairus' daughter and that is what He will do. He goes to Jairus' house. He did not have to, but that is what Jairus wanted. He also puts His hand on the dead child. That is what Jairus asked Him to do. Then He says "Little girl, I say unto thee arise" (Mark 5:41). And she rose up from the dead. Jesus had the patience to help this poor woman and the power to raise this child even after she was dead.

We are told that Jairus' daughter was 12 years old. The woman had this issue of blood for 12 years. That is a beautiful lesson for us. Jairus enjoyed the beauty and pleasure of seeing his child growing for 12 years. She was his joy and he loved her. This poor woman was an outcast from society. She was not a leper, but she was treated like one. There is a whole chapter given to the uncleanness of anyone with an issue of blood. Leviticus 15:19–26 tells us that they are unclean and any one or any thing that touches them is unclean also, as long as they have this running bloody sore. She had it for 12 years. She was most likely divorced and ostracized from her own children. Unlike Jairus, she could not hug her children and have the joy of seeing them growing. But she had faith, even to touch His clothes. That is all it took. That is all it takes now, faith in Jesus. If I may but touch Him by faith I can be made whole from my sins.

He has an unchanging purpose for us, and the power to make it work, and the patience. He has a lot to do in me still. He needs the patience. One thing was necessary. Jairus asked Jesus to come with him. That is what we need to do. Ask Jesus to come into our lives and go with us through this life. He is willing and waiting for us to ask. Ask Him.

BEAM 116

WHO'S IN CHARGE HERE?

ROMANS 12:1–2

If you skip chapters 9 through 11 of Romans you would not notice it. It is like 9 through 11 are a great parenthesis. The thought of Romans 8 continues right on in chapter 12. Chapters 9 through 11 are about the nation of Israel. God is not through with Israel yet. They are in a stage of dormancy, or blindness. One day the blindness shall be taken away from her eyes and she shall see that Messiah already came and she did not recognize Him. Paul says that "blindness in part is happened to Israel, until the fulness of the Gentiles be come in," that is until the church is complete and raptured away (Romans 11:25). He says "in part" because he himself was a Jew and saw that Jesus was the Christ or Messiah, the Anointed One of Israel. The church started out Jewish but soon became mostly Gentiles. There are Jewish Christians today. Israel is part blind.

Look at the ending of chapter 8 and the beginning of chapter 12. In chapter 8 Paul says that nothing can separate us from the love of Christ. He names everything that could possibly be thought in some way to separate Christians from Christ. There are none. Read Romans 8:35–39. Nothing, nothing coming, nor nothing past, nothing can separate us from Christ once we have come to Him by faith. Then look at the opening of chapter 12. "I beseech you therefore, brethren by the mercies of God that ye present your bodies a living sacrifice, holy, acceptable unto God, which is your reasonable service." God in His grace has provided that nothing can ever separate the believer from the Savior. So it is reasonable to offer Him our bodies for service. We are to be living sacrifices on the altar. That's where it becomes tough.

In the Old Testament, the animal was killed and then placed on the altar. He could say nothing about it nor could he do anything about it. He was dead. He could not complain that the fire was too hot. He could not crawl over to the edge of the altar where it might be a little cooler. He was dead. But those days are gone. We are saved to serve. We are living saints who need to be living servants of Him Who saved us. We are His feet, His hands, His mouth. We are His body here on earth. He works through us to reach a lost world.

The problem is that we, who believe on Him for salvation, still want to do things our way. But our way is not His way. Some time, after we have been saved, we come to the place where we realize that our way is not the best way. We owe Him everything. What He wants us to do is for His glory and for our good.

We come to the place where we abdicate our rule and give ourselves over to Him, without reservation. How can a soldier say that I will serve if it is not dangerous, or if I do not have to sleep in foxholes? Does a soldier say I will serve if I get a good pension? We are to be completely given to Him Who completely gave Himself for us. If we cannot do that, then we cannot be His soldiers. We may keep on trying to work out things for ourselves until we see the light. He only accepts volunteers in His army.

The time will come, if we are willing to see the light, when we will see that we have been in charge too long. We need to turn our lives over to another and let Him be in charge. He will not lay upon us more than we can handle. He knows how frail we are. He knows our weaknesses and our ignorance. He will do us good. Besides owing this to Him, He knows all things, the end from the beginning, so that He can guide us right. And what does Paul add to this verse? We are not to look like the world, or think like the world, or act like the world (12:2). And by doing so we can "prove what is that good, and acceptable, and perfect will of God." Why settle for anything less than perfect? Who's in charge? He does not club us over the head to take over our lives. He patiently waits for us to come to our senses where we realize we need another boss. He cannot be our boss until He is first our Savior. So what are we waiting for? Put Him in charge and find out what a perfect boss He is, and what perfect means.

BEAM 117

ASSURANCE–YOU CAN KNOW

1 JOHN 5:13

What is assurance anyhow? The Apostle John writes his Gospel to tell us how we can be saved. Chapter 21 is an addendum to the book so the end of chapter 20 gives us the reason for writing the Gospel. He states "But these are written that ye might believe that Jesus is the Christ, the Son of God, and that BELIEVING YE MIGHT HAVE LIFE through His name" (John 20:31). He is giving a record that Jesus is God in the flesh. He starts out that way and ends that way. "In the beginning was the Word, and the Word was with God, and the Word was God" (John 1:1). That is the start. Chapter 20 is the ending. In both, he declares that Jesus is God. John writes his Gospel so that by believing we might be saved.

He then writes another book that tells us that WE CAN KNOW THAT WE ARE SAVED. Some may feel that you cannot know you are saved until you die. Then you will find out. It's too late then. There are many places in the Scriptures where we read about someone knowing they were saved, while still living in this world. Paul, for one, says that he and Timothy were, that's past tense, saved. 2 Timothy 1:8–9, "According to the power of God, Who hath saved us, and called us with an holy calling." John also states it this way, "And this is the record, that God hath given (past tense again) to us eternal life, and this life is in His Son" (1 John 5:11).

Peter says "the God of all grace, who hath called us (past tense) unto His eternal glory by Christ Jesus, after ye have suffered a while, make you perfect, stablish, strength, settle you" (1 Peter 5:10). No, we are not perfect yet, He still has a work to do in us, but He has promised to finish that work which He has begun. "Faithful is He that calleth you, Who also will do it" (1 Thessalonians 5:24).

However, when we give in to our old sinful nature, as Paul tells us about in Romans 7, and do those things that we know we should not do, the doubts come. Peter must have had some doubts when he denied that he even knew the Lord. Then the Lord Jesus gave special mention of Peter when He sent word to His disciples so that Peter would not feel that he was lost again, or lost for ever. In Mark 16:7 the angel sends the message to His own, "But go your way, tell His disciples and Peter that He goeth before you into Galilee." The Lord made a special reference to Peter so Peter would not give up, because he denied he even knew his Lord.

John tells us "If we say that we have fellowship with Him, and walk in darkness, we lie, and do not the truth" (1 John 1:6). That's the word, FELLOWSHIP. We cannot have FELLOWSHIP unless we are walking with Him. And we cannot walk with Him if we walk in darkness. He is Light. That is where the assurance comes in that John is speaking of. John says "He that hath the Son hath life" (1 John 5:12). There is that past tense again. But if we do not walk in the light, if we do not live like a Christian should, then we do not have fellowship with our Savior. That is where the doubts come in. We talk to ourselves. If I am a Christian why do I do those things that I should not do? Why I am not different from the unsaved? Am I truly a Christian? I wonder? Did I really put my trust in Jesus? That is when we have no assurance. We are not sure.

John wants us to know that we may not feel like a believer should, and we may not live like a believer should, but we are still saved, if we have believed. "These things have I written unto you that believe on the name of the Son of God, that ye may KNOW that ye have eternal life, and that ye may (continue to) believe on the name of the Son of God." Sometimes we may not feel like it, but if we have believed, we have a present possession; eternal life. It is all because God saves by grace through faith. That is it. We do nothing to earn it. We just receive it. What a gracious God we have! Is He yours?

BEAM 118

HE STAYED TWO MORE DAYS

JOHN 11:6

Why? Why did He wait two more days? This is when He heard that Lazarus was sick, very sick. This is the Lazarus that Jesus loved. I am sure Lazarus loved Jesus, and would have come quickly if Jesus had been sick However, strange as it may sound, the sisters send the message to Jesus that "He whom thou lovest is sick" (John 11:3). Then Jesus stays two more days where He is. This seems to be strange behavior. Why not go as fast as you can when the one you love is sick?

After spending two more days where He is, Jesus says let us go again into Judea. His apostles are now alarmed because they said those people in Judea sought to stone Jesus. Now go back there again? Yes, He says, let's go. "Our friend Lazarus sleepeth, but I go, that I may awake him out of sleep" (John 11:11).

The apostles really get confused here and so do a lot of "religious" people today. There is nothing in the Bible about "soul sleep" but sleep is used for the believers' bodies, when they die. They are said to "sleep" in Christ. In fact our word "cemetery" comes from the Greek word "coemeterium" which means "sleeping chamber." The saints' bodies sleep, waiting for the day when their bodies shall be awakened from the sleeping chamber. When you sleep, it is temporary, and you expect to wake up again. So it is with our dead bodies. And don't they look like they are asleep when you see them in their coffin?

Paul writes to the Corinthians in 15:51 "We shall not all sleep, but we shall all be changed." He speaks about the resurrection of the saints' bodies at the return of the Lord Jesus. Some saints shall be alive at that time. They shall not die, or be asleep, but they shall be clothed with new glorified bodies, while those who died shall have their "sleeping" bodies raised from the dead. The apostles did not understand this at that time and thought Jesus was talking about bed rest. Why hurry to awaken someone who is sleeping? But that is another beautiful story. Why did Jesus wait two more days to go to Lazarus?

This is one of the most beautiful stories in the Scriptures. It would not be, if Jesus had gone immediately. True, Lazarus might have been dead when they got there, but now they arrive and Lazarus has been dead four days. What can be done for someone who has been dead four days? Only the power of Almighty God could bring back life to a dead corpse, a four day old dead corpse. And that is what happens. Martha says her brother's body must be stinking now. It was in a hot climate, without the Egyptian embalming. Whew!

But Jesus says "take away the stone." Then he simply calls "Lazarus come forth" (John 11:43). Only God could do that. This miracle may exceed all the others, although in some sense a miracle is a miracle and all miracles are physical impossibilities. But four days? And Lazarus is not limping or crawling along the ground. He is not needing any help with a cane or wheelchair. He is whole and healthy again. Because of this miracle many believed on Jesus (John 12:9). His enemies could not deny it.

Martha and Mary may have wondered why Jesus did not come swiftly to their aid. We may wonder also why the Lord does not answer the prayer we have prayed for so long. It may have made them wonder how much Jesus loved Lazarus. He loved him exceedingly. He loves us exceedingly. We may not understand the long wait, but we can know that He loves us and has a loving purpose in what seems like a delay to us.

God's delays are not denials. One day, He says, "All that are in the graves shall hear His voice and shall come forth, they that have done good, unto the resurrection of life; and they that have done evil unto the resurrection of damnation" (John 5:28–29). We are going to be in one or the other. Which one will it be? Doing good is believing on the Lord Jesus Christ and receiving life. Doing nothing will cause us to be in the wrong resurrection, unto damnation. Hear Him now and you will be sure to hear Him later when He calls your body to come forth.

BEAM 119

JUDAS

RABBI, IS IT I?

MATTHEW 26:25

Some years ago I had a problem with Judas. It looked to me like he was one of the twelve, so he was a disciple and follower of Jesus. Then he betrayed the Lord. This looked like someone who was saved and got lost again. This bothered me for quite some time. It took a long time, and some Bible study, for me to see the light. There is never any evidence that Judas ever was a believer. Yes, he was with the Lord and with the other eleven, but he himself did not believe. He may have been in it for the money. There wasn't much money, but a thief is a thief. John the Apostle writes that Judas "was a thief and had the (money) bag, and bare what was put therein" (John 12:6). He was a clever thief because none of the other eleven suspected him of thievery. It was afterwards they realized what Judas had been doing.

When the time came for the arrest of Jesus and His sacrifice for our sins, he told the twelve that one of them would betray Him. Each of the eleven asked "Lord is it I?" (Matthew 26:22). Except Judas. He said "Master, is it I?" (Matthew 26:25). That may not seem like much evidence but what Judas said was Rabbi, which means "my teacher." He did not say Lord, the word is "kurios," like the others. Paul tells us in 1 Corinthians 12:3 "That no man speaking by the Spirit of God calleth Jesus accursed; and that no man can say that Jesus is the Lord (that is the word "kurios") but by the Holy Ghost." Judas never said Lord, or "kurios." He said rabbi or teacher. When I realized that, I knew I was onto something.

When Peter made his statement about believing that Jesus was the Christ, the Son of the living God, he said "we believe." Jesus corrected him immediately in John 6:68–70. He pointed out that one was going to betray Him. Here again Judas is not numbered among those that Peter said believed Jesus was the Messiah.

Later, when Jesus washed His disciples' feet, He said "Ye are clean, but not all." John writes "For He knew who would betray Him, therefore said He, Ye are not all clean" John 13:10–11). Here again Judas is not among the believing twelve.

Judas is a picture of those who go along with the crowd but never have had a new birth. He would be like someone today who joins a church, pays his bills, gives to the offering, is baptized, and perhaps sings in the choir. All of this means nothing without a new birth. One might even be on the board of deacons, or in the pulpit speaking. This is difficult for those who are not into the Scriptures to comprehend. Men in the pulpit not saved, not true believers? Yes, it happens. And then they become heads of their denomination. How awful! Paul told us it would happen in the last days.

Jesus told us about those who "Say Lord, Lord" but are not true believers. He said "many will say to me in that day, Lord, Lord have we not prophesied (that is preached) in thy name? And in thy name have cast out devils? And in thy Name done many wonderful works? And then will I profess unto them. I never knew you: depart from Me ye that work iniquity" (Matthew 7:22–23). Some are in the pulpit because their parents thought it might be nice. They have a son who is a doctor and another who is a lawyer. It would be nice to have a minister in the family. Some may feel that they have not done anything wrong to need a savior. These may be the hardest to reach. If we do not believe we are lost, we are not going to ask for salvation. If we are not drowning, we are not going to ask for a life preserver. No, Judas was never a believer. But the door is open to all who believe, even a Judas, if he wanted to enter the door. Have we entered? He is the Way, the Truth, the Life. Come on in. Not Rabbi, but Lord!

"And this is the Father's will which hath sent Me, that of all which He hath given Me I should lose nothing, but should raise it up again at the last day" (John 6:39).

BEAM 120

ALL IS VANITY

ECCLESIASTES 1:1–3

What is this book all about anyway? (Have you ever read it?) It starts out by saying “all is vanity” (Eccl. 1:1–3) and it ends by saying “all is vanity” (Eccl. 12:8). Webster says this word “vanity” means “something that is vain, empty, or valueless.” Then why write a book about nothing? Because mankind does not see the valuelessness of what mankind seeks out of life.

Mankind seeks money, fame, honor, prestige and strives to live here as long as possible to maintain this honor and fame and wealth, etc. Paul said that the love of money, not the money itself, but the love of money is the root of all kinds of evil (1 Timothy 6:10). Paul also tells us that men shall be “lovers of their own selves” and “lovers of pleasure” (2 Timothy 3:2, 4).

Men will give money to keep their name alive. They buy painted windows for a church that they may never bother to attend. They give money for hospitals, parks, public buildings, and streets to have them named after them. Giving is good if it given in the name of the Lord and for the right purpose.

But “all is vanity.” Man is here for a little while. James says like a vapor that appears for a little while and then vanishes (James 4:14). And then we leave all of the honor, wealth, prestige, and give an account to Him Who gave us this honor and wealth. What have we really done in this world?

Years ago I read about the richest man on earth. He was a billionaire when there were few multimillionaires. This man was richer than anyone could imagine. But then I read where he said he had never known a happy day in his life. This is hard even for me to believe. Not one happy day! Wow! You would think that a man could find some happy days with his yacht, or his winter home, or summer home. What good did all of that money do him? “All is vanity.” We leave our pleasures and our wealth, and all of our projects, and go on to the Righteous Judge of all the Earth. What does our wealth mean to Him?

The gold is His, the silver is His. He says He owns the “cattle upon a thousand hills," and every beast of the forest (Psalm 50:10). It is all His. And we can have it when we become members of His family.

So what are we struggling for? To make a name for ourselves? To amass wealth? To get honor and praise of men everywhere? We leave all of this. "All is vanity." But there is a beauty here also. What are we worth? God so loved this world of self-centered, honor-seeking, proud sinners that He gave His Son to die in their place so that they might have all of the righteousness of His Son (2 Corinthians 5:21). Love for those who are so unlovely! What a love this is! And at what price? "Herein is love, not that we loved God, but that He loved us, and sent His Son to be the propitiation for our sins" (1 John 4:10). And what does it cost us? The price of faith, believing what God says simply because God said it.

How much is that painting worth? Twenty dollars or a million? Well, it depends on how much someone is willing to pay for it. If I had some so-called art, a painting that looks horrible to me, I'd be glad to get rid of it. You cannot tell if he is riding a horse or a camel, if he is riding frontward or backwards, does he have two legs or six? You can buy it from me, cheap.

But how much is it worth? You cannot tell. Someone else may pay a fortune for it. It depends on how much someone is willing to pay. Our souls must be of tremendous value then, because look what Jesus was willing to pay for them. Do we thank Him for that? We should.

"How much better is it to get wisdom than gold!" (Proverbs 16:16)

BEAM 121

SEW AND SEWS

DORCAS

ACTS 9:39

Here is a beautiful story of a resurrection done by Peter to a woman named Dorcas. Dorcas means "gazelle." She is also called Tabitha which means the same thing. Different dialects. She is also called something else. The word for "disciple" used here is a feminine, the only place it is used in the Scriptures. She is a feminine "disciple" of Christ. She was a woman full of good works and almsdeeds which she did (Acts 9:36). What she did looks like sewing. She sewed coats and garments which the women of Joppa loved. She was loved so much, the women wept because Dorcas was now dead.

The other disciples heard that Peter was nearby in Lydda so they sent for him. I do not know what they expected him to do but they must have had some hope to even send for him to come, perhaps to give a eulogy. Peter follows the example of the Lord Jesus when He came to the home of Jairus. Jesus put them all out except Peter, James, and John, who came with Him. Then He raised Jairus' daughter. Peter puts them out. Then he kneels down and prays. God hears his prayer. Peter then turns to Tabitha and says "Tabitha, arise (Acts 9:40). And she does. There are still doubters today who claim the Book was written by men and has mistakes in it. No one argued with Peter about the genuineness of this miracle in the name of Jesus.

The Bible is quite full of miracles that were done in the beginning of the New Testament to show that this message of Christianity was genuine and true. Later on, in this same book of Acts, Paul also raises one from the dead. In Acts 20:10 he raises up Eutychus from the dead. This was proper since it happened while Paul was preaching to them well into the night. He probably started after dinner. Eutychus was sitting in a window in an upper chamber, the third loft. There were many lamps on so the heat went up to Eutychus. It got to be too much for Eutychus and he fell asleep and then fell down to his death. It must have been very high and no straw to shield his fall. So Paul goes down to Eutychus and restores him to life. So much for long sermons. But today we can fall asleep in the pew and not get hurt.

But what has all of this to do with me or you? From what we read Tabitha, or Dorcas, made her sewing her gift to the Lord. We can assume that she gave away many a coat or garment to cover the poor and the needy. This was her ministry. She did what she could. Alms giving was most likely from the garments she sewed, if the person could afford to pay for it. That money would be given to the poor. If the person was too poor, then the garment went to the poor without pay. She was a wonderful worker and loved by many who mourned her death. So what does this say to us? We do not have to stand up on Sunday and preach from a pulpit. We do not need to take a text for our sermonizing. Whatever she had she used for the glory of God. If we can sew, we can sew for the Lord. If we are a plumber, we can use our plumbing for the Lord. If we are an automobile mechanic, we can use our mechanical knowledge for the Lord.

What is it we have? What is our gift or special talent? Remember how God asked Moses what it was he had in his hand (Exodus 4:2)? Moses said a rod, that is, a stick. Then God told him to use it for the Lord.

What is that in your hand? A needle? Then use that needle for the Lord. Is it a shovel? Use that shovel for the Lord. Whatever it is we have, it was given to us by the Lord and we can give it back to Him in service. Yes, she sewed, for the Lord. We can sing for the Lord. We can paint for the Lord. I knew a house painter who was a faithful witness for the Lord. He was not a "star" or a famous person. But when he died there were dozens of people whose houses he painted, even including the Mayor of the city, who came to his funeral because of this simple house painter's testimony for the Lord. So sew for the Lord, paint for the Lord, paper hang for the Lord. "And whatever you do in word or deed, do all in the name of the Lord Jesus, giving thanks to God and the Father by Him" (Colossians 3:17).

BEAM 122

THE JUDGMENTS

PLURAL THAT IS

Hasn't everyone heard about the judgment? Even non-church goers have some idea that there is a judgment coming. They may be trusting in their being "good" when they think about it. However, there are many Bible teachers that talk about "The Judgment." I was in a Sunday School class as a visitor when the subject was "The Judgment." I asked which one? The teacher thought I was talking about the seven letters to the seven churches in Revelation 1 and 2. Or, maybe he thought I was nuts.

There are really seven judgments in the Scriptures and we should be familiar with them. Three of them are for the believer. Then, there are the other four. All of these judgments concern different people or places or times. We should not be surprised at the number seven. Isn't it the number of completeness, or some would say the perfect number? So let's look at these judgments.

1. The believer's past judgment. This is the judgment where the penalty for sin was accomplished by Christ on the cross. If we are believers, then we also died with Him on that cross. That is our first judgment. Paul says in Romans 6:6–9 "Knowing that our old man is crucified with Him, that the body of sin might be destroyed . . . for he that is dead is freed from sin . . . Now if we be dead in Christ . . . death hath no more dominion." That is a past judgment for believers, at the cross. That is where the penalty for our sins was paid for by Christ.

2. The believer's present judgment. This judgment is one that goes on all through our lives. It is for us to judge ourselves. This judgment is for fellowship. We cannot walk in darkness with Him Who is the Light. If we sin, and we will, then we confess our sin and are cleansed to stay in fellowship with Him. If we ignore this judgment then He must judge us. Sometimes the sins may be flagrant and so unbecoming a saint of God that He judges, and He may bring sickness upon us, or even death. Paul tells us that we should judge ourselves. "For this cause many are weak and sickly among you, and many sleep (are dead) for if we would judge ourselves we should not be judged.

But when we are judged we are chastened of the Lord that we should not be condemned with the world" (1 Corinthians 11:28–32). We are not lost, but we may lose our witness and a reward. We do lose fellowship with the Savior. But He provides for us. "If we confess our sins, He is faithful and just to forgive us our sins, and to cleanse us from all unrighteousness" (1 John 1:9).

3. The believer's future judgment. This takes place after the believer leaves this world, either by death or by Rapture. There will be a Judgment Seat of Christ, before which we all appear. This is not for salvation, or finding out if we are lost. That penalty was paid. This judgment is to reward the believer and grant him according to what he did while on earth. "For we must all appear before the judgment seat of Christ; that every one may receive the things done in his body, according to that he hath done. Whether it be good or bad" (2 Corinthians 5:10).

This Judgment Seat is called the Bema, which is the name given to the judgment seat at the Olympics. This is only for believers. Only believers are alive and can run the race. Dead men cannot run and are not allowed to compete. The Olympics gave out some crowns of leaves. He will give out more permanent and glorious crowns. We are told that there is one Foundation, Christ. We may build on that foundation things like gold, silver, precious stones, or some wood, hay, and stubble. Those precious stones and silver and gold will not be hurt by the fire. The wood hay and stubble is what I did in the flesh. It will go up in smoke. Yet we are told that "If any man's work shall be burned he shall suffer loss, but he himself shall be saved yet so as by (through) fire" (1 Corinthians 3:12–15). We are not lost again but we may lose His "Well done thou good and faithful servant."

4. The judgment of the Gentiles. This takes place when He returns to earth to reign for 1000 years. Matthew 25:31–33 tells us how, when the King returns, He will separate the sheep from the goats among the nations, i.e. the Gentiles. Their judgment will depend on how they treated Israel.

5. The judgment of the nation Israel. Israel shall be judged also when the Messiah returns. Ezekiel 20:35–38 tells us how He will bring Israel into the wilderness as He did when He brought them out of Egypt, and He will purge out the rebels from among them.

6. The judgment of the angels, including Satan. After the 1000

year reign of the Messiah He lets Satan out of the bottomless pit, where He put him for the 1000 years. Even when there has been peace on earth and good will toward men for a 1000 years, there will still be some rebellious people who do not want Jesus to reign over them. Satan gets a little time to round them up for a final battle. The devil is then cast into his final place of punishment, a lake of fire and brimstone, to be tormented day and night for ever and ever (Revelation 20:10). Fallen angels also will be sent with him and the saints shall judge the angels (1 Corinthians 6:3).

7. The Great White Throne Judgment of the lost. "And I saw a great white throne, and Him that sat on it . . . and I saw the dead, small and great, stand before God . . . and whosoever was not found written in the book of life was cast into the lake of fire" (Revelation 20:11–15). This is the judgment of the lost who have rejected God's mercy and grace and rejected the Lord Jesus. They also are sent into the lake of fire where Satan is, and for whom this lake was prepared. This place was not made for the lost but for Satan, but those who follow him will end up with him. (Matthew 25:41). Don't be there.

That is the end and final judgment. No more rebellion, no more chances, no more willfulness of sinful man. It is over, done, finished. Eternity without sin, suffering and death can go on and on and on and on. The saints rejoice in the glory of God forever and forever and forever

Be with the Lord, by faith, so you will be with Him for ever and ever. It's by grace through faith. Be there!

"And I saw a new heaven and a new earth; for the first heaven and the first earth were passed away; and there was no more sea" (Revelation 21:1).

BEAM 123

PAUL'S LABOR PAINS

GALATIANS 4:19

Yes, that is correct. Many times women tell their husbands, or other men, that men just do not know what it is like to give birth to a child. How right they are. And most men, if not all, are glad it is that way. It is painful. Yet, here is the Apostle Paul not only saying he gave birth to believers in Galatia but that he is giving birth to them a second time. This is not saying that he bore twins. This is saying that he birthed some children and he has to do it all over again with the same children. What kind of labor is this?

Paul's normal greetings in his letters are usually friendly and thankful. He says to the Romans "I thank my God through Jesus Christ for you all" (Romans 1:8). In 1 Corinthians 1:4 he says "I thank my God always on your behalf." To the Ephesians He remarks that I "cease not to give thanks for you, making mention of you in my prayers" (1:16). Likewise he states "I thank my God upon every remembrance of you" (Philippians 1:3). In the Galatian letter, however, there is a noticeable difference. There was some trouble there and Paul comes directly to the point.

The Gospel he had preached to them was now so polluted that it was no longer the Gospel. "I marvel that ye are so soon removed from Him that called you into the grace of Christ unto another Gospel, which is not another" (Galatians 1:6–7). Then he states in strict terms "But though we, or an angel from heaven, preach any other gospel unto you, than that which we have preached unto you, let him be accursed" (1:8). That is mighty strong language. There is only one Gospel. By grace through faith.

But this error, which they have heard and some have listened to, is about the very heart of the Gospel. Either we are saved by grace alone, through faith, plus nothing, or we have been listening to a false gospel, which Paul says "is not another" gospel, but a false and corrupt religion (1:6–7). That teaching, that says we must keep some kind of a law, or some kind of religious standards, is the great divider among believers and non-believers. Even some true believers, when they are babes in Christ, believe they must live up to a certain standard of religious principles or they are lost again. They have been taught that. There had been some legalists, called Judaisers, who told the Galatians that faith was not enough. They also had to keep the Law of Moses, or at least be circumcised.

Paul says to them "O foolish Galatians, who hath bewitched you that ye should not obey the truth?" (3:1). This is important doctrine. Either we are saved by grace through faith plus nothing, or we are trusting our own goodness before God to help us make peace with God. Since this is the heart of the Gospel, it is like starting over again with the ABC's of the Gospel. Paul says he labored in birth pangs once to bring them to Christ, now he must labor a second time. Whew! Twice for the same babies! He wants to form Christ in them (4:19). That is what salvation is all about. Not just saving sinners from an eternal hell but "that He (Jesus) might be the firstborn among many brethren" (Romans 8:29). God wants more than one Son in heaven, but they must be perfect, as His only begotten Son is. So He gives us the righteousness of Christ by grace. The Holy Spirit comes to abide in the believer and leads him to grow in the Word so that we become more like Him. You hear people say "He looks just like his father." That is what Paul wants people to say about the Galatians and us. I wonder if anyone ever says that about me? But now he must start over again and teach the ABC's of the Gospel.

Christ cannot be formed in us until He is first found in us. We must be made alive before we can grow. This is where the birth pangs come in. Paul wants to present us perfect. "And the very God of peace sanctify you wholly; and I pray God your whole spirit and soul and body be preserved blameless unto the coming of our Lord Jesus Christ" (1 Thessalonians 5:23). Anything less than salvation by grace through faith is another gospel, which is a false gospel. Stick with Paul. His Gospel is by grace alone.

BEAM 124

CHARGE IT, PLEASE

PHILEMON

Aren't you glad you live in a plastic society? You do not have to carry around a wad of dollar bills anymore. "Just put it on my credit card."

The Book of Philemon tells us a story of what may be the world's oldest charge account. Philemon was brought to the Lord by the Apostle Paul. This same Philemon had a slave who stole something and then ran a thousand miles away to get lost in the big city–Rome. This was a desperate act. Slaves had no rights under Roman law. They had no rights of appeal. Greeks spoke of slaves as "animated tools."

There was no such thing as murdering your slave. A slave was your property. You can do anything you want to do with your own "tool." That is all he was, just a tool. The worst manner of execution was reserved for runaway slaves, or rebellious slaves, and the worst of criminals. They were crucified. About a year before this was written, while Paul was in Rome, and perhaps Onesimus also was there, a Roman Senator, Pedanius Secundus, was killed by a slave. The law demanded that all of the slaves of the household should be executed; men, women and children. There were so many in this household, 400, that even the Romans thought it harsh punishment. But the Law demanded it and the Senate, the highest court of appeals, said the law must be carried out. All 400 were put to death, innocent men, innocent women, and innocent children.

By chance (?) this fugitive, Onesimus, heard Paul preaching the Gospel while Paul was a prisoner in Rome and he was led to the Lord. He was still an escaped slave with a price on his head. Paul, as an apostle, could have ordered Philemon to take him back. That was not the path Paul chose. Instead he says "If he has harmed you in any way, or stolen anything from you, charge me for it, I will pay it back" (vs.18 TLB).

This is more than a happy-ending story. It contains the heart of the Gospel.

Substitute the Lord Jesus for the Apostle Paul.

Substitute God the Father for Philemon.

Substitute me, and you, for the runaway slave.

What do you have now?

Do I owe God a great debt of sin, which I can never repay? Do I have a death sentence hanging over me? Have I no hope of ever paying what I owe? Yes to all of the above. But the Lord Jesus says "Whatever this sinner owes, put it down to My account, I will pay it." He will pay it. And He did. When He went to the cross He paid what I owed. He was made "sin for us, Who knew no sin; that we might be made the righteousness of God in Him" (2 Cor. 5:21).

What a beautiful story. The world's oldest charge account! You can charge it to Him. Have you opened your account yet? He is still waiting to give you your credit card that says "Paid in Full." The debt must be paid either by you or by Him. There is no way you can pay it. He has already paid it. You can have your card now. Have you received Him yet? No credit card till you do.

"For what saith the scripture? Abraham believed God, and it was counted (accredited, put down on his account, logged in the ledger) unto him for righteousness" (Romans 4:3).

"But to him that worketh not, but believeth on Him that justifieth the ungodly, his faith is counted (imputed, put down to his account) for righteousness" (Romans 4:5).

BEAM 125

SEEING GOD

"Blessed are the pure in heart, for they shall see God"

MATTHEW 5:8

Is He saying that we shall really see God? It sure sounds like it. But why is it I do not see this taught anywhere? Oh, yes, I am told that those who are "pure in heart" shall see God, in the person of the Lord Jesus. But would this be saying anything? The impure in heart saw Him, even some very impure scoundrels saw Him.

There were Pharisees and Scribes and Lawyers who argued with Him and clamored for His death. There were self-righteous hypocrites who wanted Him put to death. They saw Him. So does the Lord Jesus mean that the "pure in heart" shall see Him? What would that teach then?

Some, in fact many ministers do not want to say anything about being lost, or the hell that awaits those who die still lost, but Jesus said more about it than anyone else. Look at what He says about those people who were seeing Him. "Woe unto you, scribes and Pharisees, hypocrites for ye compass sea and land to make one proselyte, and when he is made, ye make him twofold more the child of hell than yourselves" (Matthew 23:15). Or this, "Woe unto you, scribes and Pharisees, hypocrites, for ye are like unto whited sepulchres, which indeed appear beautiful outward but are within full of dead men's bones, and of uncleanness," (Matthew 23:27). "Ye serpents, ye generation of vipers, how can ye escape the damnation of hell? (Matthew 23:33).

Yet, this generation of snakes saw Jesus and contended with Him constantly. Are these "the pure in heart" that shall see God in the person of Jesus? What then would that be saying? If they can "see God" by seeing Jesus, then anyone should be able to "see God." What would that say? Nothing, absolutely nothing. Am I alone in this? Do angels see God? Of course. Jesus said "take heed that ye despise not one of these little ones, for I say unto you, That in heaven their angels do always behold the face of my Father which is in heaven" (Matthew 18:10). Ok, so we are not angels, and never will be, but if angels behold the face of the Father, Who Is Spirit, why cannot the saints, after they are given their new eyes? Do the saints behold angels? Of course they do, when God fixes their eyes so they can behold angels. Joseph and Mary both saw angels. God fixed their eyes temporarily so they could.

When Stephen was being stoned to death he looked up to heaven and saw "the Son of man standing on the right hand of God" (Acts 7:56). Now how did Stephen know it was God? He saw Jesus and someone alongside of Jesus. If that Someone were the Holy Spirit then he was still seeing someone who is spirit.

Why are we so afraid to admit there is a problem here, that seeing God is not the same thing as the pure in heart seeing Jesus? We cannot see God with these eyes, now. Paul was blinded after he saw the glory of Christ. But somehow, he was able to "see" Christ in His resurrected glory. We will have bodies that are not subject to the same laws that they now are. What does it say? "The pure in heart shall see God." Not any heart that we have now. Our hearts are not pure.

How does a can of worms look to you? Ugh! Unless you are a fisherman. They may tempt you to go fishing. But ask your wife what she thinks of that can of dirty slimy crawling worms, Ugh! "You have these for bait? Don't come near me with them." Our hearts are worse than that. Look at what comes out of our hearts. "For from within, out of the heart of men, proceed evil thoughts, adulteries, fornications, murders, thefts, deceit, lasciviousness, an evil eye, blasphemy, pride, foolishness: All these evil things come from within, and defile the man" (Mark 7:21–23). Have I left out anything?

This is what man's heart is like! I think the worms look better. I'd rather have the worms. I do not mean to defend Satan but he does get blamed for a lot of things that come out of the evil heart of man. So the can of worms needs to be cleaned up.

That is just what salvation does for us. It gives us a new heart, one that is pure. "If any man be in Christ, he is a new creature; old things are passed away; behold, all things are become new" (2 Corinthians 5:17). I am sure glad of that. My old heart is not fit for heaven, much less to behold God. But I have a new heart in Christ. With that heart, and no worms, I can some day, when I get my new eyes, behold the face of God. Yes, the Father on the throne. What a gracious and loving God He is to grant such mercy to an undeserving sinner. Praise be the Lord!

BEAM 126

WHAT CAN BABIES DO?

MARK 10:15

In Mark 10:15 the Lord Jesus said "Anyone who refuses to come to God, as a little child (paidion), will never be allowed into His kingdom" (TLB). That word "paidion" was used for infants. The Lord Jesus was a "paidion" of eight days old when He was circumcised (Luke 2:21).

What does this mean? How can we become like a baby? It is almost like the question Nicodemus asked in John 3:4 when he said "How can a man be born when he is old?" Good question. Well how can we become babies again, and what can babies do if we become babies? It cannot clean itself, it cannot bathe itself, it cannot clothe itself. What can it do for itself? Nothing. He must absolutely depend on someone else to do all for him. A "paidion" can do absolutely nothing for itself. It must rely on someone else. Everything must be done for it.

We must become like that. We must completely depend on Jesus Christ Who has done all of the work of salvation for us. As long as we believe we can help God save ourselves, we are not yet able to receive the gift of life. We must depend on Him alone.

When we do, He will cleanse us from all sin. 1 John 1:7: "The blood of Jesus Christ His Son cleanseth us from all sin." Babies cannot clean themselves.

He will clothe us. In 2 Corinthians 5: 1–2, Paul says that we are in an earthly house, our bodies, that he calls a tabernacle after the Old Testament Tabernacle, which was a tent. These are temporary abiding places. He says we have a building from God, a permanent building, which is a glorified body. He wishes to be clothed with this building, which is from God. Tents are all right for camping out on a vacation but who wants to live in a tent permanently? We have better buildings. In John 14:2 Jesus said "In My Father's house are many mansions . . . I go to prepare a place for you." He will clothe us with a better body and a permanent body that will not know sin, suffering, pain, death, and the things connected with this earth. And all done for us by another, Who has given us His righteousness for our sins (2 Corinthians 5:21).

He will feed us. The children of Israel ate manna in the wilderness. But they still died. He says He is the true, the living Bread from heaven. Whoever eats of that bread will live forever (John 6:58). What more can He do? Yes, babies can do nothing for themselves. Someone must do it all for them. It is natural for a mother to care for this infant she has brought into the world. But God loves the unlovely, the sinful, the willful, the rebellious. He loves and gives Himself to care for sinners.

It is hard for grown men to become babies in their hearts. That is the problem. Babies cannot resist your help, but grown people can refuse to be helped. They think they are good enough, they are not as bad as some, or they will try harder to be "good." All to no avail. "All we like sheep have gone astray; we have turned every one to his own way; and the Lord hath laid on Him the iniquity of us all" (Isaiah 53:6). "As it is written, There is none righteous, no not one" (Romans 3:10).

What a beautiful story. God is willing to care for our every need. But we must become like babies.

"By grace are ye saved through faith . . . it is the gift of God" (Ephesians 2:8). We get it when we get small enough to receive it.

BEAM 127

IGNORANCE IS NO EXCUSE

"Because thou knewest not the time of thy visitation." These words of the Lord Jesus were spoken during that last week as He approached the Holy City as the triumphant King of Israel. The people at that time cried out "Blessed be the king that cometh in the name of the Lord" (Luke 19:38). But Jesus wept bitterly instead of rejoicing in what is called a triumphant entry. He said if Jerusalem "hadst known . . . the things which belong unto thy peace" (Luke 19:42). The good things that should happen to Jerusalem. Peace with the surrounding nations, the Gentiles. Jerusalem is to be the center of worship for the whole world. The ruler of the whole earth would be at Jerusalem. No, not New York, nor Paris, nor London, nor Moscow would be the center of political power, nor religious power, but little old Jerusalem. But now there is a judgment coming.

He gives a foretaste of what is coming. Jerusalem would be leveled to the ground, completely destroyed. Not one stone left upon another (Luke 19:44). And this did happen. In AD 70 the Roman general Titus wreaked havoc upon Jerusalem. The Roman Emperors were tired of all the trouble and rebellion this city had caused. His armies destroyed it as Jesus said, and it stayed destroyed for hundreds of years.

Jesus said the peace of Jerusalem was lost and destruction came instead of peace because "Thou knewest not the time of thy visitation." That time was when He came to Jerusalem and offered Himself to Jerusalem as her king. Yes, they shouted Hosannas when He came riding into the city, but a few days later they were yelling "Crucify Him, crucify Him." Is that fair? That they should be punished for not knowing? Can they defend themselves by saying that they were ignorant of the importance of that time? Not so.

Ignorance is no excuse BECAUSE there is no excuse for ignorance. She should have known. Jerusalem had the words of God's prophets who foretold what would happen. They told that one would be born of a virgin. He would be born in Bethlehem, that He would come into the city riding on a donkey. They had the Scriptures, and they had His miracles, and His words. "Never man spake as this man."

"Which of you convinceth me of sin?" (John 8:46). Here was a challenge. No one, not even His worst enemies, could show any sin in His life. Who else but Messiah could stand up to such a test? "Before Abraham was I AM" (John 8:58). Here was His claim to be God, the I AM of the Old Testament, the One who sent Moses into Egypt to bring out His people.

He raised the dead, one who was dead four days. He gave sight to the blind, He stilled the boisterous waves of the storm. He could create food before their eyes and feed thousands with a little lad's lunch. He came from the tribe of Judah, from the line of David, to bring salvation to them. A forerunner, John the Baptist, cried out that this One was the Messiah and John said the Lamb of God which taketh away the sins of the world (John 1:29). And they knew that John the Baptist was a man sent from God. What more did they need? They had no excuse.

And what is our excuse? We have the Word of God that was written by some forty men, over a period of some 1500 years, overseen by the Holy Spirit, and given by inspiration of God (2 Timothy 3:16) so that it is without error. We have an empty tomb that tells us that He is risen. We have the Holy Spirit Who creates a new life in those who believe the message. We have nearly 2000 years of the church which is built upon the One Foundation, the Rock Jesus. We have the testimony of millions of sinners who have come to Him and have had their lives changed. Ignorance? We have no excuse. Let us rejoice in knowing the time of OUR VISITATION. He has come. He is risen. He has ascended. He will return. Are we alive in Him? If they had no excuse, we have less. Messiah has come. Hosanna!

BEAM 128

WHY ARE WE HERE?

1 CORINTHIANS 10:31

The most famous of all catechisms, the Westminster Confession, put together centuries ago by men of God, and used for generations by Bible believing churches, begins with a question, "What is the chief end of man?" It then gives the answer to that question. "Man's chief end is to glorify God and enjoy Him for ever."

The word "glory" comes from the word "doxa" which we recognize in doxology or paradox. It can mean brightness, as in Acts 22:11 when Paul was blinded by the brightness of Christ's glory. It can mean "splendor, radiance, magnificence," anything that catches the eye, such as in Matthew 6:29, where we read of the splendor of Solomon and his court. It can mean "honor," like in Romans 3:23 where we read that all have sinned and come short of the glory of God.

Let us look at the first part of that statement. How can I, who am but the dust of the earth, glorify God?

I glorify God by WHAT I SAY.
"Whoso offereth praise glorifieth Me" (Psalm 50:23)

Matt. 12:34, "out of the abundance of the heart the mouth speaketh." James 3:10, "but the mouth of man speaks both blessing and cursing." The cursing should not be. Peter tells us, in his first epistle that we are a holy priesthood, chosen "to offer up spiritual sacrifices, acceptable to God by Jesus Christ" (1Pet 2:5). We are priests offering up praises to God. My words can glorify God.

I glorify God by WHAT I DO.
This is the principle for all of life.

"All things are naked and opened unto the eyes of Him with Whom we have to do," the writer of Hebrews tells us (Heb 4:13). There are no secrets. There is nothing hid from His eyes, so we live as in His presence always.

"Whether therefore ye eat, or drink, or whatsoever ye do, do all to the glory of God" (1 Cor. 10:31). There are no little things that are "too little" to pray about. Remember how even Joshua was fooled by the Gibeonites. (Joshua 9)

I glorify God by HOW I SUFFER.

When Lazarus suffered and the Apostles wanted to leave immediately to see him cured, the Lord stayed two more days. The Lord Jesus said that Lazarus' suffering was not unto death, but for the "glory of God, that the Son of God might be glorified thereby" (John 11:4). Because of Lazarus' death, many believed on the Lord Jesus. Should Christians get sick? Are they out of God's will? Is it a sign that God does not love us? Ask Lazarus.

See in Eccl. 9:1–4 how wrong values by man are placed upon the outside circumstances.

"All things come alike to all; there is one event to the righteous, and to the wicked; to the good and to the clean, and to the unclean" (Ecclesiastes 9:2). The rain falls on the good and the evil. How do I receive it?

I glorify God by WHAT I AM.

"Herein is my Father glorified, that ye bear much fruit, so shall ye be my disciples" (John 15:8). "Ye are the light of the world" (Matt 5:14). Light shines, it cannot help it. "The fruit of the Spirit is love, joy, peace, longsuffering, gentleness, goodness, faith" (Galatians 5:22). Are we glorifying God? We can, by all that we say and do and suffer and are. "Praise ye the Lord. Praise the Lord, O my soul. While I live will I praise the Lord: I will sing praises unto my God while I have any being" (Psalm 146:1–2). "Give unto the Lord, O ye mighty, give unto the Lord glory and strength. Give unto the Lord the glory due unto His name; worship the Lord in the beauty of holiness" (Psalm 29:1–2).

BEAM 129

THE UNPARDONABLE SIN

MATTHEW 12:31

Oooh! This is sounding so theological. So deep. But let's make it simple, if we can. There are theological discussions of just what this unpardonable sin is and it can get complicated. Nothing is more complicated than a theologian when he sees a simple passage of Scripture.

I have heard a number of deep theologs talk about how this sin was calling the miracles of Jesus the work of Satan. And the verses are given. Matthew 12:31 states "Wherefore I say unto you all manner of sin and blasphemy shall be forgiven unto men; but the blasphemy against the Holy Ghost shall not be forgiven unto men." Does this mean that they, who called His miracles the work of Satan (verse 24), had committed this unpardonable sin? But would it be like the Lord Jesus to warn them of something after it was too late to do anything about it? Hardly. This would not fit into His character. Other theologs insist that we today cannot commit this unpardonable sin. On what grounds? Are there not some who today would deny His miracles just like those Pharisees did? They say it is all the work of demons, it is all a hoax. Especially those of another religion altogether.

But what does the Scripture say elsewhere. Acts 10:43 reads "To Him (Christ) give all the prophets witness that through His name whosoever believeth in Him shall receive remission of sins." Another verse that bears light upon this deep subject is Acts 13:39. This verse states "And by Him (Jesus) all that believe are justified from all things from which ye could not be justified by the Law of Moses." So what sin is not forgivable, which is the same thing as being unpardonable? Once more take a look at it. "They that believe are justified." And the other one, "Whosoever believeth in Him shall receive remission." So according to these verses the one sin that is unforgivable or unpardonable is . . . not believing.

Maybe I am too naive or not able to comprehend the deep deep theological revelations of Scripture. But I do not believe Jesus would warn people of some unforgivable sin which they had already committed and it was already too late for them to do anything about it. What good would that do?

Can you really picture the Lord Jesus saying, "Oops! Sorry about that! You did it and there is nothing I can do about it. If I had just spoken a little sooner, perhaps this would not have happened. After all, I knew what you were going to say before you said it, since I am the Great I Am of Scripture, the God of Israel. I know all things before they happen. I was ten minutes too late. Sorry about that!"

But what does Matthew 12:31 have to do with this sin that is unpardonable? It is a warning. If they continue to go on with this attitude of unbelief, if they continue to resist the evidence of the Holy Spirit, if they continue to deny the very works of the Savior, they will continue to harden their hearts, like Pharaoh did, and eventually die in unbelief. That is unpardonable, that is unforgivable. It is the unbelief that cannot be forgiven. And ignorance is no excuse, for there is no excuse for ignorance. They could have known and should have known. We also have no excuse. We can know and should know.

You know how we get callouses? You can keep pressing against your skin until it builds up a thick layer to resist what hurts. You keep building up until it doesn't hurt any longer. You can do this with your conscience also. Paul writes about those last days ""Speaking lies in hypocrisy, having their conscience seared with a hot iron (1 Timothy 4:2). If we keep on resisting the message, our conscience will build up a layer of resistance till it no longer bothers us when we hear the preacher giving forth the message of salvation. Then we are on dangerous ground. We may discover our error too late. It's over. It's done. We are finished. Kaput! Unbelief is unforgivable. And it is so unnecessary.

BEAM 130

GIVING ALL—HOWEVER SMALL

MARK 12:44

"Did you see that? Did you see how much Yitzaak gave? Wow! He must really love Adonai."

This is what many a person must have thought as they watched the rich men of the rich families toss money into the offering bowls. Many of them made the coin clang out loud so their giving was seen and heard of men. They also loved to be seen praying, so they made long prayers. This showed to the world that they were very religious men and very generous men. Jesus told us that we should not make a show of our giving, or our praying.

Matthew 6:1–2: "Take heed that ye do not your alms before men, to be seen of them: otherwise ye have no reward of your Father which is in heaven. Therefore when thou doest thine alms, do not sound a trumpet before thee, as the hypocrites do in the synagogues and in the streets that they may have glory of men. Verily I say unto you, They have their reward." Yes, they have been paid in full. They wanted to be seen and heard of men and they got just what they wanted. But they did not have any reward from God.

Some people like to show how much they love the Lord, whether they do or not, by showing people how much money they give, or how long they can pray in public. There is nothing wrong with praying in public, if we do it unto the Lord. The pastor of the church may lead the congregation in a public prayer. Nothing wrong with that. There may be an offering plate passed around and we give to the Lord's work. It should be done as inconspicuously as possible, but it is public. We do not show our trust in the Lord, or our religiosity by how much we give. We should not compare what we give with what others give. There could be some poor widows, barely struggling to pay all their bills and still give a little to God's work.

Some rich people may give a small fortune to have their names remembered by donating church windows with their names inscribed on them. There have been extremely wealthy men who have left fortunes to build churches, or colleges. This is all right also, if it is not done to keep their name alive. The purpose of giving should be to give to Him for His work, and it is to be given according to our means. Paul says we should give like someone sowing his field. "But this I say, He which soweth sparingly shall reap also sparingly, and he which soweth bountifully shall also reap bountifully" (2 Corinthians 9:6).

What did the Lord say when a poor widow threw in 2 mites? A mite was as small a coin as you could have, 1/8 of a cent. We can hardly buy anything with a penny any more. She gave two mites to the temple, a fourth of a cent. Yes, that was it. And some people want to cheat her out of half of her giving by speaking of "The Widow's Mite." It was two mites. But how can two mites be greater that all the rest of the giving put together? There must have been several shekels of silver, or maybe even gold, given in the temple coffers. How come?

It was because the poor widow, and He does call her "poor," tossed in all she had, and He does say she gave "all" she had. She could have rationalized and said "I will give half of what I have to the Lord's work." She might even have said, "The Lord knows I do not have much so I cannot give. He will understand." No! She gave "ALL her living." Somehow the Lord would provide, she thought.

That is what counts. It is not how big our gift is. Is it our all? No, it does not have to be all of our money. Our money is now His money anyway. Are we giving Him all our lives that He has saved by giving His ALL for us? It may not be much, my little life, but is ALL of it given to Him. What is better, the little reward of men's praise that we get down here, or His "Well done thou good and faithful servant" up there? She gave her ALL, however small it looked in men's eyes. What a beautiful story! Are we doing like she did? Are we giving everything we have to Him? He gave everything for us.

BEAM 131

COUNTING THE COST, IF YOU CAN

LUKE 14:28

How much does the Lord Jesus cost? Is He for sale? And, if He were, would I have enough to buy Him? I thought I was completely bankrupt, lost in sin, and dead in my sins, having no hope and without God (Ephesians 2:1, 12, 13). My righteousnesses, that is the very best that I have, my righteousnesses are as filthy rags in God's sight (Isaiah 64:6). This is what God says. My neighbors might think I am a nice guy and my friends (both of them) might think I am a good guy. But God has a different standard. His standard is absolute perfection, nothing less. My filthy rags are the best I can offer God. Let's not talk about the worst things I have to offer Him.

That word "filthy" is used of the rags that were used by lepers to cover their putrefying sores, and their mouths. It is also used for menstrual cloths used by women. Ugh! Let's move on. I remember years ago seeing one of my best friends on a Sunday morning. I must have caught him by surprise because he had a chest full of medals. He looked like a young General Patton decorated with a bar and about six, or maybe eight, medals hanging from that top bar. He looked embarrassed. I can see why now. I asked him what all those bars meant. He looked rather sheepishly at me and almost in a whisper said, "These are for six years of perfect Sunday School attendance." No wonder he was embarrassed. From the language he used I never thought he went to Sunday School. What righteousness! Filthy language, but perfect Sunday School attendance. That should impress God!

Suppose I come before God and say to Him "Look at me Lord, look at me. I have attended Sunday School perfectly for six years. Aren't I a good boy, Lord? Huh?" God says "Rags. Filthy rags."

It takes more than what my neighbors think is a "good person" to meet God's demands. He demands absolute 100 per cent perfection. So how can I buy Jesus, if He were for sale? I cannot.

Yet I have heard many times, from the pulpit, that we, sinners that is, must count the cost before we come to Him. If that were true then salvation is not a gift of God's grace. Ephesians 2:8–9 must be wrong when it states that it is "By grace are ye saved through faith, and that not of yourselves, it is the gift of God, not of works lest any man should boast." So what is the Lord Jesus talking about when He says we must count the cost? Simple enough. If we count the cost it means our everything, but not to be saved. **COMING TO HIM** means salvation. He told us that if any man come to Him He will in no wise cast out that one (John 6:37). But to be a disciple, that is another story. That is **COMING AFTER HIM**. Salvation is a free gift of God's grace. We cannot earn a gift. We earn a salary for what we have worked for. We do not have to be ashamed to take our pay check if we have done our job. It is what the boss owes us. A gift is another matter. It costs nothing to become a Christian. It costs everything to be a disciple, a follower of Christ.

Who is it that is building a tower and fighting a war (Luke 14:28–33)? It is the Lord Himself, not us. He is building His church. He is in a battle with that spirit enemy, Satan. The question is can He depend on us? We must give Him our all. When General Eisenhower was planning the invasion of the European mainland he needed to know how many he could absolutely depend on. Suppose he had a small army of a few thousand men who told their commanding officer that they would like to help General Eisenhower, but they did not like fighting. Guns scared them. You could get hurt shooting guns. "If it's all right with you, Sir, we would stay here in England and sort the mail or ship food packages over to France. We're afraid of guns, Sir." What would Eisenhower say to them? They cannot be his soldiers. He cannot use them in the war. "I need men I can count on. Men who will risk their all in battle," He would say.

That is what this passage is all about. We cannot buy Jesus. We have nothing to buy Him with. He is not for sale. But He is asking for us to count the cost to follow Him. It costs nothing to be a Christian. It costs everything to be His disciple and follower. So what is the answer? Do we just come to Him and let someone else fight the battle? Or do we take up His cross and follow after Him, not counting the cost because it costs everything? We should be wholly committed to our Savior and give all we have as followers. Saved by grace, saved to work, soldiers giving our all to Him, Who gave His all for us. That is what it costs!

BEAM 132

WHAT MUST I DO?

ACTS 16:30

From the many religions, and many churches, one would think that there is a real problem about how one gets to heaven. It really comes down to two simple things, two simple ways that are taught. There may be hundreds of religions teaching various ways to get to heaven but they all teach basically one approach. You must somehow appease an angry God. You must DO SOMETHING FOR GOD to turn away his wrath. The other approach is to RECEIVE SOMETHING FROM GOD Who has already received the sacrifice of His Son. He GIVES the gift of eternal life to sinners.

If God were to ask us to do something difficult, like pushing a peanut down the highway with our noses for a half mile, we would all get to the store today and buy some peanuts. We might get the largest ones or the roundest ones, but we would have highways loaded with people trying to earn their way to heaven. But if it is not that complicated, then we have trouble getting agreement. Even churches do not accept the simple plan of salvation. We are taught by some that we must be baptized, or we must join their church, or we must live up to a certain standard that the church sets for us. You would think that the true answer is difficult to dig out of the Scriptures. It is a deep deep subject. Hmm!

Yet, the very question of what one must do to be saved is in the Bible, and the answer is given in the Bible, and it is not hard to find it in the Bible. It is Acts 16:30. The jailor was responsible to keep Paul and Silas and any other prisoner. Keep meant just that. He forfeited his life, under Roman law, if he allowed one prisoner to escape. Paul and Silas had been beaten and thrown in jail. Around midnight these two evangelists, these new folk, these Christian preachers, started singing while in jail Acts 16:25). They may not have sounded like opera singers or popular singers or crooners, but they were happy enough to be beaten for the Lord Jesus that they started singing.

Nothing is said about the singing waking anybody up. When the earthquake struck it was different. It shook the prison so violently that the doors were thrown open. That would seem to be enough but this was no ordinary earthquake. It actually loosed the prisoners from their handcuffs. Now that is a special earthquake! The guard naturally thought the prisoners would not be hanging around the jailhouse now. They had a break. "Let's get going," he could hear them screaming, in his mind anyway. Rather than have Rome kill him, he thought it best to take his own life. He is about to commit suicide when Paul yells out, "Do thyself no harm for we are all here" (Acts 16:28). Why the other prisoners did not run away I cannot explain. Perhaps Paul's preaching got to them also. They were all there, all of them.

So the jailor is stunned. No one ran away! No one escaped! Wow! What is it about these two "Christian preachers?" That is when it came home to him. They had something he did not have. Something he needed, something he may have searched for for years. So he asks the question "Sirs, what must I do to be saved?" (Acts 16:30).

And the answer is given. "Believe on the Lord Jesus Christ, and thou shalt be saved, and thy house" (Acts 16:31). No, you do not have to raise your hand. You do not have to come forward. You do not have to join a church either, or sing in the choir, or give money to the church. It is a free gift. One only has to take the gift that God offers. Faith is the handle that receives the free gift of God's grace. That is all. But it must be done if we are to have eternal life. We must believe. And if any man comes to Him in faith, He has promised never to leave that person, never, ever (Hebrews 13:5). Many have never asked the question. The answer is clearly given. Only a theologian could miss the point here. Please, don't you miss it. You ask, Paul answers. "Believe on the Lord Jesus Christ and thou shalt be saved" (Acts 16:31).

BEAM 133

REJOICE, ALWAYS
I COMMAND YOU
1 THESSALONIANS 5:16

John 11:35 reads "Jesus wept." This verse is considered by many to be the shortest verse in the Bible. And in some respects that is true. But if you were to see the original language you would find a verse that is even shorter. John 11:35 has two words and 9 letters, in the English. 1 Thessalonians 5:16 has two words and 15 letters, in the English.

In the original language, however, John 11:35 has three words and 16 letters. 1Thessalonians 5:16 has two words and 14 letters. But that may be immaterial to the subject at hand. What is not academic is that 1 Thessalonians 5:16 is a command. It is imbedded among other commands.

We are commanded by Paul to rejoice evermore. But how can I always rejoice? I have troubles. I have worries. I am getting older. I have pains. Will I be able to pay for the nursing home? How can I always be rejoicing? Wouldn't I look foolish? In the next verse Paul says that we are to "Pray without ceasing." That word in the original is used to describe someone who has a hacking cough. Even under the worst conditions, someone in that state is not always coughing. But he still has the cough, even when he is not coughing at that moment. We should always be in a prayer attitude. We should always be in a state where we are aware of God's presence and listening for His direction, not audibly, but through the Word which we should constantly have in our hearts. That means we do not have to always be on our knees or prostrate before Him to be talking to Him. Pray-ers in the Scripture could look up to heaven, as Solomon did, and pray with their eyes open. There are various positions of prayer. But the attitude should always be there, like the cough, even if we are not audibly speaking words that others could hear. So then we may take the same attitude about rejoicing. We may not always be laughing, or even smiling, but the joy should be there always. So, what have we to be joyous about? Let's see.

We already have eternal life. We do not have to wait until we die to find out if we have it. God gave it to us as a free gift of His grace. He has promised not to take back His gift. He has promised never to leave us nor forsake us. God has given us the righteousness of Christ in exchange for our sins. He has said He has gone to prepare a place for us and He will come again and receive us unto Himself.

He has said there is a day coming when we will have new bodies that will know no pain, suffering, or death. He said a day is coming when all tears will be wiped away from our eyes. He has said there is such a beautiful and wonderful place waiting for us that we cannot fully imagine how beautiful it will be.

He has said our sins will be remembered against us no more. What else do we need?

In John 5:24 we have all three tenses used to give us joy. "He that heareth My word, and believeth on Him that sent Me HATH everlasting life (present tense), and SHALL NOT come into condemnation (future tense), but IS PASSED from death unto life (past tense)."

Psalm 37:23 "The steps of a good man are ordered by the Lord: and He delighteth in his way."

Proverbs 3:5–6 "Trust in the Lord with all thine heart; and lean not unto thine own understanding. In all thy ways acknowledge Him, and He shall direct thy paths."

Nehemiah 8:10 "For the joy of the Lord is your strength."

Psalm 68:4 "Sing unto God, sing praises to His name; extol Him that rideth upon the heavens by His name JAH, and rejoice before Him." Christians should be the happiest people in the world. Are we? Rejoice in the Lord! It's an order.

BEAM 134

IN THE FAMILY

JOHN 3:3, 1 Peter 1:23

If you saw the movie "Ben Hur" you may remember that Judah Ben Hur was adopted into the Roman family, the Roman who was captain of the ship that Hur was an oarsman on. This was the Roman style. We ordinarily think of adoption as something that is done to children, children who may not have any living parents, or are unwanted by their parents. In the Roman culture it was quite possible to be adopted as an adult. When a Roman did adopt an adult, he was signifying to the Romans that this adult was his heir and had his title as a member of his family. He could pass on all his wealth to this adopted adult heir.

This is one way to enter into a family. There are two other ways also. We are most familiar with the child who is born into the family. He is the joy of his parents and they gladly make him a part of the family and the family's estate. There is one other way to become a part of a family and that is not hard to see. We all know that we are in the family when we marry into a family. Without going into the in-laws (or outlaws), we become part of a new family when we marry.

What is all this about? Does it matter? It is a beautiful story about how we, poor sinners without hope, get into God's family. We get into God's family not just through one avenue but all three.

THE FIRST WAY: Jesus told Nicodemus "Except a man be born again he cannot see the kingdom of God" (John 3:3). Peter tells us just how this is done (in case some one might think it is by being baptized). Peter writes "Being born again, not of corruptible seed, but of incorruptible, by the word of God, which liveth and abideth forever" (1 Peter 1:23). The water is used in Scripture as a cleansing agent. Again in John 15:3 Jesus said "Ye are clean through the word which I have spoken unto you." So, by hearing the Word and heeding the Word, there is a new birth and we are in the family. If we are children, then we are heirs with Christ and joint heirs with Him, Paul says in Romans 8:17.

THE SECOND WAY: But we are also in the family through marriage. Right now it is an engagement but the wedding is coming.

Paul writes in 2 Corinthians 11:2 "I am jealous over you with godly jealousy, for I have espoused you to one husband, that I may present you as a chaste virgin to Christ." He is telling us we are engaged to Christ so we should act like it. That is the first step in a Scriptural wedding, the engagement. In most cases the engagement is done by others than the two who are to get married. In Genesis 24 we have the arrangement of Rebekah and Isaac done by a servant of Abraham. In our case it is the Holy Spirit that arranges for our engagement. He brings us to Jesus. And again, whatever the husband has is now shared by the bride. The second part of the wedding is the coming together of the two individuals. This is the union and will be done when Jesus returns. This puts us in the family a second way. And, whatever the husband has is also inherited by the wife, and shared by her.

THE THIRD WAY: The third way, as you might expect, is by adoption. Yes the church is adopted into the family of God. We read that "When the fulness of time was come, God sent forth His Son, made of a woman, made under the Law to redeem them that were under the Law, that we might receive the adoption of sons" (Galatians 4:4–5). Under Roman law the adopted child was made a legal heir of the family and the family fortune. So likewise we are to inherit what is the Son's.

All of this by grace. What a beautiful story. We poor, lost, helpless, and hopeless souls receive eternal life and the riches of Christ. We are in the family by faith. That is all we need! Are you in?

"Ye are blessed of the Lord which made heaven and earth" (Psalm 115:15).

"And if ye be Christ's, then are ye Abraham's seed, and heirs according to the promise" (Galatians 3:29).

BEAM 135

REPENT

WHAT DOES IT MEAN?

MATTHEW 21:29

This is something we all must do. Repent or else! But what does it mean? Is it being sorry? People believe that repentance is being sorry for something we did. We should not make this a difficult thing to understand. We must repent. But just what is it that we must do?

Judas Iscariot, who betrayed Jesus for a little silver, repented, in one sense. Judas repented himself when he saw things were not going the way he planned. Then he cast down the 30 pieces of silver and went out and hanged himself. The rope must have broken because we read that falling headlong he burst asunder in the midst, and all his bowels gushed out (Acts 1:18). What a way to die. But was he saved? Not at all.

We read in Acts 1:25 where Peter says Judas "by transgression fell, that he might go to his own place." No Bible teacher I know of would think this means with the Savior he betrayed. He has gone to a place of the dead, called "Sheol" in the Old Testament, and "Hades" in the New Testament, where he waits for the resurrection of the lost, when they stand before the Lord in Judgment. But "he repented himself." This is NOT the kind of repentance we MUST do.

Repentance may be accompanied with sorrow and grief, but that is not what the word means. Paul writes in 2 Corinthians 7:10 that "godly sorrow worketh repentance to salvation, not to be repented of, but the sorrow of the world worketh death." There is a sorrow of the world. Someone may be sorry he got caught after he robbed that bank, or stole that car, or had an adulterous relation with that woman. Sure they are sorry. Who wouldn't be. For a while you feel you have it made, and then you have to spend time in a jail for many years, or worse. Sure they are sorry. But they are a sorry lot. They have not repented in the Bible sense.

One could go into the various Greek words and the different shades of meaning. It is not necessary. It is so simple. The Lord Jesus tells us what the meaning is. Look at what He says. He says a certain man had two sons, and he came to the first one and said, "Son, go work in my vineyard." This son answered and said "I will not." That was a rather sharp and hard answer to give one's father. Then the man came to the second son and said the same thing. This second son said "I will, Dad," but he didn't go. Then we read in Matthew 21:29 that the first son, who said "No way," afterwards "repented and went." That is as simple as it can get. He changed his mind and went out into the father's vineyard.

That is what it is all about, that is what it means. The second son may have been sorry later but that is not repentance. The first son turned about, changed his mind, and went in the opposite direction. This is what it means to us. We live our lives in our own way. We may not be robbers or criminals. We may be what the world calls "good," but we are dead to God, lost in our sins, heading toward that Hades or hell that Judas went to. Then we hear the Word. The Holy Spirit touches our hearts and minds so that we really begin "To hear the Word," like we never heard it before.

Oh sure, we heard it with our ears, but that is as far as it got. Now, in some way we do not understand, it has gone farther than our ears. It has reached our innermost being. We call it the heart, but we do not mean that blood pump. We mean our personal being, our inside, our spirit. Now the light dawns. Now we turn around and start facing God. We start listening to His word, His will, His Savior, and know that He died for us. We have repented. We have turned about and now are face to face with God our Savior. We have repented. It is as simple as that. Have we done it? If not, turn around! About face!

"Or despisest thou the riches of His goodness and forebearance and longsuffering; not knowing that the goodness of God leadeth thee to repentance?" (Romans 2:4).

BEAM 136

ALL THINGS ARE POSSIBLE TO HIM THAT BELIEVETH (MARK 9:23)

FAITH–REALLY WORKS

Works do not work. Titus 3:5 states that it was "not by works of righteousness which we have done, but according to His mercy He saved us." Works of righteousness, or any other kind, do not work. But faith works.

Faith enlightens us to SEE THE INVISIBLE. It was by faith that Moses forsook Egypt, "by faith he forsook Egypt not fearing the wrath of the king: for he endured, as seeing Him who is invisible" (Hebrews 11:27). How can these poor eyes behold Him who is invisible? Faith does that. Not only does faith let us see what is unseeable but—

Faith endows us with knowledge to KNOW THE UNKNOWABLE. Paul prays in Ephesians 3:17–19 "by faith that ye . . . may be able to comprehend . . . and to know the love of Christ, which passeth knowledge." It is past knowledge, but I can know it? That is beyond my understanding already. Maybe I need more faith. By faith I can know what is unknowable! Not only does faith allow me to see what cannot be seen, and to know what is too great to be understood but—

Faith enables us to DO THE IMPOSSIBLE. "Through faith also Sara herself received strength to conceive seed, and was delivered of a child when she was past age, because she judged Him faithful who had promised" (Hebrews 11:11). Sarah was well past menopause at ninety years of age. Her husband was one hundred years old, and most likely well past the age of (N)iagara? Hebrews 11:12 says Abraham was "as good as dead." But God said they would have a son. Sarah once laughed at God's promise, but later she called her son Izaak (Isaac), which means laughter. She once laughed in unbelief but now she laughs because God's promise came true. A "dead" Abraham becomes a father! They did what was impossible. And from Abraham and Sarah sprang as many children as the stars in the sky in multitude.

Faith really works. Have your tried it? Without faith it is impossible to please God (Hebrews 11:6). Faith in a falsehood does not change a falsehood. Faith must be in what God has declared to be true. That is the kind of faith that is saving faith. That kind of faith makes it possible for us to see the invisible, understand the unknowable, and to do the impossible. How beautiful it is that those of us who have poor eyesight, and poor knowledge, and poor strength to do anything with that poor knowledge and poor sight, can do it all by faith.

Try it. You'll like it.

"If ye have faith as a grain of mustard seed, ye shall say unto this mountain, Remove hence to yonder place; and it shall remove: and nothing shall be impossible unto you" (Matthew 17:20).

"Now faith is the substance of things hoped for, the evidence of things not seen" (Hebrews 11:1).

"Who through faith subdued kingdoms, wrought righteousness, obtained promises, stopped the mouths of lions, quenched the violence of fire, escaped the edge of the sword, out of weakness were made strong etc. etc.," (Hebrews 11:33–36).

"Fight the good fight of faith, lay hold on eternal life, whereunto thou art also called, and hast professed a good profession before many witnesses" (1 Timothy 6:12).

BEAM 137

TITHE OR NOT TO TITHE? THAT IS THE QUESTION

2 CORINTHIANS 9:6–7

The teaching of the tithe, like the teaching of baptism, separates some congregations from others. This should not be. The tithe, one tenth that is, was part of the Law of Moses. Israel was to trust that God would supply their every need. Every third year they were to bring their tenth, or tithe, to the storehouse and it was to be given to the Levites, the priests, who had no land of their own, and the widows and the fatherless, and strangers. One of God's plans to take care of welfare recipients was by the tithe. In Deuteronomy 14:28–29 we read "At the end of three years thou shalt bring forth all the tithe of thine increase the same year, and shalt lay it up within thy gates; And the Levites, (because he hath no part nor inheritance with thee,) and the stranger, and the fatherless, and the widow, which are within thy gates, shall come, and shall eat and be satisfied; that the Lord thy God may bless thee in all thy work of thine hand which thou doest." It was a requirement under the Law of Moses.

The Lord Jesus condemned those scribes and Pharisees who were so particular about paying a tithe but omitted weightier matters of the Law (Matthew 23:23). Remember, man was not made for the Law nor the Sabbath, but the Sabbath was made for man (Mark 2:27).

However, in the new dispensation of the church age the church is not under the Law. We are to give freely as the Lord has blessed us. "Every man according as he purposeth in his heart, so let him give; not grudgingly, or of necessity, for God loveth a cheerful giver" (2 Corinthians 9:7). That should be enough right there. We are not to give by necessity. Under the Law you HAD to give. It was commanded that you had to give a tithe. Not so under grace. There is no teaching in the New Testament that puts the church under the Law of Moses or under the tithe. Someone will go to Genesis 14:20 where Abraham gave a tenth to Melchizedek. However, there is no command anywhere mentioned. If it is not commanded, then it is a free will offering. You can give two or four tenths if you wish, but it still is not a tithe. It is a free will offering. I am told that LeTourneau, the man who owned an earth moving equipment company, gave nine tenths to the Lord's work and kept one tenth for himself. That still does not make nine tithes. It was a free will offering.

Paul says that we are to lay aside on the first day of the week "as God hath prospered" us for the work of the church (1 Corinthians 16:2). If we give a tenth it should not be called a tithe. Let's not go back under the Law again. This does not mean we should give less, as Christians. Paul reminds us that there is a reward coming and we should be aware of it. "He that soweth sparingly shall reap also sparingly, he that soweth bountifully shall reap also bountifully" (2 Corinthians 9:6). So the more we sow the more we reap. That makes sense. There are some widows living off a meager pension that may not be able to give. Leave her alone. We are to give as God has prospered us. He does not want her to go hungry in order to give to His work.

There is something else that we should be aware of. God does not ask unbelievers to support His work. God never asked the Philistines to send material to build Solomon's temple. We should practice this also.

The offering plate should be like the communion plate; for believers only. How different it would be if pastors told the visitors that they are not to feel that they should give to the work of the Lord. They should be told that they are to receive from the Lord, instead of giving to Him. It is for believers to give to support God's work. So let us give. Not grudgingly. God does not want even believers giving if they are going to begrudge the gift. Give cheerfully, if you can give. If you cannot, God knows your circumstances. "And God is able to make all grace abound toward you, that ye always having all sufficiency in all things, may abound to every good work" (2 Corinthians 9:8).

BEAM 138

NUNC DIMITTIS

NOW LETTEST THOU DEPART

LUKE 2:29

This is from the Latin and is what Simeon said in his Aramaic, or Hebrew. "Lord, now lettest Thou Thy servant depart in peace, According to Thy word." Luke has a number of words that have been used in Latin to sing the praises of God. We have the angel speaking to Mary and saying "Hail, thou that art highly favoured, the Lord is with thee: blessed art thou among women" (Luke 1:28). This has become the "Hail Mary" or Ave Maria used in some church services.

In Luke 1:46 Mary responds with "My soul doth magnify the Lord." This gives us the Magnificat, another confession used in some churches. Then there is the basis for the Gloria Patri in Luke 2:14, where a multitude of angels were SAYING, not SINGING, "Glory to God in the highest and on earth peace, good will toward men." There is nothing here about angels singing but it makes for better Christmas carols.

There is one more that is of particular beauty. It is the "Nunc Dimittis" spoken by Simeon. We read that Simeon was a just and devout man who was waiting for the consolation of Israel, which is the Messiah, or the Christ. We can understand that he was an old man who had been waiting for years to see the Lord's Savior. We read that God had revealed it to Simeon, by the Holy Spirit, that he should not die before he had seen the Lord's Christ (Luke 2:26). What a wonderful promise! To see the Messiah before death. Death would not hold fear if one could see the Lord's Messiah first.

We do not know how long he waited and prayed, but on a certain day he was led by the Spirit to come in to the temple. It just so happened (?) that Mary and Joseph were bringing Jesus before the Lord in the temple to offer unto the Lord a sacrifice for the cleansing of Mary. Under the Law of Moses she was unclean for forty days. Mary and Joseph came at this time. Simeon was just lucky, right? Uh huh. It was all determined by God. The Spirit revealed to Simeon that this child was the Messiah, the deliverer of Israel, the Anointed One of God, the Savior. Simeon takes Jesus up in his arms and blesses God for His wonderful grace.

He says "Lord, now lettest thou thy servant depart in peace, according to Thy word: for mine eyes have seen Thy salvation." He says that this child is "A light to lighten the Gentiles," and he was Jewish, "and the glory of Thy people Israel" (Luke 2:29–32). What a wonderful thing to allow this old gentleman to hold this baby and see the Lord's Messiah. We do not know how long Simeon lived after this but we can suppose it was not long. But he could die happy and in peace. He saw God's "salvation" when he saw baby Jesus. That is what He truly is, God's salvation given to a world to save sinners.

So what? What does this have to do with us? Notice that it was "I have seen Thy Messiah, now let me die in peace." It cannot be the other way. There can be no peace if we die without seeing God's Messiah. We, of course, see Him by faith after hearing the Word preached to us. If we have seen Him as our Savior and redeemer, then death holds no fears for us. To be absent from the body is to be present with the Lord, 2 Corinthians 5:8. "Into thine hand I commit my spirit; Thou hast redeemed me, O Lord God of truth" (Psalm 31:5).

So what? The question remains. Have we seen God's Messiah? We dare not go out of this world until we have. If we have, then "O death, where is thy sting? O grave, where is thy victory? But thanks be to God, which giveth us the victory through our Lord Jesus Christ" (1 Corinthians 15:55–57). If we have seen Him, we can depart in peace. God's "salvation" is Jesus Who died for us on the cross.

BEAM 139

GROW UP

HEBREWS 5:11–6:2

Are we babes in Christ? Well, what are we eating, milk or meat? How can you tell the difference?

The writer of Hebrews tells us that he could not talk about a lot of things because the hearers, and that may include us, had not grown up enough to be able to handle it. He states that everyone "that uses milk is unskillful in the word of righteousness: for he is a babe" (Hebrews 5:13). Babies do not have their teeth yet so they cannot handle meat truth.

He says that these people should have been teaching the word of God, but instead were in need to have someone teach them. Yes, it is wonderful to see a little baby. It is tragic for that little baby to stay a baby. He says that we need to grow up. "Strong meat belongeth to them that are of full age" (Hebrews 5:14). So what are these milk truths that we have been nursing on for too long? He tells us.

"Therefore leaving the principles of the doctrine of Christ, let us go on unto perfection; not laying again the foundation of repentance from dead works, and of faith toward God" (6:1). Some people keep on repenting from dead works over and over again and again. Faith toward God. We needed that when we first came to the Lord Jesus. That was a first. It should not be a continual first. Move on!

Then there is the doctrine of baptisms. Baptism was an outward sign that united the church to tell a world that we had taken our stand with Christ and were believers. Now it divides the church over which way it should be done. Then there was the laying on of hands. This did not pass any mystic power to the one being anointed. It was simply a way of blessing one. It was done by Jacob when he laid his hands upon the sons of Joseph. In Genesis 48:17–19 Joseph tries to correct his father because the right hand held the greater blessing and Joseph thought his father had made a mistake and put his left hand on the older son. But Jacob knew what he was doing. His right hand was on Ephraim.

Then there is the belief in a resurrection of the dead. That may sound like a real meat truth but this writer calls it milk truth. Let's go on he says. Surely we believe in the resurrection of Christ or we have no foundation. What is Christianity without the resurrection? Just another religion. Let's go on.

And eternal punishment. Many do not want to believe this. A loving God, sending people into a punishment that lasts forever and ever! That's what His word says. Sometimes we wish it were not so. Even a Hitler should have some end to his suffering. But the Scripture does not teach it. The punishment goes on and on and on. Let's move on. Let's grow up. Peter tells us "As newborn babes, desire the sincere milk of the word, that ye may grow thereby" (1 Peter 2:2). But don't keep on drinking from the bottle.

Babies are beautiful, all of them. It is a blessing to watch them grow, learning new things each week. Trying to say words that they are not sure the meaning of, but they try. Then crawling, and trying to stand, and walking on their own. What blessings they bring to their parents and grandparents. But if they do not grow, it is a tragedy.

Years ago, when I was a young lad, the gang of us would play on a vacant lot up the street. We never had much money. We even invented games. If no one had a ball we would sail bottle caps to the batter. We learned to hit bottle caps, too. One day, when I was alone in the vacant lot, practicing, I heard some weird and awful sound coming from the house next to the empty lot. It sounded like a gorilla but I did not think anyone would have a pet gorilla. I heard the same sound several times after that, but still did not know what caused it.

One day I was at the lot again and alone. Again I heard this awful roar that sounded like some animal. I looked at the window of the corner house and then I saw it. "It" was a young boy, who looked to be about 12 or 14, who was sitting by the window in a super large highchair. His mother was giving him something, food or medicine. He let out a few more roars. Even at my young age I felt sorry for that mother.

Children are beautiful. But if they remain children for years and years it is a tragedy. This mother had her burden to care for a child who never grew up. We must grow up. If we remain children some day something will come into our lives and God will not be able to speak to us about it. We may lose our job, or have to move to another city. We may have some illness or some loved one may get an incurable illness. We may lose a loved one. God will want to speak to us and He will not be able, because we never grew.

"Let the Word of Christ dwell in you richly in all wisdom" (Colossians 3:16). "Study to shew thyself approved unto God, a workman that needeth not to be ashamed, rightly dividing the word of truth" (2 Timothy 2:15). "Be ready always to give an answer to every man that asketh you a reason of the hope that is in you with meekness and fear" (1 Peter 3:15). "But speaking the truth in love, may grow up into Him in all things, which is the head, even Christ" (Ephesians 4:15). "But grow in grace and in the knowledge of our Lord and Savior Jesus Christ" (2 Peter 3:18).

We need to grow some teeth after we have had the milk truths, and get our teeth into some meat truths. Let's grow up. We have been babies long enough. And how does a baby grow? He doesn't grit his teeth, or gums, and say "From now on I am going to grow." No. He does what comes naturally. He feeds off the milk for a while. Then he gets those teeth and wants solid food. Let's grow. Let's get into the solid meat of the Word and grow. Stop being a baby.

BEAM 140

A PLACE FOR HIS HEAD

JOHN 19:30

In Luke 9:58 we read "Foxes have holes, and birds of the air have nests; but the Son of man hath not where to lay His head." This tells us something about the poverty of the Lord Jesus and His followers. He lived off the gifts of friends who gave to Him and His followers. As someone has said, He never wrote a book, or took public office, or received an inheritance. He was poor from the beginning. His trade was carpentry but He left all of that when He went public with His message, when He was about the age of thirty. He was invited to dinners and at least one wedding. He could have created food, as He did on one occasion when He fed thousands with a boy's lunch. But He was poor.

His whole life was one of doing without what many call the necessities of life. He did not have them. No luxury. No real place in this world to call home. Born in a stable and never getting to the top of the business world. He said animals had more, in some respect. They had some place that they could call home. It could be a hole in the ground or a nest in a tree. Whatever it was, and wherever it was, they had a home. He was never "at home" here. His home was above.

There is an interesting light shed on His statement about not having a place to lay His head. The word used for "lay" is the Greek word ***klino***. It is used seven times in the Scriptures. Twice for having no place to lay His head. But it is used in another place that may not be evident from reading the English. It is in John 19:30 where on the cross, when the penalty for sin had been paid for and Jesus cried "It is finished," He bowed His head and gave up the ghost. That word "bowed" is the word ***klino,*** that was used for having no place for His head.

This says that Jesus had no place to lay His head but found a place on the cross. That is a beautiful story. The creator of the universe, the Son Who has all things given to Him from the Father, Who is King of kings and Lord of lords, Who was poor in this world's goods and had no place to rest His head, found a resting place on the cross. There He found a resting place. There He could lay His head.

Light came into the world "and men loved darkness rather than light because their deeds were evil" (John 3:19). The world had no place for Him. In fact, the world hated Him. He said "If the world hate you, ye know that it hated Me before it hated you" (John 15:18). He had no place to lay His head. He had no place to call His own. He found a place at the end when He was on the cross. Only after it was all finished, then did He have a place to bow, or lay, His head on the cross.

Oh yes! He had no home here. His home is in heaven, where He came from. We have a home there. He is preparing it for us. Better than we have ever seen on earth. A mansion. "In My Father's house are many mansions; if it were not so, I would have told you. I go to prepare a place for you" (John 14:2). I have never lived in a mansion. Few people have. Some churches provide a house for their pastor. It is called a manse, a short form of the word mansion. Some of those "manses" are dumps that should be torn down. What He has in store for us is greater than we can imagine. A true, live, honest to goodness, mansion. And there is no rent to pay. The deed is given to us. Yes, because He left His mansion above to come down here and have no place to lay His head, until He got to the cross. And these mansions are just part of His Father's house. What must that house look like?

What a gracious and loving Savior! And He did it for the unworthy, the sinners of this world, including me. How about you? He did it for you. Now we sinners can rest in Him and His finished work on the cross. The least we can do is thank Him. Have we?

BEAM 141

JOHN, THE GREATEST

LUKE 7:28

John the Baptist, the greatest prophet? What about Isaiah, or Jeremiah, or Daniel? How can this be? The Lord Jesus said so. And then He says "he that is least in the kingdom of God is greater than John." Wow! Explain this to me.

The Lord Jesus said "the Law and the Prophets were until John: since that time the kingdom of God is preached" (Luke 16:16). So John was at the end of a long line of prophets. Yet, Jesus said there were none greater than John. This must be because John was the forerunner and introducer of the Messiah, the Elijah that was to come. In Matthew 17:11–12 the Lord Jesus said that Elijah was to come first and restore all things but Elijah had indeed already come, in the person of John. If they, the nation of Israel, would have received Jesus as Messiah, then John would have been the Elijah that was to come. Since they did not receive Him, then the Old Testament Elijah will come again and restore all things and be the forerunner of the Messiah when He comes back the second time. Now that Jesus the Messiah has come, the kingdom is preached. John, by baptizing and preaching that Jesus is the Messiah, is classified as greater than all other prophets.

John, the second cousin of Jesus, pointed Him out as "the Lamb of God which taketh away the sin of the world" (John 1:29). John lost his life by being true to his calling as the identifier of Jesus as Messiah. And yet the Lord said that "he that is least in the kingdom of God is greater than he" (Luke 7:28). How can this be? So many, many Christians do not sacrifice their lives for the Master's sake. Some do not sacrifice at all. How can they be better? We must think of weddings now. John said "He that hath the bride is the bridegroom: but the friend of the bridegroom, which standeth and heareth Him rejoiceth greatly because of the bridegroom's voice: this my joy is fulfilled" (John 3:29). In other words, John the Baptist considered himself to be the best man at the wedding. The church is the bride. Which is greater, the bride or the best man? There would be no comparison as far as the bridegroom is concerned. He is marrying the bride, not the best man.

The Church is called His bride and Paul says he engaged us, the church, to Jesus the bridegroom in 2 Corinthians 11:2. The word used there means to "be fitted together." Paul says we should act like it. If you are engaged to be married you remain true to your fiancé. So being engaged is greater than being the best man. The apostles shall have a special place of honor in the coming kingdom. He says they shall sit on twelve thrones judging the twelve tribes of Israel (Luke 22:30). But the bride has a place of honor. She sits on the throne with the Lord of all of the earth as His special bride.

If we are children of God, then we are "heirs; heirs of God, and joint-heirs with Christ; if so be that we suffer with Him, that we may be also glorified together" (Romans 8:17). If we are joint-heirs, then everything He has we have. That is so tremendous that it is hard to comprehend. He is the Lord of all and King of kings. He is the creator of all things and everything is His. Every knee shall bow to Him and every tongue shall confess that He is Lord (Philippians 2:10–11). And the least in the kingdom of God shall share all of this. Yes, that is greater than being the identifier and forerunner of the Messiah. What a wonderful gracious God we have. That a Holy and Righteous God would even save unworthy sinners is a marvel of grace. So wonderful, it is hard to comprehend. But to bring them into His glory and seat them on thrones in glory like the Lord Jesus, and to have these unworthy sinners share in His glory! That is beyond imagination. What love! Have we thanked Him for it? Have we received it? Don't wait. Who knows what tomorrow brings. Now is the day of salvation. Tomorrow is nearer than we think.

BEAM 142

WASHING AND BATHING

JOHN 13:9–10

There is a beautiful and comforting story in this passage. The Lord Jesus took the towel and water and started to wash the disciples' feet. He did this as an example. The disciples were occupied with who would be the highest ranking officers in the coming kingdom. The natural man of course thinks of his own glory and pleasure and power. Like all of us do until we have a new birth. They forgot the common courtesy that when you came into a house someone met you with a basin and a towel to wash the dust from your feet. This was usually some servant of the household. No one wanted to take the position of a servant, so no one did the washing. So the Lord and Master of them all did the servant's job. It was an example of humility. Just as the Master took the humble job, so they should also take an example of His humility and put pride away and serve one another. It was an example.

Peter did not feel right about having his Lord wash his feet and said he would never let Jesus wash his feet. Now the Lord said something that we all should learn from. He said "If I wash thee not, thou hast no part with Me" (John 13:8). Then Peter said he would not only have his feet washed but all of him, feet, hands, head, all. Then the Lord Jesus said that "He that is washed, needeth not save to wash his feet, but he is clean, every whit" (John 13:10). He used two different words here. Without knowing this we may miss the point.

First, notice that He said if He did not wash Peter's feet, Peter would have no part WITH Him. He did not say IN Him. That would be an entirely different matter. That would imply that Peter might need to get saved again and again. IN ME stands for salvation. WITH ME stands for service. There would not be the fellowship and service WITH the Savior. He used one word, "nipto," which means to wash a part of the body, such as the hands, or the feet. He used another word, "louo," which means to take a bath. He is saying that if one is bathed, "louoed," he only needs to have his feet "niptoed" to be completely clean. Louo stands symbolically for salvation. We are cleansed once for all from our sins by the blood of Christ, once we believe. We are louoed once. But we can be niptoed every day.

After we are saved we need constant niptoing, a washing of a part of the body. Those apostles may have had a bath in a local pool. There were few places to get a bath. But then they would have to put on their sandals and walk home. What happened along the way? They picked up some dust. When they arrived home, they needed that basin at the door to cleanse their feet. The walk through the streets gathers dust and some dirt on the feet of the individual. It is a picture of our walk in this world. We pick up some dirt from this world. Believers also sin, some more or less. But we get dirty just by being in this world and walking through it in our daily lives. We live in a dirty and wicked world. Just look at the newspaper. But we do not get BATHED again; we are not saved over again. We confess our sins and are cleansed from our daily walk.

Eternal life is eternal and a gift not taken back by God. But to walk with Him in the light we need to confess our sins and be cleansed so we may continue to walk in the light with Him. "If we confess our sins (written to believers) He is faithful and just to forgive us our sins, and to cleanse us from all unrighteousness (1 John 1:9). That is the nipto of washing to get the dirt from this world off us. The louo, the bath, we have one time when we trust the Lord Jesus and are completely saved forever.

What a beautiful story. Just get the dirt off. We do not need a second bath. We have had one and that one lasts. But we do need the washing of the feet to keep completely clean. Are you bathed? You have to be louoed first before the niptoing does any good. Bathe and then wash is the proper way.

"Now ye are clean through the word which I have spoken unto you" (John 15:3).

BEAM 143

THREE CROSSES

LUKE 23:43

Here is perhaps the best example of a deathbed repentance. It is the dying thief nailed to a cross alongside Jesus. We should never wait when we hear the gospel message. We have no guarantee that we will have another chance to hear it gain. But this man had not heard the message before, so it is not quite the same as a deathbed turning about. This might be called a first time turning. But first, look at that great question of life. It is again, "How is a sinner saved?" What do we learn here?

In Luke 23 we do not have the thief asking how to be saved. He most likely held little hope that a wretch like he was could be saved by a holy God, not after all he did. But the big question of life is still there at the cross. "How does a sinner get saved?" I would say this is a case of "WHAT CAN I DO to be saved?" I am nailed to a cross. I can do nothing now. It all centers around Jesus Christ, and what we do with Jesus Christ.

There were two thieves who were crucified along with Jesus. At first they both mocked Him and insulted Him like the crowd was doing. Then one of them listens to how Jesus answers the crowd and realizes that this One is different. He hears Him forgive the crowd that is yelling at Jesus. He listens, and looks, and something happens. He sees that this One is the looked for Messiah. He is the One that did miracles, healed the sick, gave sight to the blind, raised the dead. He sees that this one does not return hatred for hatred.

He believes that this One is the one true Savior of Israel and all sinners. All three are nailed to crosses and all this one thief can do is to turn to Jesus and say "Lord, (Already he is addressing Jesus as Lord) remember me when thou comest into thy kingdom" (Luke 23:42). He does not ask to be saved. He may have held little hope for something so precious. He has lived a wicked and ungodly life of crime. He may think he is not worth saving. All he asks is to be remembered. And he says when Jesus comes into His kingdom. Whatever the crowd may have yelled, this man thought this One dying on a cross, just like he was dying on a cross, would some day be alive again and have that kingdom He spoke about. Yes, that took faith to see one dying like you are and yet believe that the death you see is not the end for this One. Here is a man who believes in the resurrection of Jesus before it happens.

But what could this one dying thief do to help God save him? Nothing. He could not give money, not even a tithe of a tithe. He could not join a church. He could not do any good deeds, like remembering the poor. All he could do was to believe, and that he did. The Lord Jesus says to this one, "Verily (that is truly) I say unto thee, to day shalt thou be with Me in paradise" (Luke 23:43). Is believing all there is to it? What did this one do, but believe. And he was to spend the last part of that horrible day with this Savior in paradise, the place where the saved people went when they died. That was before the death of Jesus. After Jesus' death Paul says to be absent from the body is to be with Christ. (2 Corinthians 5:8). This thief was the first to be absent from his body and to be with Christ in paradise. Yes, believe on the Lord Jesus Christ and thou shalt be saved. That is it. That is all of it. What a savior!

"But to him that worketh not, but believeth on Him that justifieth the ungodly, his faith is counted for righteousness" (Romans 4:5).

There were three men dying on crosses. To the world they may have all looked alike. Physically they did look like three criminals being executed for their crimes. However, there was a tremendous difference between each one of them. If this is old stuff to you, perhaps we can review it for beginners.

There was one who had no sins ON him, although he still had sin IN him. This would be the thief who turned to Jesus and believed on Him just before that thief died. His sin nature was still there IN him. The sins he had ON him were placed ON Jesus so that this thief could now enter into paradise with Jesus. His sins would be gone forever.

There was another thief who did not believe. He is to be pitied. His sins were still IN him and still remained ON him. He went to another place to await the coming Great White Throne Judgment. He had his opportunity, just like we have. He ignored it. We, also, will join him if we ignore our opportunity to come to the Savior.

Then there was one more Person dying. He was in the Middle of the three. He had no sin IN Him because He is sinless. But He had sin

ON Him. That may sound odd, but His sins that were ON Him were my sins and your sins and the sins of the other thief who believed. And, all the sins of the world were placed ON Him. Yes, the spotless and sinless Son of God became sin there on the cross FOR US. He took our sins ON Him so that we would not have to have them ON us any longer. That is true for every one who believes. But without faith IN HIM, we still have our sins IN us and On us.

Let's not go on carrying that awful weight of transgressions around with us any longer. Put it On Him. He invites us to do that very thing. What a loving Savior!

"Surely, He hath borne our griefs, and carried our sorrows . . . But He was wounded for our transgressions, He was bruised for our iniquities . . . and the Lord hath laid on Him the iniquities of us all" (Isaiah 53:4–6).

BEAM 144

WHO KILLED JESUS?

ACTS 4:27–28

There has been much discussion about who it was that killed Jesus. Can we answer this old and difficult question? Different groups come up with different answers. Some groups condemn other groups or races. There should be some understanding of the ground rules. There were many atrocious crimes done by the Nazis under Hitler's rule. That does not mean that German people today are guilty of those crimes. The Rape of Nanking makes even the Nazis look good in comparison, but that does not make the people of Japan today guilty of the executions that were committed. So with that in mind let us look at what the Scripture says.

Peter, that good old Apostle that we love, says some things about the death of Jesus that should clear up the matter. This is from the new Apostle Peter, after he has been filled with the Holy Spirit. In Acts 4:26 he states it this way. First he gives the context from David. He quotes from Psalm 2:2. "The kings of the earth set themselves and the rulers take counsel together against the Lord and against His anointed." This makes it clear that the kings killed Jesus. That would mean Herod and Pontius Pilate, and even Tiberius Caesar. So the Romans did it.

Peter also says that "the rulers were gathered together against the Lord and against Christ." So this would include Annas the High Priest and Caiaphas the High Priest. It was Caiaphas who said that they must do something with Jesus. You can guess what that means. His enemies admit that He had done many miracles. Caiaphas said that they must do something with Jesus, for if they left Him alone "the Romans shall come and take away both our place and nation" (John 11:48). It's all about money, like Paul was to say later. The love of money. That sin grabs most people. So the high priests and other priests killed Jesus.

But the Jews also were guilty. They followed these priests knowing full well that it was evil. "The chief priests and elders persuaded the multitude that they should ask for Barabbas, a murderer, and destroy Jesus" (Matthew 27:20). So the elders killed Jesus. And the multitude killed Jesus, also. Peter also says that the Gentiles, and the people of Israel were gathered together to kill Jesus. So the nation of Israel, at least those who were in Jerusalem for this Passover feast, and that was a lot of them, killed Jesus. And the Gentiles who cried out for His blood, they killed Jesus.

Jesus came into the world to seek and to save that which was lost (Luke 19:10). So sinners were responsible. Sinners killed Jesus. He came to save them by dying on the cross. So you and I killed Jesus.

But Peter also says something else that really makes this a tough nut to crack. He says God killed Jesus. Yes, he says all of these people, Jews, Romans (or Gentiles), priests, Judas, crowds shouting "Crucify Him" were doing what God had "determined beforehand to be done." So God planned it and did it. And man planned it and did it. Was man responsible? Yes he was. Those men did what they wanted to do–kill Jesus. Did God do it? Yes, He did what He had determined back in eternity to do. Is God sovereign? Yes, He is. Was man free, at least in choosing to kill Jesus? Yes he was. No one made him do it. They did what they wanted to do and they freely did what they wanted to do. And yet God worked in it all to do what He had planned to do. Is this hard to understand? It sure is. We may never understand it on this side of the curtain of death. Both are taught. God saves by grace. Man is responsible for being lost. Men killed Jesus. God killed Jesus. But it was all done to save sinners. He came to seek and to save that which was lost. Are you lost? You do not need to stay that way. It was all done to save poor sinners by grace. Have you thanked Him for it?

BEAM 145

YOU CAN'T TAKE IT WITH YOU, RIGHT?

LUKE 16:25

That's what they say. Can 50 million Americans be wrong? How about 30 million church-going Americans? You certainly do not carry out of this world any riches or wealth. If we get buried with gold rings we had better know the undertaker. There are such things as grave robbers. We cannot take our books or inventions, if we had any, with us. Edison had over a thousand patents I am told, but he had to leave them. So is it true that we cannot take it with us? It depends on what "it" is. There is one thing that we do carry out of this world and it is not a nice story to talk about. We do take memories with us.

The story is so horrible that many a preacher does not even want to think of preaching about it. But many Bible preachers can be wrong, also. Here is one place where we are told that we do carry out something. It is often called a parable about the rich man and the beggar, Lazarus. But the Scripture never says it was a parable. Many, many times we read that the Lord Jesus spoke a parable. Not here. This is a story that was told about a certain rich man. We are told that this rich man had five brothers, so it might have been told so that they would not come to the same place where this brother was who had died.

The rich man had everything of this world's goods. Clothed in purple and fine linen and eating the best meals, he had everything. Isn't this what many believe life is all about? Eat, drink, and be merry, for tomorrow we die. And the beggar, Lazarus, he was waiting for the crumbs that were thrown out by the rich man. Anything at all was good enough for him. And oh yes, like Job, he was full of sores. The dogs came and licked his sores. Might not be as good as alcohol or iodine, but it was better than nothing.

I am sure you have heard this story. Both men die. The beggar dies and we are told the angels carry him to Abraham's bosom. This would be the name of the place where souls went before the cross and Jesus' death. In the Old testament it is called "Sheol," the place where the dead go. In the New Testament it is called "Hades." That word may lead some to think of "hell" but not so. All the dead went to the place of the dead, Sheol, or Hades. There was a separation there between those who had believed and had been saved, and those who did not believe. In contrast to the beggar's death, we read simply that the rich man died and was buried. Nothing about angels. Then the rich man suffered torment. He cried out for just a bit of water to cool his tongue. Here is the answer. "Son, remember that thou in thy lifetime receivedst good things" (16:25).

It is a terrible thing to think about, but we must face the facts or we may end up like that rich man. "Son, remember." We take our memories with us. How awful that will be when we think about all of the opportunities we had. We will remember how someone spoke to us about our Savior. We will remember how our mother prayed for us, or some Christian friend told us about the Redeemer. We will remember how that sermon made us think about receiving Jesus as our own. We will remember how we put off making any decision. We will remember how we thought we had plenty of time. Oh, the horribleness of it all. Oh, how different it could have been, if . . . But it will be too late. We cannot change it then. Even if Lazarus wanted to help, he could not. There was a great gulf between the two men. No one could cross over. But the memories! They will be with us and remain with us forever! What a horrible thought. Let's change that right now. Let's not put off till tomorrow what we had better do today.

"He, that being often reproved hardeneth his neck, shall suddenly be destroyed, and that without remedy" (Proverbs 29:1). Let's not put it off any longer, "Believe on the Lord Jesus Christ and thou shalt be saved, and thy house" (Acts 16:31). Remember all those things that have been said about the Savior? We will keep on remembering them. Let's be in the right place when we remember them. We do take our memories with us. Let's make them blessed memories, not brutal.

BEAM 146

ANDREW THE INTRODUCER

OH, TO BE LIKE HIM

Almost everyone has heard about Peter. It is so nice to read about someone who trips up and blunders every so often. It gives us hope, at least it gives me some. Maybe you don't need it. I do. Few people know anything about Andrew. When Jesus first started His ministry He attracted to him Andrew as one of His followers. In fact Andrew, and the other disciple, wanted to know where Jesus was living or staying at that time. Jesus said "Come and see" (John 1:39). They spend a night with Him. The first thing Andrew does next day is to find his brother Peter and tell him that the two had found the Messiah. "And he brought him to Jesus" (John 1:42).

A little later we see Andrew again introducing someone to the Lord Jesus. The crowd had been following Jesus because they saw the miracles He did. Jesus went up into a mountain with His own. But the crowds still followed Him and wanted to see miracles which Jesus did. Only they did not bring any meals with them. It was getting late and they were getting hungry. They thought that some of the crowd might faint on their way home if they did not get food. But where would they get it out in the wilderness?

Then Andrew, who always seems to be addressed as Simon Peter's brother, says "There is a lad here which hath five barley loaves and two small fishes, but what are they among so many?" (John 6:9). He mentioned it like he expected Jesus to do another miracle. Here he is again introducing this lad with his lunch.

Once more we see Andrew the Introducer at work. There were some Greeks that came up to worship at the feast. They have heard about this Jesus and they wanted to see Him. Again, it is Andrew who is the introducer. He brings them to Jesus (John 12:22). Jesus says now is the time for Him to be glorified. And the Father speaks out from heaven and says He will glorify Him again (John 12:28). The people heard this and some thought it thundered, while others thought an angel spoke to them (John 12:29).

He is the Introducer, always bringing someone to Jesus. And it does not seem hard for him. He does not get into a theological debate. He simply says "Come and see." That is a good way to do it. Come and see for yourself, if any good thing can come out of Nazareth. This is what we all should be doing, introducing someone to Jesus.

We do not hear much else about Andrew but we do have something the Lord said about those who may come along late and try to do a little something for His name.

He told about some laborers in the field. They made a bargain to work for so much pay. Later in the day others came along and they went into the fields to work. They did not bargain but they trusted the landowner, who said he would give them what ever was right. Later on he did the same thing to other laborers. They trusted him to give them what was right, no haggling over the salary. They would work for whatever the master thought was right. When the day ended he gave the latecomers a day's wages. The ones who worked half a day got a full day's wages. Then the ones who worked all day got a day's wages (Matthew 20:10–11). They complained because they worked longer than the others. But they bargained and got what they bargained for. The others simply trusted their boss to do what was right. So the Lord said that "the last shall be first, and the first last" (Matthew 20:16).

Andrew may not have made the headlines like other apostles, but he may be one of those last that will be first. Wish I could be like the Introducer. And I can, if I really want to. So can you. Andrew said "We have found the Messiah" (John 1:41). We ought to be able to say that.

BEAM 147

WHAT'S IT TO YOU?

JOHN 21:22

Peter wanted to know what John was going to do. Jesus had just told Peter something about how Peter would die. He said essentially that Peter, at this time, can do what he wants, more or less. He can dress himself and he can go where he wants. But the time will come, and time keeps coming, when Peter will not be able to dress himself and go where Peter wants. John tells us that Jesus spoke of Peter's death and the glory Peter would give God by his death. So it was quite natural for Peter to wonder how things would go with John. "What shall this man do?" he asks (John 21:21). This is where the Lord Jesus tells Peter to mind his own business, so to speak, and not be bothered about John. He is saying "What's it to you? You have your job to do. That job is to follow me. Don't bother about John."

What's it to you? We should not bother ourselves with how these other folks are doing or how they got to where they are. We can spend countless days and even years wondering why it happened to them and not us. How was it that Mozart could compose such beautiful music that has thrilled millions for centuries and it didn't happen to me? Why is it that Michelangelo could do such fantastic carving in Florence? Why didn't I receive such a gift? I could have done that for the Lord, too.

Why was Shakespeare given such marvelous talent to write such beautiful lines in poetic dramas but not me? And Beethoven? Why did he go deaf? He could have done even more if he could have heard. And the list goes on and on. There are musicians and painters and builders. How about that Brooklyn Bridge? And the Golden Gate? And Edison with all his inventions? Maybe you don't care for Shakespeare or Mozart. How about those evangelists? Why did Spurgeon get such ability? How about Moody? We could go on and on. But what is that to you, the Lord says to Peter. You have one job to do–follow me.

They say the grass is always greener on the other side of the fence. Sure it is, because the cows are on this side of the fence and they are eating grass on this side. Of course the other side is greener. There are no cows over there. But the lord put us on this side of the fence.

But what is the point? The Lord gives to all His children gifts. Some have bigger receptacles for them than others of us. It is what we do with what we have that counts. In Matthew 25 the Lord Jesus tells us about the kingdom of heaven. He says it is like a man who before he goes away calls his servants and gives to them some money, talents. He does not give them all the same amount. "To every man according to his several ability" (Matthew 25:15). He gave one five talents, another two, and another one. When he returned, the man with five doubled his five, the man with two doubled his also. They both received the same reward. "Thou good and faithful servant." It did not matter that one had five and the other had two. They both did what they could with what they had. Except the man who got one talent. He said he hid his talent in the earth. He had his talent taken away and given to the one who had ten.

So it does not matter if we only get a pound to work with, or two pounds. Some of us may only get 4 ounces. Are we using what we have? That is the question. Never mind Mozart or Moody. What do we have? Are we using it for God's glory? That is what counts. Some cannot carry a tune in a bucket, so if we cannot sing in the choir maybe we can put the chairs up there where the choir can be seen better. What are we doing with what God has given us? And what is our neighbor going to do? None of your business. "Follow Me," He said. Don't bury that little bit of ability you have been given. It is given by the Spirit as He wills (1 Corinthians 12:4–7). "But the manifestation of the Spirit is given to every man to profit withal." We all have something given to us to glorify God. Let's not bother about the other fellow. Just follow Christ. Use what we have to glorify Him with it. Don't bury it. Use it for His glory.

BEAM 148

MARY UNDERSTOOD

JOHN 12:1–9

Time and time again we read where the apostles did not know what Jesus meant. From the beginning, Jesus had difficulty getting people to understand Him. Even as a child His parents did not understand that He would be in the temple, hearing, and asking questions of the priests when he was only twelve (Luke 2:49).

His disciples did not understand what He said about leaven (Matthew 16:9–11). They did not understand His discourse about the shepherd and the sheep (John 10:1–6). When He made what is called His triumphal entry into Jerusalem they did not understand that (John 12:16), but remembered these things after His resurrection.

When He talked to them about His crucifixion and resurrection, they were completely dumbfounded. It seems clear enough to us, on this side of the cross, but not to them. In Luke 18 He spells it out clearly and fully. He said they were going up to Jerusalem and there He "shall be delivered unto the Gentiles, and shall be mocked, and spitefully entreated, and spit on, and they shall scourge Him and put Him to death: and the third day He shall rise again" (Luke 18:31–34). They understood none of these things. Sure, they did not want to hear bad news, who does? But He told them in advance and told them He would rise again from the dead. He also said that "all things that are written by the prophets concerning the Son of Man shall be accomplished." If they were Bible students they would have known. But they were humble men, not scholars. However, they should have heard what He said would happen, even if they did not know the Scriptures.

Again, in Mark 9:31, He foretells His death and afterwards His resurrection upon the third day but we read "But they understood not that saying, and were afraid to ask." No question is too stupid to ask, I think. At least in theology it is not. But they did not ask and did not understand. This is the way it went. Once more, in Luke 9:44–45, He tells them to "Let these sayings sink down into your ears; for the Son of Man shall be delivered into the hands of men. But they understood not this saying." They spent much time with Him during those three years of His earthly ministry and did not understand much of what He taught.

Mary, however, had far less time with Him, yet she seems to be the only one who understood what He was talking about. Just before He was arrested and tried and crucified, she comes to Him while He was at Bethany in the house of Simon the Leper. She came unto Him with an alabaster box "of precious ointment, and poured it on His head, as He sat at meat" (Matthew 26:6–7). This woman was Mary, the sister of Lazarus whom Jesus raised from the dead (John 12:1–8). Alabaster is the stone from which the cruse is made. It contained precious ointment. This may have been a dowry. Some maids kept one that was set aside for their wedding. It was valuable. Judas, the betrayer, said it could have been sold for 300 pence. That would be equal to 300 days salary, according to the workman's daily salary of a penny a day, in their money. Almost a year's salary. She pours it on Jesus. Some of His disciples said, "Why was this waste of ointment made?" (Mark 14:4). Judas, I am sure, was the one who led the others in saying this.

Can anything given to the Lord Jesus be called a waste? How could anyone say that? But Jesus says, "She hath done what she could: she is come beforehand to anoint my body to the burying" (Mark 14:8). Mary understood when no one else did. She poured her most precious possession upon Him. She understood He was going to die. She was anointing Him for His burial. She did what she could. Have we? What have we given Him? What have we to give? It is not the size of the gift, but how much are we giving of what we have. Whatever is given to Him is not a waste. Mary knew. She gave Him her most precious possession. Do we? He deserves our very best. Nothing given to Jesus is a waste.

"Sing unto the Lord, bless His name; shew forth His salvation from day to day. Declare His glory among the heathen, His wonders among all people" (Psalm 96:2–3).

BEAM 149

THE BRAZEN SERPENT

NUMBERS 21:8

JOHN 3:14–15

Not many people like snakes. There are a few that handle them, but they are by far the minority. This was the animal that Satan used to seduce Eve in the Garden. It did not look like the snakes we see today, because one of its punishments was to crawl on it's belly. It was sentenced to eat dust all the days of it's life (Genesis 3:14). It was cursed above all cattle and every beast of the field. It must have been a beautiful creature before, but that is what sin did to it for lending its body to Satan for the temptation.

When Israel complained again, for the umpteenth time, and spoke against God and Moses, the Lord sent fiery serpents among the people and they bit the people and many of them died (Numbers 21:5–6). The people then came to Moses and confessed that they had sinned and asked Moses to pray for them to take away the serpents. And Moses prayed to God for these rebellious people. Then the Lord told Moses to make a serpent of brass and put it on a pole for the people to look upon. If they did, they would be saved from the snake bite. Moses did just that and those who looked were saved.

In John 3:14 the Lord Jesus says that just as Moses lifted up that serpent on a pole that whosoever looked upon it lived, so would He be lifted up so that whosoever looks upon Him would have eternal life. That is a simple statement with some simple facts taught. For one thing the people did not have to understand why it was a serpent, nor why it was of brass, nor why it was lifted up on a pole. All they had to do was to look at it. That was all, just look at it. That in itself did say something. If they looked at it, they were showing faith, they believed Moses and what he said about that serpent. After all if a tarantula bites you, you might think of a doctor or medicine. You would hardly think of making another tarantula out of play dough to help heal you. All they had to do was to look. That was it.

So what does this mean to us? Jesus was to be lifted up, only it would be a cross instead of a pole. He would be in the likeness of sinful flesh, like that brazen serpent, which looked so much like the real serpents that bit them. He would be in the form of sinful flesh, but without sin. Brass was a metal used in the altars on which sacrifices were made for sin. It becomes a metal that speaks of judgment. Sin was to be judged. The sins that were on us would be placed on Him, on the cross, so that God's holiness and righteousness would be executed against sin, only it would be executed upon the innocent One instead of the guilty ones, like those murmuring Israelites who complained, complained, complained, and then were spared their proper judgment (2 Corinthians 5:21). All it took was faith to look. They did not have to understand why it was brass. What a relief for us.

We do not have to understand all of the deep things of theology and some even deeper things that theologians dream up. We do not have to understand limited atonement, or substitutionary atonement, or atonement. We just have to come to the Lord Jesus by faith. They just had to look. We just have to believe. We do not have to understand why He died, nor why it was three days before He rose again. We do not have to know about the Rapture or what a rapture is. We just have to come by faith to One who died for us. For "whosoever believeth in Him should not perish, but have eternal life" (John 3:15). That's all. How simple God makes it. Ignorance, then, will be no excuse. We do not have to know much. Just believe on Him. That's it. Not believe about Him. We can believe that He lived, just like we believe that Washington lived and died. But we are not saved by Washington. He is simply a fact of history. Believing facts of history does not save anyone. Believing ON Him is a committal. We commit ourselves to Him as Savior and rest in His finished work on the cross. Believe ON him and be saved. We believe that He died on that cross to save sinners, which we are. What a gracious God to provide a way for us to be cleansed from our sins and have eternal life. Look to Him in faith like they did and have eternal life.

BEAM 150

SINS? GO WHERE?

Just where do our sins go? Sins contaminate us like leprosy contaminated the lepers of old. They bring us down to a horrible end too, like leprosy did to those who had that terrible disease. But what does the Bible say about our sins and just where do they go when they are removed from us?

Buried in the depths of the sea.

"He will subdue our iniquities, and Thou wilt cast all their sins into the depths of the sea" (Micah 7:19).

I do not know just how deep that sea is, but it is deep enough to put them away from me for ever.

He blots out our sin.

"I have blotted out, as a thick cloud, thy transgressions, and, as a cloud, thy sins; return unto Me; for I have redeemed thee" (Isaiah 44:22). Clouds are beautiful things, but not the dark clouds. When they vanish, or evaporate, you cannot put that same cloud together again. A new one? Yes. But the old one is gone forever. He will wipe out our sins like that cloud.

Put behind God's back.

"For Thou hast cast all my sins behind Thy back" (Isaiah 38:17). This is figuratively speaking of course.

We do not think of God as having a front face and a rear view. But the teaching is beautiful. When we were lost in our sins we could not come to God because our sins stood between God and us. So He must judge us. Now, He is saying with our sins behind Him He sees no sin in front of Him as we approach a Holy God. There is nothing in between to hinder our drawing near.

Remembered no more.

"For I will forgive their iniquity, and I will remember their sin no more" (Jeremiah 31:34). A forgetful God? Impossible! But when it comes to our sins that are forgiven, God loses His memory. He will remember them no more. I still remember mine and it is a burden. But if He forgets, the time will come when He will wipe out my memories too, and I will remember them no more.

As far as the East is from the West.

"As far as the East is from the West, so far hath He removed our transgressions from us" (Psalm 103:12).

I am glad He did not say "as far as the North is from the South." What happens when I go north? I go up through Canada and then through Arctica, then the North Pole. Then I go through Russia, then Kazakhstan, then India. Hey! Wait a minute! I am heading south now. I was going north. So I keep going south through Antarctica then the South Pole, then Argentina. Hey! Wait a minute! I am heading north again. How long does this go on? You see there is a limit on going north and south. Not so, going east. You can go east and go east and go east and you will still be going east. You can go east forever and still be going east. He is saying our sins are gone completely forever, never to be met again.

There is one condition for our sin removal. "Without shedding of blood there is no remission" (Hebrews 9:22). That word remission means a "sending away." There is no sending away of our sins, if we have not believed on Him and had His blood applied to our lives by faith. If we have trusted Him, then look at the list. Our sins are buried, blotted out, put behind His back, remembered no more, and removed from us forever. All it takes is faith.

"He that believeth on the Son hath everlasting life: and he that believeth not the Son shall not see life; but the wrath of God abideth on him" (John 3:36).

"I had fainted unless I had believed to see the goodness of the Lord in the land of the living. Wait on the Lord; be of good courage, and He shall strengthen thine heart; wait, I say, on the Lord" (Psalm 27:13–14).

Contact George Miller
or order more copies of this book at

TATE PUBLISHING, LLC

127 East Trade Center Terrace
Mustang, Oklahoma 73064

(888) 361 - 9473

Tate Publishing, LLC

www.tatepublishing.com